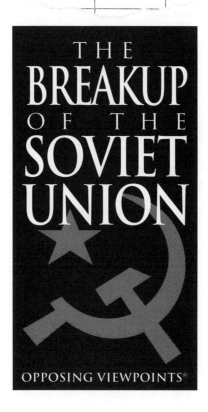

THE
BREAKUP
OF THE
SOVIET
UNION

OPPOSING VIEWPOINTS®

Other Books of Related Interest in the Opposing Viewpoints Series:

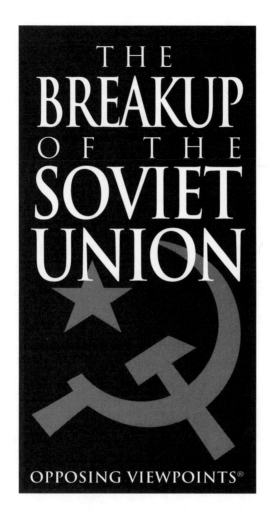

THE BREAKUP OF THE SOVIET UNION

OPPOSING VIEWPOINTS®

David Bender & Bruno Leone, *Series Editors*

William Barbour, *Book Editor*
Carol Wekesser, *Book Editor*

OPPOSING VIEWPOINTS SERIES®

Greenhaven Press, Inc.   PO Box 289009   San Diego, CA 92198-9009

Library of Congress Cataloging-in-Publication Data

The Breakup of the Soviet Union : opposing viewpoints / William Barbour, book editor ; Carol Wekesser, book editor.
    p.   cm. — (Opposing viewpoints series)
    Includes bibliographical references and index.
    Summary: A collection of articles debating issues related to the collapse of the former Soviet Union, the future of the region, and America's foreign policy there.
    ISBN 1-56510-068-9 (alk. paper) — ISBN 1-56510-067-0 (pbk.)
    1. Soviet Union—History—1985-1991. 2. World politics—1989- . 3. United States—Foreign relations—Former Soviet republics. 4. Former Soviet republics—Foreign relations—United States. 5. Former Soviet republics—Economic policy. 6. Former Soviet republics—Ethnic relations. [1. Soviet Union—History—1985-1991. 2. World politics—1989- . 3. United States—Foreign relations—Former Soviet republics.]
    I. Barbour, William, 1963-   . II. Wekesser, Carol, 1943-   .
III. Series: Opposing viewpoints series (Unnumbered)
DK286.B75   1994
947.085'4—dc20   93-1809
                                          CIP
                                          AC

"Congress shall make no law . . . abridging the freedom of speech, or of the press."

First Amendment to the U.S. Constitution

The basic foundation of our democracy is the first amendment guarantee of freedom of expression. The Opposing Viewpoints Series is dedicated to the concept of this basic freedom and the idea that it is more important to practice it than to enshrine it.

Contents

Chapter 3: How Should the U.S. Respond to the Breakup of the Soviet Union?

Chapter 4: What Policies Would Strengthen the Republics' Economies?

Chapter 5: What Measures Would Reduce Ethnic Conflict in the Republics?

Why Consider Opposing Viewpoints?

"The only way in which a human being can make some approach to knowing the whole of a subject is by hearing what can be said about it by persons of every variety of opinion and studying all modes in which it can be looked at by every character of mind. No wise man ever acquired his wisdom in any mode but this."

John Stuart Mill

In our media-intensive culture it is not difficult to find differing opinions. Thousands of newspapers and magazines and dozens of radio and television talk shows resound with differing points of view. The difficulty lies in deciding which opinion to agree with and which "experts" seem the most credible. The more inundated we become with differing opinions and claims, the more essential it is to hone critical reading and thinking skills to evaluate these ideas. Opposing Viewpoints books address this problem directly by presenting stimulating debates that can be used to enhance and teach these skills. The varied opinions contained in each book examine many different aspects of a single issue. While examining these conveniently edited opposing views, readers can develop critical thinking skills such as the ability to compare and contrast authors' credibility, facts, argumentation styles, use of persuasive techniques, and other stylistic tools. In short, the Opposing Viewpoints Series is an ideal way to attain the higher-level thinking and reading skills so essential in a culture of diverse and contradictory opinions.

In addition to providing a tool for critical thinking, Opposing Viewpoints books challenge readers to question their own strongly held opinions and assumptions. Most people form their opinions on the basis of upbringing, peer pressure, and personal, cultural, or professional bias. By reading carefully balanced opposing views, readers must directly confront new ideas as well as the opinions of those with whom they disagree. This is not to simplistically argue that everyone who reads opposing views will—or should—change his or her opinion. Instead, the series enhances readers' depth of understanding of their own views by encouraging confrontation with opposing ideas. Careful examination of others' views can lead to the readers' understanding of the logical inconsistencies in their own opinions, perspective on why they hold an opinion, and the consideration of the possibility that their opinion requires further evaluation.

Evaluating Other Opinions

To ensure that this type of examination occurs, Opposing Viewpoints books present all types of opinions. Prominent spokespeople on different sides of each issue as well as well-known professionals from many disciplines challenge the reader. An additional goal of the series is to provide a forum for other, less known, or even unpopular viewpoints. The opinion of an ordinary person who has had to make the decision to cut off life support from a terminally ill relative, for example, may be just as valuable and provide just as much insight as a medical ethicist's professional opinion. The editors have two additional purposes in including these less known views. One, the editors encourage readers to respect others' opinions—even when not enhanced by professional credibility. It is only by reading or listening to and objectively evaluating others' ideas that one can determine whether they are worthy of consideration. Two, the inclusion of such viewpoints encourages the important critical thinking skill of objectively evaluating an author's credentials and bias. This evaluation will illuminate an author's reasons for taking a particular stance on an issue and will aid in readers' evaluation of the author's ideas.

As series editors of the Opposing Viewpoints Series, it is our hope that these books will give readers a deeper understanding of the issues debated and an appreciation of the complexity of even seemingly simple issues when good and honest people disagree. This awareness is particularly important in a democratic society such as ours in which people enter into public debate to determine the common good. Those with whom one disagrees should not be regarded as enemies but rather as people whose views deserve careful examination and may shed light on one's own.

Thomas Jefferson once said that "difference of opinion leads to inquiry, and inquiry to truth." Jefferson, a broadly educated man, argued that "if a nation expects to be ignorant and free . . . it expects what never was and never will be." As individuals and as a nation, it is imperative that we consider the opinions of others and examine them with skill and discernment. The Opposing Viewpoints Series is intended to help readers achieve this goal.

David L. Bender & Bruno Leone,
Series Editors

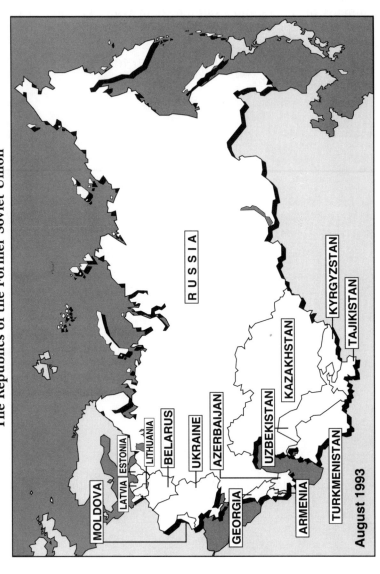

The Republics of the Former Soviet Union

RUSSIA

MOLDOVA
LATVIA
ESTONIA
LITHUANIA
BELARUS
UKRAINE
AZERBAIJAN
GEORGIA
ARMENIA
UZBEKISTAN
KAZAKHSTAN
KYRGYZSTAN
TAJIKISTAN
TURKMENISTAN

August 1993

Introduction

"Russia is at a painful turning point. . . . Its people stand at the junction of their authoritarian traditions and their novel experiment with political freedom."

David K. Shipler, *The New York Times Magazine*, April 4, 1993.

With the breakup of the Soviet Union, the all-pervasive ideology that prescribed and controlled every sphere of Soviet life for over seventy years—Soviet communism—has been swept away. As Russian philosophy professor Igor Shamshchev says, "The whole mentality that was built over all these years [of communism] was destroyed, and in its place there is practically nothing." The people of the former Soviet republics must now redefine themselves as individuals, as communities, and as newly independent countries. While some wish to revert to traditional ethnic identities, large numbers are looking to the West for political, social, and economic direction. The leaders of most of the republics, supported by the majority of their citizens, say they are committed to Western-style governments and economies.

In the Russian Federation, seen as the indicator of the region's future, leaders have instituted drastic reforms aimed at establishing U.S.-style market capitalism. They have freed prices from central control and begun privatizing state-run enterprises—transferring them to private ownership. This sudden birth of capitalism has transformed the streets of Russian cities into teeming marketplaces where entrepreneurs strike deals and citizens peddle goods, activities that were illegal under communism. According to journalist Elizabeth Shogren, many young people have enthusiastically adopted the Western ideal of individual initiative. Some are succeeding: As reporter Andrew Kopkind put it, "A very few have very quickly become very rich."

Polls show that most Russians support such reforms, and many Western observers share their optimism. Columnist Mona Charen notes that it will take time to undo the effects of seventy years of an inefficient Soviet command structure, but capitalism is already "thriving at the grassroots level." Professor Martin Malia agrees: "Real prices—not administrative directives—are now the norm for economic activity," and privatization is "gaining momentum."

13

Russian scholar Nina Balyaeva concludes that "Russia shows many signs of being able to manage this transition [to democracy] thoughtfully and carefully."

While the majority of Russians support reforms, most have found that capitalism is less attractive than they had been led to believe. "Western reality comes as a shock to most Soviets," says commentator Leonid Goldin, "who have seen only black-and-white pictures of it before." Not only has hyperinflation sent prices soaring, but capitalism has led to new problems, such as unemployment, homelessness, and increased crime. Furthermore, the end of communism has meant the end of social benefits, such as free health care, education, and transportation. One Russian citizen quoted by the *Christian Science Monitor* sums up the transition from Soviet communism to Western capitalism: "Before [the collapse], there were some guarantees and protection. Now you have to take care of yourself." People are learning, says Goldin, that "the American way of life and thinking . . . , on inspection, turn out to be not so attractive, after all."

While reforms have reduced living standards for most Russians, they have benefitted the *nomenklatura*, the former Communist party and bureaucratic elite class. The ideology of Soviet communism has been officially rejected, notes Kopkind, but the actual distribution of privilege and wealth has changed little. Members of the *nomenklatura* still retain positions of power in politics, business, and the military, and are using their influence to their advantage. Ownership of many state-run enterprises has simply been transferred to their erstwhile directors, a process cynically referred to as "*nomenklatura* privatization." Thus Russia's conversion to capitalism is seen by many as a massive and corrupt get-rich-quick scheme orchestrated by the government. As Russian commentator Yuri Burtin puts it, "The government itself is evolving into a statist, post-communist plutocracy"—a centralized government of the wealthy, much like the situation under communism.

Regardless of whether democracy and capitalism succeed in the former Soviet republics, the region's future is likely to be as tumultuous and complex as its past. The viewpoints in *The Breakup of the Soviet Union: Opposing Viewpoints* examine the forces and events that led to the collapse of the Soviet Union and the consequences of the empire's disintegration. The book explores the following issues: Why Did the Soviet Union Collapse? How Will the Breakup of the Soviet Union Affect the World? How Should the U.S. Respond to the Breakup of the Soviet Union? What Policies Would Strengthen the Republics' Economies? What Measures Would Reduce Ethnic Conflict in the Republics? The viewpoints presented in this book will provide valuable insight into the region's policies, recent history, and relationship with the West.

Why Did the Soviet Union Collapse?

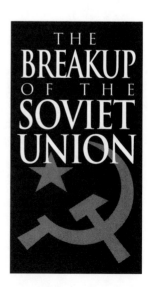

Chapter Preface

Although many factors contributed to the collapse of the Soviet Union, some commentators argue that it was external pressures that weakened the Soviet economy and undermined the ideology of communism. Former U.S. president Ronald Reagan's stern military posturing and harsh ideological attacks are among the elements credited with forcing the Soviets into decline. Reagan intentionally and successfully exploited "the psychological vulnerabilities of totalitarianism," according to his speechwriter Anthony R. Dolan, by calling the Soviet Union an "evil empire" and "the focus of evil in the modern world"—verbal lashings that were also used to justify an escalation of the arms race that the faltering Soviet economy could ill afford to match.

It is likely that many Soviet citizens perceived Reagan's rhetoric as simplistic and naive, as did many Americans. However, some contend that the West did influence the demise of the Soviet Union—by example, rather than by manipulative pressure. More powerful than Reagan's moralistic verbiage, say Daniel Deudney and G. John Ikenberry, was "the appeal of Western affluence and permissiveness. . . . Western popular culture—exemplified in rock and roll, television, film, and blue jeans—seduced the communist world far more effectively than ideological sermons."

Others, however say factors internal to the Soviet system led to the empire's self-destruction. Michael Mandelbaum asserts that Mikhail Gorbachev's reforms destabilized central control, undermined the credibility of communism, and weakened the Soviet economy. John P. Maynard, on the other hand, argues that the very basis of the Soviet economic system was inherently inefficient and corrupt. Because it achieved full employment by giving people "jobs doing nothing," says Maynard, and wasted its resources on non-productive enterprises—such as the Communist party, the KGB, and the military—the colossal bureaucracy failed to produce enough valuable goods to keep its economy afloat.

Soviet communism, the foundation of the Soviet system, was flawed as well, contends correspondent Bob Abernethy: It failed "because of its naive view of human nature. Its ideologists believed that we flawed human beings could be made perfect by social engineering, and that those accomplishing this miracle would not themselves be corrupted by their power."

Many factors influenced the pace and shape of events in the Soviet Union as it broke apart. The roles of external pressures and internal conditions are among the topics debated in the following chapter on the causes of the collapse of the Soviet Union.

"We in the West made a contribution to the fall of the Soviet system."

U.S. Democracy Contributed to the Collapse of Soviet Communism

George Urban

George Urban, the author of the following viewpoint, is the former director of Radio Free Europe, a privately managed radio service created to provide information from the West to citizens behind the Iron Curtain. Although he believes that the main cause of the Soviet Union's collapse was the inadequacy of the socialist system, Urban argues that the West accelerated the empire's decline. By building up its military, providing an example of wealth and freedom, and by reaching out to countries under communist control, Urban says, the United States contributed to the collapse of the Soviet system. Particularly successful, according to Urban, were the effects of Radio Free Europe (RFE) and Radio Liberty (RL).

As you read, consider the following questions:

1. What does Urban mean by saying George Orwell's prediction was wrong?
2. According to the author, how did the SDI project hasten the decline of the Soviet Union?
3. How did Radio Free Europe use ideas and culture against the Soviet Union, according to Urban?

From George Urban, "After the Fall," *The Heritage Lectures* series, September 24, 1991. Reprinted with permission.

Did the Soviet system collapse under the pressure of democratic capitalism, or did it fall under the weight of its own absurdities, or both?

It would be flattering for many of us to think that we have done it, and it is in some significant ways true to say that we accelerated, even if we did not cause, the extinction of the Soviet model of "socialism." But the principal cause of the landslide in 1989 and in 1991, of the sudden collapse of Sovietism in the former U.S.S.R. must, in my view, be ascribed to the evils inherent in the system itself—to oppression, officially sanctioned violence, institutionalized lying and all-pervasive poverty. These were the hallmarks of Soviet socialism since its inception in 1917, and both Boris Yeltsin and Mikhail Gorbachev said as much on ABC television (September 6, 1991). "This experiment conducted on our soil was a tragedy," Yeltsin observed, to which Gorbachev added: "The model that was brought about in our country has failed, and I believe this is a lesson not only for our people but for all peoples." Nothing more significant has been said in the political world since Marx published the Communist Manifesto in 1848.

But we should go beyond Yeltsin and Gorbachev. What 1989 and 1991 have shown is that peoples that lived under despotic rule for half, or almost three-quarters, of a century, and have known nothing but distorted history; people who were denied the right to meet, to discuss and to worship in freedom; people who were debarred from any knowledge of alternative ways of thinking and being—that these people nevertheless carried in their souls an indelible imprint of freedom, truth and morality. They toppled an outwardly impregnable dictatorship because they knew in their bones that the wrong they had been made to suffer was too great to be suffered any longer. Whatever the social scientists may be telling us, it was basically as simple as that. It is Mikhail Gorbachev's historic achievement that, wittingly or unwittingly, he undermined the legitimacy of the Soviet system; but it was the nations of the Soviet empire and of Central and Eastern Europe that took the system by the throat and flung it (in the language of Marx) onto the dustheap of history.

Ideology Buried Itself

Not so many years ago, Nikita Khrushchev warned us "we will bury you." History has chosen to go down a slightly different road. It was the Marxist-Leninist ideology that buried itself. It died (Hugh Trevor-Roper tells us) "quite suddenly, after a short spasm, in its own bed, apparently from natural, or at least internal, causes. It has reached its term— threescore years and ten—made its confession and passed away."

There is cause here for celebration though not for gloating.

The expiry of the system is proof enough that George Orwell's prediction was mercifully wrong, brainwashing and coercive persuasion do not ultimately work. The mind of Man is not an empty slate on which dictators and collective despotisms can inscribe their programs for us. Big Brother cannot watch all the people all the time. "Genghis Khan with the telegraph" is an antiquated threat in the age of high technology. Between the fall of 1989 and August 1991, liberty gained a whole range of fresh overtones which history will remember as surely as the French and American Revolutions.

Dick Wright reprinted by permission of UFS, Inc.

But in what sense can it be said that we in the West made a contribution to the fall of the Soviet system? We did so, as I see it, in at least three different ways.

First, American rearmament under President Reagan, and especially the SDI [Strategic Defense Initiative] project, conjured up for an already declining Soviet economy the prospect of so heavy an extra burden that the Soviet leadership was propelled to surrender Moscow's outposts in the colonial empire as well as its glacis in Central and Eastern Europe. In one important sense, *glasnost* and *perestroika* too were Gorbachev's responses to this pressure, although a strong argument can be made to show that

Mikhail Gorbachev, Eduard Shevardnadze, Aleksandr Yakovlev and other radicals had been intending to reduce or eliminate imperial over-extension in any case, recognizing that the Soviet Union was no longer in a position to take on the entire capitalist world plus China without inviting self-destruction. To put it in another way: President Reagan had caused the U.S.S.R. to spend itself into near-bankruptcy; and when bankruptcy began to loom, the U.S.S.R. sent itself into liquidation.

By Example

The second way in which we hastened the demise of the Soviet system has been by example: the mere existence of relatively rich and relatively free capitalist countries, side by side with the Soviet Union and its satellites, carried its own message. The spirit of rebellion grew from nothing more dramatic than geographic proximity. This was, of course, especially true of Western Europe where wealthy and on the whole well-managed countries such as Austria, Germany, the Scandinavian nations, Belgium, Holland, offered daily and highly damaging standards for comparison. What could be bought in Germany, spoken in France and printed in Holland could not be bought, spoken or printed in the U.S.S.R. or Poland. With *glasnost*, the abolition of jamming, growing economic links, cultural cross-fertilization and international travel, it proved no longer possible to isolate the Soviet system from the rest of the real world. Something had to give—and it did.

We can now see why Stalin and the Stalinists were, from their point of view, right to segregate their empire from the rest of humanity; for as soon as the Soviet model of Communism came to be exposed to the light of day, it withered and brought the empire down with it. Those who ignore human nature have no choice but to look to the police state as their natural ally.

Our third contribution to the fall of the Soviet system has been a deliberate policy of identification with the nations under Communist tutelage. Back in the early 1950s, far-sighted Americans recognized the need to equip Western—especially U.S.—foreign policy with a psychological arm to enable us to talk to the peoples of the extended Soviet empire. Radio Free Europe and Radio Liberty were born under that dispensation.

They turned out to be (if I may say so as an interested party) one of the most successful political investments the U.S. has ever made, for much of World War III was fought and won in terms of ideas and culture—the very tools which these two Radios used on our behalf in the worldwide spiritual contest better known as the "Cold War." What was their function? They helped to prevent national consciousness from being wiped out by the homogenizing influence of Marxism-Leninism—they helped to prevent Poles from being deprived of their history, Estonians of their culture, Ukrainians of their language and the Russian nation from being identified with the claims and practices of Communism.

Domestic Attack

Let me say in passing that surrogate broadcasting (for that is how it has come to be known) did not carry universal approval, least of all by the American Left. Frequently, the two stations were under severe domestic attack. . . . We were accused of being "anti-Communist," of wanting to jeopardize the integrity of the Soviet state, of pitting polemical arguments against Soviet ideology. Hideous sins, these, don't you think? From time to time strange guidelines were imposed on us under the pressure of the liberal establishment—guidelines which some U.S. legislator would, I'm certain, now be happy to see expunged from the record. One of these said: "RFE/RL have no mandate to advocate the establishment or disestablishment of a particular system, form of state organization, or ideology in the areas to which they broadcast"—please mark the wording: the disestablishment of any particular system or ideology. . . .

I remember Senator Claiborne Pell telling me with some irritation in the 1970s: "What are these radios about at a time of detente? You don't want to stir things up in Eastern Europe, do you?" or words to that effect. So our broadcasters had to do their jobs with one arm tied behind their backs. They had no difficulty dealing with the Soviet system, but they did have a hard time fending off the suspicions and vituperations of certain congressmen and the liberal press. Sometimes it was a war on two fronts—on the Elbe and the Potomac—of which the one fought along the Iron Curtain often struck me as much the less demanding.

The question that now has to be addressed is whether our victory means peace for the foreseeable future; more particularly whether the attempt to instill democracy in the former Soviet empire is likely to succeed and promote world peace. . . .

We certainly have a stake in democratic rule and a prosperous free-market economy throughout the lands of the former U.S.S.R. What is more, we can, if we so choose, have a limited but important influence in bringing these things about.

"Socialism collapsed in the USSR under its own weight despite the help it constantly received from the West."

Soviet Communism Collapsed on Its Own

John P. Maynard

The author of the following viewpoint argues that Western leaders do not deserve credit for the Soviet Union's demise. By providing economic and technical assistance, says the author, the United States helped the Communist party remain in power throughout—and up to the very end of—its reign. The author contends that the true causes of the Soviet Union's collapse were the inherent flaws of socialism—inefficient bureaucracy, nepotism, and the denial of human freedom. The author fears that the West is gravitating toward a similar system in which bureaucracy and big government undermine traditional values. John P. Maynard is the pseudonym of a congressional staff member who requests anonymity.

As you read, consider the following questions:

1. Why, according to the author, is the media not focusing on the failure of socialism in the Soviet Union?
2. In what ways does Maynard think that the Soviet Union was a "perfect" socialist society?
3. According to the author, in what ways are the United States and Western Europe becoming socialist?

From John P. Maynard, "What's Sad About the Soviet Collapse," *Conservative Review*, April 1992. Reprinted with permission.

Watching the former Soviet Union collapse has been a dismaying process. Not that there are any regrets about the demise of the USSR. What is dismaying is the manner in which the collapse is being viewed, or not being viewed, as the case may be.

First, it is dismaying to see so many of our leaders, from the President on down, patting themselves on the back for achieving victory in the cold war. "We won!" they proudly exclaim.

But, it is hard to see how anyone can seriously claim "We won," when we, the West, were primarily responsible for keeping the Soviet Union alive for over seventy years. We did not win. They lost—notwithstanding our efforts to keep them alive!

Let us put things in perspective. Karl Marx was honored for doing precisely what he did: develop theories of left-wing economics and class warfare, inciting internal dissension within free nations, destroy the aristocracy *and* the middle classes or "bourgeoisie," and so make it possible for the proponents of an international socialist world order to gain total power over the "proletariat."

There was no spontaneous communist revolution by the people in Russia in 1917. There was a Bolshevik coup that had been years in building, and that drew valuable support from the socialist network that spread into many corners of the free capitalist world. Even anti-Czarist capitalists aided Lenin and Trotsky with loans. Some helped finance Japan's war against Czarist Russia, and others are alleged to have funded the indoctrination of Russian POWs [prisoners of war] by Marxists into the basic tenets of communism before they were returned to Russia.

Western Help

No sooner was the Bolshevik tyranny in place, than it faced instant failure and tottered on the brink of collapse. But, who came to the rescue? The Free World organized a famine relief mission in 1921. Although a mission of charity, this served to defuse the possibility of a major uprising against the new Marxist rulers, who had only recently murdered the Czar and his entire family, as well as slaughtering tens of thousands of police and innocent peasant farmers who did not wish to give up their land. Western industrialists from Germany, the U.S. and Britain helped reconstitute Russian industry under Lenin's so-called New Economic Policy (NEP), only to find the NEP summarily abandoned and all capitalist investment seized.

After the Soviets enjoyed this temporary economic reprieve, thanks to assistance from charitable Westerners, unwise entrepreneurs, and outright sympathizers in the West, Stalin appeared on the scene and proceeded to starve and otherwise massacre literally tens of millions of Russian and Ukrainian peasant farmers. The Western governments had all the information about the massacre, but generally refused to acknowledge that it was happening.

Reprinted by permission of Cartoonews, Inc.

Franklin Roosevelt came to the aid of the Soviet tyrants many times, beginning in 1933 when he extended diplomatic recognition to the Stalinist regime, and continuing into World War II not only with the supply of war material—which could be understood in the wartime situation—but in a multitude of other ways which we are only now coming to hear about. Most disgraceful was Yalta, when against Churchill's objections, Roosevelt agreed to hand over the entire eastern half of Europe to brutal Marxist depredation under Stalin.

Notwithstanding the Cold War and the U.S. containment policy, every U.S. President since Roosevelt has in some way provided economic and technical assistance which has in effect served to keep communism alive. Most recently, when the 'evil empire' began to break up, official U.S. policy was to preserve the Soviet empire intact—denying freedom and self-determination to the various different peoples that had been forcibly incorporated into it. George Bush did his best to keep Gorbachev in power. While Aleksandr Solzhenitsyn had been excluded from the White House, and Yeltsin received a very cool welcome, Gorbachev was welcomed—the same Gorbachev who even after he had come to power, continued to fund Gus Hall, the leader of the puppet U.S. Communist Party that caused so much campus disruption in the U.S. during the 60's and 70's.

Likewise, when the Slovenes and Croats sought independence from an unreformed Marxist government in Belgrade—which deliberately used its armed forces against civilians as the Soviet government had done in Hungary—Washington did all in its power to discourage them. So also it sought to dissuade the Latvians, Lithuanians and Estonians from demanding their independence when Gorbachev, already tottering but still proclaiming himself to be a Marxist, refused to yield to their demands.

Unusual? Not at all. As the *Los Angeles Times* recently reported, two of Saddam Hussein's biggest financial and technology-transfer supporters were George Bush and James Baker—right up to the eve of the war. The reader might say that Saddam Hussein was different. But was he? The Baathist party was strongly socialist, and Saddam Hussein was as cruel a socialist dictator as any of the Soviet leaders since the Bolshevik revolution—which is saying something. The Soviet Union, of course, had been behind the communist revolution that had murdered the Hashemite royal family when it seized power in a bloody coup which put Marxist leaders in control of Iraq and led to the seizure of all Western property—including the oil wells. Saddam's Baathists inherited this revolution, and the Soviets became the chief supplier to Saddam Hussein of arms and military advisors.

Aiding Soviet Military

It has been the same with Tanzania and a dozen other socialist states, which had ruined their own economies but have been kept alive with U.S. and other Western taxpayer's money. Although the Soviet leadership kept its people poor in order to build up the Soviet military and subsidize revolution in numerous targeted non-communist societies, the Soviet war machine was itself at times aided by U.S. technical and financial assistance. The much propagandized arms control negotiations were another good example of U.S. politics in action. There was little actual arms control but there were agreements under which the Soviets benefitted from U.S. financial and technical assistance. Consider, for example, the Basic Principles of Relations that was signed as part of SALT [Strategic Arms Limitation Talks] I, which opened the door for increased economic and technical assistance in the 1970s, or the technical assistance meetings that accompanied the signing of the INF [Intermediate Range Nuclear Forces] Treaty in 1987.

U.S. financial and technical assistance was undoubtedly used to build up the Soviet military machine. While Americans shouldered massive military expenditures for forty years to counter the Soviet threat, the Soviet economy was aided, consciously or otherwise, by U.S. Presidents and Western industrialists and merchants like Armand Hammer, as well as by other diverse Western financial interests. Ford Motors even constructed and financed the factory that built the large military trucks used by the Soviets in their invasion of Afghanistan.

Now, our leaders have the gall, the audacity, to say "We won." Nuts! We won about as much as we won in Vietnam. Socialism collapsed in the USSR under its own weight *despite* the help it constantly received from the West.

Socialism Its Own Undoing

But even more dismaying is the fact that so little attention is being focused on the reasons why the Soviet Union failed in spite of assistance from the West. The collapse of the Soviet Union is a living example of the effects of socialism—which is precisely what the Soviets called their system. The inefficiency, bureaucratic incompetence, inherent nepotism, and the deadening absence of human freedom which kills the soul, were the causes of its collapse.

While some recognition has been given to the fact that the socialist system caused its own collapse in the Soviet Union and satellite central and eastern Europe, few voices are heard pointing to the danger inherent in the ongoing spread of socialism in the West. One reason why no attention is being focused on the relevance of the collapse of socialism in the Soviet Union is that many in the West—in the media especially—are themselves still socialists at heart. These people have tremendous influence in the government and—through the media and the large non-profit foundations—in academia.

Socialism equates to big government, government controls, and a governing elite that pulls the levers of power. The elite is able to use the machinery of government to do its dirty work. . . .

Perfect Socialism

The Soviet Union was the most socialized state of all. It collapsed because of the inherent failures of socialism and the self-deception which made its socialist rulers unable to see the fatal flaws of their own system. The Soviet Union represented the ultimate in big government, in government controls, and in a governing elite. This elite controlled the Communist Party, which controlled the government, which was a mere front and a scapegoat. Successes were credited to socialism and the Party leadership. Failures that could not be hidden were blamed on government departments. Sound familiar? Over the years, the USSR government, which produced nothing, grew and grew and grew, while the residual productive forces steadily deteriorated. This is another of the principal reasons behind the collapse: the deterioration to the point of near total destruction of the ability to produce. What happened is most aptly described in the old Soviet joke, "They pretend to pay us and we pretend to work." The Soviet Union failed because in the end there were no producers left.

Although Marxists in the West are claiming today that the Soviet regime was not a true example of socialism, the Soviet Union was in fact the perfect socialist society, with guaranteed employment and guaranteed free medical care. The schools were also free. But all these free benefits were mirages—more self-deception—because they simply did not exist. Certainly, there was employment—it was illegal to be unemployed (not to work)—so people were given jobs doing nothing. Medical care was free, but hospital conditions were deplorable, waiting lines long, and decent treatment was simply non-existent—except for the governing elite. As for higher education, if you were not in the Party, you were not eligible. . . .

The collapse of the Soviet citadel of socialism is so valuable to study because the U.S. and other Western nations are headed in the same direction, driven by many of the same forces using the same deceptive strategies which will undermine, distort, and ultimately destroy our system of values—something that has to be done to make way for big bureaucracy and socialism. The Soviet collapse provides an unparalleled opportunity for the free nations to learn to recognize the dangers inherent in socialism and big government. It is truly dismaying that this lesson does not yet seem to have had the impact it deserves on the minds of those who live in the traditionally free nations of the West.

3 VIEWPOINT

"Ronald Reagan . . . won the Cold War without firing a shot."

Ronald Reagan's Presidency Caused the Collapse of the Soviet Union

Edwin Meese III

Ronald Reagan was the fortieth president of the United States, from 1980 to 1988. In the following viewpoint, Edwin Meese III argues that Reagan's assertive policies as president caused the eventual demise of the Soviet Union and thus the end of the cold war. Meese contends that Reagan built up U.S. defenses and projected a strong image in order to force the Soviets to either back down from their military stance or face increased defense spending and domestic economic problems. Meese was an advisor to Reagan from 1981 to 1985 and U.S. attorney general from 1985 to 1988. He has since written a book, *With Reagan: The Inside Story*, and has held the Ronald Reagan chair in public policy at the Heritage Foundation, a conservative public policy research institute in Washington, D.C.

As you read, consider the following questions:

1. According to Meese, how did Reagan help Solidarity survive in Poland?
2. Why was Reagan's refusal to give up SDI at Reykjavik significant, according to Meese?

The collapse of Communism from 1989 to 1991 came as no surprise to Ronald Reagan, although he didn't think it would come quite so quickly. Throughout his career Reagan had emphasized the political, economic, and moral weakness of the Soviet Union, and the inevitable breakdown of the Marxist system if it were ever seriously challenged. As president, he mounted such a serious challenge, and devised a strategy that made the Soviet leadership painfully aware of its vulnerability.

Reagan spelled out his view of Communism in four speeches of astonishing prescience: his 1982 address to the British Parliament at Westminster, his speech before the National Association of Evangelicals in 1983, his appearance at the Brandenburg Gate of the Berlin Wall in 1987, and his talk under Lenin's statue at Moscow State University in May 1988.

Of these, the speech to the evangelicals is best known. Reagan called the Soviet bloc an "Evil Empire" and referred to Communism as "the focus of evil in the modern world." These comments were widely derided at the time as the rantings of a Cold-War ideologue. But to people living under the yoke of Soviet Communism, his words were all too obviously accurate— and they were words of hope. They showed that the American president understood their plight and was not about to accede to their subjugation.

Today, after the people of Eastern Europe and the former Soviet Union have thrown off the shackles of Communist rule, few doubt that the Soviet system was indeed an "Evil Empire" and that the world is better for its passing. If Reagan had done nothing more than proclaim this truth, while fashionable opinion was ridiculing it, he would stand vindicated before history. But the president did a great deal more than this.

Freedom Is Key

In addition to stressing the evils of Communism, Reagan stressed its inherent weakness. In his view, the two were related, since in denying freedom the Communists not only engaged in tyranny, they also crippled the creative potential of the human spirit. Reagan firmly believed that freedom was both morally and materially superior to Communism. As he put it in his Westminster speech to the British Parliament:

> The decay of the Soviet experiment should come as no surprise to us. Wherever the comparisons have been made between free and closed societies—West Germany and East Germany, Austria and Czechoslovakia, Malaysia and Vietnam—it is the democratic countries that are prosperous and responsive to the needs of their people. And one of the simple but overwhelming facts of our times is this: Of all the millions of refugees we've seen in the modern world, their flight is always away from, not toward, the Communist world.

Reagan described in the Westminster speech "the march of freedom and democracy which will leave Marxism-Leninism on the ash heap of history." He went even further in his address to the evangelicals, where he predicted Communism's imminent demise. After attacking "moral equivalence" thinking, he called for a program of resistance to Soviet imperialism, and added: "I believe we shall rise to the challenge. I believe that Communism is another sad, bizarre chapter in history whose last pages even now are being written."

At the Brandenburg Gate, Reagan asked Mikhail Gorbachev to tear down the Berlin Wall, and expanded on his vision of history. "In the 1950s," he recalled, "Khrushchev predicted, 'We will bury you.' But in the West today, we see a Free World that has achieved a level of prosperity and well-being unprecedented in all human history. In the Communist world, we see failure, technological backwardness, declining standards of health, even want of the most basic kind—too little food. Even today, the Soviet Union still cannot feed itself.

"After these four decades, then, there stands before the entire world one great inescapable conclusion: Freedom leads to prosperity. Freedom replaces the ancient hatreds among nations with comity and peace. Freedom is the victor."

Then, at Moscow State University, Reagan spoke of freedom's inevitable victory to the children of the *nomenklatura*: "It's hard for government planners, no matter how sophisticated, to ever substitute for millions of individuals working night and day to make their dreams come true. . . . We Americans make no secret of our belief in freedom. . . . Freedom is the right to question and change the established way of doing things. It is the continuing revolution of the marketplace. . . . It is the right to put forth an idea, scoffed at by the experts, and watch it catch fire among the people." Not long after, the idea of freedom caught fire among the republics of the Soviet Union.

Aggravating Their Vulnerabilities

Reagan's conviction that Communism was vulnerable was not simply theoretical. It was the essence of his foreign policy and defense strategy toward the Soviet empire. Reagan knew that the Soviet system could not command the allegiance of its captive peoples, and its economic system could not produce the goods required to shelter, feed, and clothe them. In any full-scale competition with the United States and other Western powers, therefore, Communism would be forced to choose between maintaining its empire and solving its many problems.

In contrast with prevailing liberal opinion, Reagan refused to negotiate with the Soviet Union from a position of weakness. He was not opposed to negotiations, and in his second term he was a very successful negotiator. But this was only after he had restored the strength of the American military, capitalized on our technological and economic advantages, assisted anti-Communist forces around the world, and reversed the West's posture of retreat.

Reagan's strategic goal was to force the Soviets to choose: either stand down from their continuing confrontation with the West, or face increasingly devastating pressures on the home front. He rejected accommodation with the Soviets, on the grounds that it would postpone their day of reckoning between their inherent domestic weakness and their globalist ambitions.

The president made these points frequently in his Cabinet councils. "How long," he would say, "can the Russians keep on being so belligerent and spending so much on the arms race when they can't even feed their own people?" In his memoirs, he commented on intelligence updates about the condition of the Soviet economy in the early 1980s:

> The latest figures provided additional evidence that it was a basket case, and even if I hadn't majored in economics in college, it would have been plain to me that Communism was doomed as a failed economic system. The situation was so bad that if Western countries got together and cut off credit to it, we could bring it to its knees.

If economics were a major weakness of the Soviet system, he reasoned, it was a huge advantage for our own. "The great dynamic success of capitalism," he said, "has given us a powerful weapon in our battle against Communism—money. The Russians could never win the arms race; we could outspend them forever. Moreover, incentives inherent in the capitalist system had given us an industrial base that [meant] we had the capacity to maintain a technological edge on them forever."

Curtailing the Flow

The other side of the equation was for the United States and other Western powers to stop bailing the Soviets out of their economic difficulties through subsidized credit, one-sided business deals, and technology transfer. As Reagan observed, he wanted a coordinated Western policy in which "none of us would subsidize the Soviet economy or the Soviet military expansion by offering preferential trading terms or easy credit." He also wanted to restrain the flow of products and technology that would increase Soviet military capabilities. This was the principal motive behind the battle over the Siberian pipeline, and also behind the systematic effort of the Pentagon's office on technology transfer, to impede the flow of Western computers, precision machinery, microelectronics, and other militarily useful systems to the East. The coordinated effort (headed by Stephen Bryen) at the Department of Defense to curtail such

31

transfers, both from the United States and from third countries receiving our technology, was one of the great unsung successes of the Reagan era.

A vivid example of the Reagan strategy in action was the liberation of Poland, which presaged the disintegration of the other Communist regimes of Eastern Europe. This was among the earliest of test cases for the president's effort to coordinate economic, technological, and diplomatic factors against the Soviets and their clients—and it turned out to be a momentous success.

Chuck Asay, by permission of the *Colorado Springs Gazette Telegraph*.

In December 1981, the government of General Wojciech Jaruzelski declared martial law in Poland, cracking down on the protests of the Solidarity labor union headed by Lech Walesa. Here, indeed, was the face of the "Evil Empire," and it prompted a strong response from Reagan. The nature of that response was twofold: to provide material and moral support to Walesa's freedom movement, and to put the economic squeeze on Jaruzelski and his Soviet mentors.

As has now been made public by Carl Bernstein in an article for *Time*, Reagan conducted this effort in concert with Pope John Paul II, himself a native of Poland, whom the president greatly admired and with whom he saw eye-to-eye concerning the Jaruzelski crackdown. The administration shared intelligence data on the situation with the Vatican, making certain that our policies were on the identical wavelength. President Reagan conferred directly with the Pope, while others in the administration worked closely with Catholic Church officials.

The main elements of this strategy were to keep Solidarity alive through financial aid, clandestine radios, underground newspapers, and the like. Much of this was done jointly with the AFL-CIO [American Federation of Labor-Congress of Industrial Organizations], which had a strong and obvious interest in helping sustain the Solidarity union. At the same time, sanctions against the Polish regime—and against the Soviets—added to the pressure on the Communists. Administration opposition to the Siberian pipeline, and to other economic dealings with the Soviets, was integral to this campaign.

It was, as Bernstein notes, a carefully calibrated effort, designed to keep the opposition viable and the Communists on the defensive, without provoking the kind of violent clashes that had previously led to tragic outcomes in Poland, East Germany, Hungary, and Czechoslovakia. The object was to bring irresistible forces to bear that would exploit the political and economic weakness of the Communist regime—exactly as Reagan had envisioned in his many statements on the topic. Key players in the Polish drama included CIA Director William Casey, National Security Advisers Richard Allen and William Clark, and Richard Pipes of the National Security Council.

In the end, Solidarity did survive, and the Jaruzelski government backed down in stages from its hard-line posture. In 1987, the Pope traveled to his native land, where he was acclaimed by millions of his coreligionists and countrymen, to give his personal backing to Solidarity. The days of Communist rule in Poland were numbered, and the other tottering dominoes of Eastern Europe would soon follow in its wake—as would, eventually, the dictatorship of the USSR itself.

The SDI Pressure

The battle over SDI [Strategic Defense Initiative] was another important example of Reagan's strategy. Reagan thought we should exploit our technological advantages here, not unilaterally restrain them as most liberals were recommending. He favored SDI on its own merits because he wanted to move away from a deterrence strategy that relied on nuclear weapons. He also was convinced that U.S. missile defenses would bankrupt the Soviet Union, and force it to abandon the struggle.

This is essentially what happened. Even though Gorbachev himself attempted to contend otherwise (as in his book, *Perestroika*), considerable testimony from the Soviet standpoint confirms Reagan's judgment. Some of this appears in the reporting of Don Oberdorfer of the *Washington Post*, who closely tracked Soviet attitudes on Cold War issues from 1983 to 1987.

On a 1984 trip to Moscow, for instance, Oberdorfer reports that when asked what were the most important questions facing the country, "nearly all of the 12 Soviet officials or journalists whom I met named the internal management or economy of the USSR." He quotes a former KGB official, assailing Reagan's policies, as saying, "You are trying to destroy our economy, to interfere with our trade, to overwhelm and make us inferior in the strategic field."

Oberdorfer similarly quotes Soviet Foreign Minister Andrei Gromyko as telling former Senator George McGovern that Reagan and his aides "want to cause trouble. They want to weaken the Soviet system. They want to bring it down." Such concerns became more acute, Oberdorfer notes, when Mikhail Gorbachev came to power the following year: "Gorbachev and his new team were more conscious than their predecessors of the economic troubles of the country, induced in large part by massive military spending."

These concerns were made official and overt at the Twenty-Seventh Party Congress of the Soviet Communist Party in March 1986, which declared that "without an acceleration of the country's economic and social development, it will be impossible to maintain our position on the international scene."

The Final Straw

The final straw for the Soviets, as the president foresaw, was SDI. Oberdorfer quotes Gorbachev advisor Aleksandr Yakovlev as saying: "We understood that it was a new stage, a new turn in the armaments race." If SDI were not stopped, "we would have to start our own program, which would be tremendously expensive and unnecessary. And this [would bring] further exhaustion of the country." For this reason, SDI became the focal point of U.S.-Soviet negotiations—at Geneva in 1985, and at Reykjavik in 1986.

At Reykjavik, Gorbachev agreed to reduce by half, and eventually eliminate entirely, all intercontinental and intermediate missiles—but only on the condition that the United States abandon SDI. By all reports, Secretary of State George Shultz and others in the U.S. delegation were more than willing to make the trade. Had Reagan been the passive creature popularly depicted, the offer would have been accepted on the spot—SDI would have been eliminated.

But Gorbachev—and just about everyone else—had greatly underestimated Reagan's comprehension of, and perseverance on, this issue. President Reagan understood the relevant factors concerning SDI just as well as, or better than, Gorbachev, and he was not about to trade it away, even for so enticing an offer as that extended by the Soviet leader. Since SDI threatened no one, Reagan realized that there was nothing incompatible with maintaining it as a defense while eliminating offensive weapons. So why insist on its removal?

Reagan also knew the Soviets had a lengthy history of evading arms agreements. In a world devoid of missile defenses, and with everyone else disarmed, this meant that a power possessing even one offensive missile could exert irresistible blackmail. SDI was an insurance policy against that possibility, and Reagan was not about to give it up. As he put it:

> After everything had been decided, or so I thought, Gorbachev threw us a curve. With a smile on his face, he said, "This all depends, of course, on you giving up SDI." I realized he had brought me to Iceland with one purpose: to kill the Strategic Defense Initiative. He must have known from the beginning he was going to bring it up at the last minute. "The meeting is over," I said. "Let's go . . . we're leaving."

In global-strategic terms this was Reagan's finest hour—and arguably the one that conclusively won the Cold War for the West. The president, going one-on-one with Gorbachev, not only avoided the trap set for him, but effectively turned the tables—strengthening rather than weakening the U.S. commitment to SDI. Gorbachev must have known that he had gambled, and lost.

The loss had important economic consequences. As Chief of Staff Donald Regan, an important strategist for the president's early summits with Gorbachev, later put it: "To stay in the arms race, the Russians had to spend a lot more money because President Reagan had committed the United States, with all its wealth and all its technical capacity, to developing SDI, a defensive system that made the entire Soviet missile force useless. . . . This meant that Reagan had been dealt the winning hand."

Gorbachev Abandons Struggle

Realizing that Reagan would not give up SDI or Western strength, Gorbachev soon began to abandon the struggle—as Reagan had predicted the Soviets eventually would. Indeed the election of George Bush, who had been Reagan's vice president, was followed almost immediately by Gorbachev's December 1988 announcement at the United Nations that he was ordering a unilateral cutback of 500,000 men from the Soviet armed services and the withdrawal of some tank divisions from Eastern Europe.

Gorbachev himself put it this way in a luncheon with President Reagan and President-elect Bush: "I'm not doing this for show. . . . I'm doing this because I need to. I'm doing this be-

35

cause there's a revolution taking place in my country."

From a post-Cold War perspective, the main principles of the Reagan program may seem self-evident. Viewing the rubble of the Berlin Wall, the upheavals that have transformed Eastern Europe, and the internal collapse of the Soviet regime, hardly anyone can doubt that Communism was indeed an "Evil Empire" and a failed economic system. Such points have been affirmed by the former leaders of the Communist world itself.

Yet at the time Reagan was making these statements and pursuing these policies there was nothing self-evident about them. On the contrary, he was roundly attacked both for his general analysis of the situation, and for nearly all the specific steps he took in carrying out his policy—the defense buildup, INF [Intermediate-Range Nuclear Forces] deployments, aid to anti-Communist resistance forces, curtailment of technology transfer, and SDI.

Reagan Was Right

Even in the aftermath of the Communist collapse Reagan critics were reluctant to credit President Reagan with the accuracy of his vision or the correctness of his policy. Many discussions of the Communist debacle completely ignore the impact of the Reagan strategy, attributing the demise of the "Evil Empire" to a change of heart on the part of the Communists, or to unnamed forces that somehow brought about the toppling of the system.

Perhaps the most famous example of this tendency was the issue of *Time* magazine celebrating the virtual end of Communism and proclaiming Mikhail Gorbachev "Man of the Decade." The role of Ronald Reagan in all of this was scarcely mentioned, nor was much notice given to the fact that the establishment view had been mistaken at every step along the way.

Reagan himself became a friend of Gorbachev. He knew Gorbachev remained a dedicated Communist, but he thought the Soviet leader was different from his predecessors in sincerely wanting a better relationship with the Free World and in understanding many of the fallacies of Marxism-Leninism. Reagan frequently observed that Gorbachev was the first Soviet leader he had known who did not seek the establishment of a one-world Communist state. Reagan also felt that, although Gorbachev was not necessarily a believer, deep down the Soviet leader was influenced by his Christian upbringing.

Former British Prime Minister Margaret Thatcher knew Gorbachev and Reagan well. She said Gorbachev was a man we could do business with, but she didn't credit him with the collapse of Communism. That honor was due to Ronald Reagan, whose foreign policy accomplishments she summed up at a 1991 Heritage Foundation dinner in Washington: "He won the Cold War without firing a shot."

36

"Whether Reagan is seen as the consummate hardliner or the prophet of anti-nuclearism, one should not exaggerate the influence of his administration."

Ronald Reagan's Presidency Did Not Cause the Collapse of the Soviet Union

Daniel Deudney and G. John Ikenberry

In the following viewpoint, authors Daniel Deudney and G. John Ikenberry challenge the popular notion that former U.S. president Ronald Reagan's assertive policies caused the collapse of the Soviet Union and ended the cold war. The authors argue that cold war breakthroughs resulted from Reagan's anti-nuclearism, not his military buildup, and from the recognition by both Reagan and former Soviet president Mikhail Gorbachev of their nations' mutual vulnerability to the nuclear threat. Daniel Deudney is assistant professor of political science at the University of Pennsylvania in Philadelphia. G. John Ikenberry is assistant professor of politics and international affairs at Princeton University in New Jersey.

As you read, consider the following questions:

1. According to the authors, how did the Soviet Union initially respond to the Reagan administration's military buildup?
2. What was the significance of the 1986 summit at Reykjavík, according to the authors?

From Daniel Deudney and G. John Ikenberry, "Who Won the Cold War?" *Foreign Policy* 87 (Summer 1992). Reprinted with permission.

In assessing the rest of the world's impact on Soviet change, a remarkably simplistic and self-serving conventional wisdom has emerged in the United States. This new conventional wisdom, the "Reagan victory school," holds that President Ronald Reagan's military and ideological assertiveness during the 1980s played the lead role in the collapse of Soviet communism and the "taming" of its foreign policy. In that view the Reagan administration's ideological counteroffensive and military buildup delivered the knockout punch to a system that was internally bankrupt and on the ropes. The Reagan Right's perspective is an ideologically pointed version of the more broadly held conventional wisdom on the end of the Cold War that emphasizes the success of the "peace-through-strength" strategy manifest in four decades of Western containment. After decades of waging a costly "twilight struggle," the West now celebrates the triumph of its military and ideological resolve.

The Reagan victory school and the broader peace-through-strength perspectives are, however, misleading and incomplete—both in their interpretation of events in the 1980s and in their understanding of deeper forces that led to the end of the Cold War. It is important to reconsider the emerging conventional wisdom before it truly becomes an article of faith on Cold War history and comes to distort the thinking of policymakers in America and elsewhere. . . .

Reagan's Anti-Nuclearism

Perhaps the greatest anomaly of the Reagan victory school is the "Great Communicator" himself. The Reagan Right ignores that his anti-nuclearism was as strong as his anticommunism. . . .

There is abundant evidence that Reagan felt a deep antipathy for nuclear weapons and viewed their abolition to be a realistic and desirable goal. Reagan's call in his famous March 1983 "Star Wars" speech for a program to make nuclear weapons impotent and obsolete was viewed as cynical by many, but actually it expressed Reagan's heartfelt views, views that he came to act upon. As *Washington Post* reporter Lou Cannon's 1991 biography points out, Reagan was deeply disturbed by nuclear deterrence and attracted to abolitionist solutions. "I know I speak for people everywhere when I say our dream is to see the day when nuclear weapons will be banished from the face of the earth," Reagan said in November 1983. Whereas the Right saw anti-nuclearism as a threat to American military spending and the legitimacy of an important foreign policy tool, or as propaganda for domestic consumption, Reagan sincerely believed it. Reagan's anti-nuclearism was not just a personal sentiment. It surfaced at decisive junctures to affect Soviet perceptions of American policy. Sovietologist and strategic analyst Michael

MccGwire has argued persuasively that Reagan's anti-nuclearism decisively influenced Soviet-U.S. relations during the early Gorbachev years.

A Vision of Vulnerability

Contrary to the conventional wisdom, the defense buildup did not produce Soviet capitulation. The initial Soviet response to the Reagan administration's buildup and belligerent rhetoric was to accelerate production of offensive weapons, both strategic and conventional. That impasse was broken not by Soviet capitulation but by an extraordinary convergence by Reagan and Mikhail Gorbachev on a vision of mutual nuclear vulnerability and disarmament. On the Soviet side, the dominance of the hardline response to the newly assertive America was thrown into question in early 1985 when Gorbachev became general secretary of the Communist party after the death of Konstantin Chernenko. Without a background in foreign affairs, Gorbachev was eager to assess American intentions directly and put his stamp on Soviet security policy. Reagan's strong antinuclear views expressed at the November 1985 Geneva summit were decisive in convincing Gorbachev that it was possible to work with the West in halting the nuclear arms race. . . .

Reagan's commitment to anti-nuclearism and its potential for transforming the U.S.-Soviet confrontation was more graphically demonstrated at the October 1986 Reykjavík summit when Reagan and Gorbachev came close to agreeing on a comprehensive program of global denuclearization that was far bolder than any seriously entertained by American strategists since the Baruch Plan of 1946. The sharp contrast between Reagan's and Gorbachev's shared skepticism toward nuclear weapons on the one hand, and the Washington security establishment's consensus on the other, was showcased in former secretary of defense James Schlesinger's scathing accusation that Reagan was engaged in "casual utopianism." But Reagan's anomalous anti-nuclearism provided the crucial signal to Gorbachev that bold initiatives would be reciprocated rather than exploited. Reagan's anti-nuclearism was more important than his administration's military buildup in catalyzing the end of the Cold War. . . .

Mutual Weakness

Whether Reagan is seen as the consummate hardliner or the prophet of anti-nuclearism, one should not exaggerate the influence of his administration, or of other short-term forces. Within the Washington beltway, debates about postwar military and foreign policy would suggest that Western strategy fluctuated wildly, but in fact the basic thrust of Western policy toward the USSR remained remarkably consistent. Arguments from the New Right notwithstanding, Reagan's containment strategy was not that different from those of his predecessors. Indeed, the broader peace-through-strength perspective sees the Cold War's finale as the product of a long-term policy, applied over the decades.

In any case, although containment certainly played an important role in blocking Soviet expansionism, it cannot explain either the end of the Cold War or the direction of Soviet policy responses. The West's relationship with the Soviet Union was not limited to containment, but included important elements of mutual vulnerability and engagement. The Cold War's end was not simply a result of Western strength but of mutual weakness and intentional engagement as well.

The West Did Not Win

If there is one thing Americans agree on, it is that "we won the Cold War." Unexamined and unchallenged, this simplistic notion is a reminder that we have not come so far in international relations and foreign policy. While it sounds reasonable at first—because democracy seems to be the preferred system for most of our ex-adversaries in Eastern Europe and the former Soviet Union—the claim is presumptuous, ethnocentric and insulting to the people and places it describes.

Everette E. Dennis, *Los Angeles Times*, August 17, 1992.

Most dramatically, the mutual vulnerability created by nuclear weapons overshadowed containment. Nuclear weapons forced the United States and the Soviet Union to eschew war and the serious threat of war as tools of diplomacy and created imperatives for the cooperative regulation of nuclear capability. Both countries tried to fashion nuclear explosives into useful instruments of policy, but they came to the realization—as the joint Soviet-American statement issued from the 1985 Geneva summit put it—that "nuclear war cannot be won and must never be fought." Both countries slowly but surely came to view nuclear weapons as a common threat that must be regulated jointly. Not just containment, but also the overwhelming and common nuclear threat brought the Soviets to the negotiating table. In the shadow of nuclear destruction, common purpose defused traditional antagonisms.

The Pacific West

A second error of the peace-through-strength perspective is the failure to recognize that the West offered an increasingly benign face to the communist world. Traditionally, the Soviets' Marxist-Leninist doctrine held that the capitalist West was inevitably hostile and aggressive, an expectation reinforced by the aggression of capitalist, fascist Germany. Since World War II, the Soviets' principal adversaries had been democratic capitalist states. Slowly but surely, Soviet doctrine acknowledged that the West's behavior did not follow Leninist expectations, but was instead increasingly pacific and cooperative. The Soviet willingness to abandon the Brezhnev Doctrine in the late 1980s in favor of the "Sinatra Doctrine"—under which any East European country could sing, "I did it my way"—suggests a radical transformation in the prevailing Soviet perception of threat from the West. In 1990, the Soviet acceptance of the de facto absorption of communist East Germany into West Germany involved the same calculation with even higher stakes. In accepting the German reunification, despite that country's past aggression, Gorbachev acted on the assumption that the Western system was fundamentally pacific. As Russian foreign minister Andrei Kozyrev noted subsequently, that Western countries are pluralistic democracies "practically rules out the pursuance of an aggressive foreign policy." Thus the Cold War ended despite the assertiveness of Western hardliners, rather than because of it.

The Allure of Decadence

The second front of the Cold War, according to the Reagan victory school, was ideological. Reagan spearheaded a Western ideological offensive that dealt the USSR a death blow. For the Right, driving home the image of the Evil Empire was a decisive stroke rather than a rhetorical flourish. Ideological warfare was such a key front in the Cold War because the Soviet Union was, at its core, an ideological creation. According to the Reagan Right, the supreme vulnerability of the Soviet Union to ideological assault was greatly underappreciated by Western leaders and publics. In that view, the Cold War was won by the West's uncompromising assertion of the superiority of its values and its complete denial of the moral legitimacy of the Soviet system during the 1980s. Western military strength could prevent defeat, but only ideological breakthrough could bring victory. . . .

The end of the Cold War indeed marked an ideological triumph for the West, but not of the sort fancied by the Reagan victory school. Ideology played a far different and more complicated role in inducing Soviet change than the Reagan school allows. As with the military sphere, the Reagan school presents an incomplete picture of Western ideological influence, ignoring the emergence of ideological common ground in stimulating Soviet change.

The ideological legitimacy of the Soviet system collapsed in the eyes of its own citizens not because of an assault by Western ex-leftists, but because of the appeal of Western affluence and permissiveness. The puritanical austerity of Bolshevism's "New

41

Soviet Man" held far less appeal than the "bourgeois decadence" of the West. For the peoples of the USSR and Eastern Europe, it was not so much abstract liberal principles but rather the Western way of life—the material and cultural manifestations of the West's freedoms—that subverted the Soviet vision. Western popular culture—exemplified in rock and roll, television, film, and blue jeans—seduced the communist world far more effectively than ideological sermons by anticommunist activists. As journalist William Echikson noted in his 1990 book *Lighting the Night: Revolution in Eastern Europe*, "instead of listening to the liturgy of Marx and Lenin, generations of would-be socialists tuned in to the Rolling Stones and the Beatles."

If Western popular culture and permissiveness helped subvert communist legitimacy, it is a development of profound irony. Domestically, the New Right battled precisely those cultural forms that had such global appeal. V. I. Lenin's most potent ideological foils were John Lennon and Paul McCartney, not Adam Smith and Thomas Jefferson. The Right fought a two-front war against communism abroad and hedonism and consumerism at home. Had it not lost the latter struggle, the West may not have won the former.

Liberal Ideology

The Reagan victory school argues that ideological assertiveness precipitated the end of the Cold War. While it is true that right-wing American intellectuals were assertive toward the Soviet Union, other Western activists and intellectuals were building links with highly placed reformist intellectuals there. The Reagan victory school narrative ignores that Gorbachev's reform program was based upon "new thinking"—a body of ideas developed by globalist thinkers cooperating across the East-West divide. The key themes of new thinking—the common threat of nuclear destruction, the need for strong international institutions, and the importance of ecological sustainability—built upon the cosmopolitanism of the Marxist tradition and officially replaced the Communist party's class-conflict doctrine during the Gorbachev period.

It is widely recognized that a major source of Gorbachev's new thinking was his close aide and speechwriter, Georgi Shakhnazarov. A former president of the Soviet political science association, Shakhnazarov worked extensively with Western globalists, particularly the New York-based group known as the World Order Models Project. Gorbachev's speeches and policy statements were replete with the language and ideas of globalism. The Cold War ended not with Soviet ideological capitulation to Reagan's anticommunism but rather with a Soviet embrace of globalist themes promoted by a network of liberal internationalists. Those intellectual influences were greatest with the state elite, who had greater access to the West and from whom the reforms originated. . . .

The new conventional wisdom, in both its variants, is seriously misleading. Operating over the last decade, Ronald Reagan's personal anti-nuclearism, rather than his administration's hard line, catalyzed the accommodations to end the Cold War. His administration's effort to go beyond containment and on the offensive was muddled, counter-balanced, and unsuccessful. Operating over the long term, containment helped thwart Soviet expansionism but cannot account for the Soviet domestic failure, the end of East-West struggle, or the direction of the USSR's reorientation. Contrary to the hard-line version, nuclear weapons were decisive in abandoning the conflict by creating common interests.

On the ideological front, the new conventional wisdom is also flawed. The conservatives' anticommunism was far less important in delegitimating the Soviet system than were that system's internal failures and the attraction of precisely the Western "permissive culture" abhorred by the Right. In addition, Gorbachev's attempts to reform communism in the late 1980s were less an ideological capitulation than a reflection of philosophical convergence on the globalist norms championed by liberal internationalists. . . .

In the end, Reagan partisans have been far more successful in claiming victory in the Cold War than they were in achieving it.

"Glasnost, democratization and perestroika—had in the end subverted, discredited and all but done away with . . . [Gorbachev's] Communist Party."

Political Reforms Caused the Collapse of the Soviet Union

Michael Mandelbaum

In the following viewpoint, Michael Mandelbaum argues that the Soviet Union collapsed due to three of Soviet leader Mikhail Gorbachev's reforms: *glasnost*, democratization, and *perestroika*. *Glasnost* freed restrictions on the flow of information, easing the terror which had kept citizens obedient. Democratization allowed the Soviet people, via elections, to express their lack of respect for and disgruntlement with the Communist party. *Perestroika* increased the government's spending while reducing its income, intensifying the country's severe economic crisis. In the end, says Mandelbaum, Gorbachev destroyed the system he had tried to reform. Mandelbaum is a professor of American foreign policy at Johns Hopkins University's Paul H. Nitze School of Advanced International Studies in Baltimore.

As you read, consider the following questions:

1. According to the author, how did democratization backfire on Gorbachev?
2. How did Gorbachev's anti-alcohol campaign hurt the economy, according to Mandelbaum?
3. Why does Mandelbaum believe Gorbachev deserves the Nobel Peace Prize he received in 1990?

From Michael Mandelbaum, "Coup de Grace: The End of the Soviet Union." Reprinted by permission of *Foreign Affairs*, Autumn/Winter 1991/1992. Copyright 1992 by the Council on Foreign Relations, Inc.

On August 24, 1991, three days after the collapse of an attempted coup by a group of high Soviet officials in Moscow, Marshal Sergei Akhromeyev killed himself in his Kremlin office. Mikhail Gorbachev's special adviser on military affairs left a suicide note: "Everything I have worked for is being destroyed."

Akhromeyev had devoted his life to three institutions: the Soviet army, in whose service he had been wounded at Leningrad in 1941 and through whose ranks he had risen to the position of chief of the General Staff (1984-88); the Communist Party, which he had joined at 20 and on whose Central Committee he had served since 1983; and the Union of Soviet Socialist Republics itself, officially founded a year before his birth in 1923. In the wake of the failed coup all three were disintegrating.

The armed forces were divided and disgraced. Entire units had refused to take part in the coup. A number of the troops sent to besiege the Russian parliament building—where a crowd that ultimately numbered 100,000 had gathered to defend the Russian president, Boris Yeltsin, and his government—defected to Yeltsin's side. After the coup had failed Defense Minister Dimitri Yazov and his deputy, Valentin Varennikov, were arrested. Yevgeny I. Shaposhnikov, the newly appointed minister, announced that 80 percent of the army's officers would be replaced because they were politically suspect.

The Communist Party was shattered. As jubilant crowds cheered, statues of communist heroes were pulled down all over Moscow. Gorbachev, shortly after his return from his ordeal in the Crimea, resigned as leader of the party, dissolved the Central Committee, ordered an end to party activity in the military, the security apparatus and the government, and told local party organizations that they would have to fend for themselves.

The union of 15 republics was itself dissolving. In Moscow people began to wave the blue, white and red flag of prerevolutionary Russia. The republics scrambled to declare their independence, the Ukrainian parliament voting for full independence by 321 to 1. For 75 years the vast stretch of Eurasia that was the Soviet Union had been tightly, often brutally controlled from Moscow, which had come to be known as "the center." The president of Armenia, Levon Ter-Petrossian, declared that "the center has committed suicide.". . .

Gorbachev the Destroyer

How did it happen that a mighty imperial state, troubled but stable only a few years before, had come to the brink of collapse in 1991? Who and what were responsible?

The chief architect of the Soviet collapse was Mikhail Gorbachev himself. During the August 1991 coup, as a prisoner of the junta in his Crimean villa, he was the object of a struggle between the partisans of the old order and the champions of liberal values. But it was Gorbachev who had, in the period between his coming to power in 1985 and the fateful days of August 1991, created the conditions that had touched off this struggle.

The Soviet leader had created them unintentionally. His aim had been to strengthen the political and economic systems that he inherited, to strip away their Stalinist accretions and make the Soviet Union a modern dynamic state. Instead he had fatally weakened it. Intending to reform Soviet communism he had, rather, destroyed it. The three major policies that he had launched to fashion a more efficient and humane form of social-ism—glasnost, democratization and perestroika—had in the end subverted, discredited and all but done away with the network of political and economic institutions that his Communist Party had constructed in Russia and surrounding countries since 1917.

Relaxed Controls

The policy of glasnost relaxed bureaucratic controls on infor-mation, broadened the parameters of permitted discussion and thereby enabled the people of the Soviet Union to say more, hear more and learn more about their past and present. Gor-bachev's purpose had been to enlist the intelligentsia in his campaign to revitalize the country and to generate popular pres-sure on the party apparatus, which had resisted the changes he was trying to make. He plainly wanted to encourage criticism of his predecessor, Leonid Brezhnev, and to resume the campaign against Stalin that Nikita Khrushchev had launched but that Brezhnev had ended.

Glasnost, however, did not stop there. The sainted Lenin, and even Gorbachev himself, came in for critical attention. Gor-bachev wanted to foster a reassessment of some selected fea-tures of Soviet life. Instead glasnost called all of it into question, including, ultimately, the role of the general secretary of the Communist Party.

More broadly, the people of the Soviet Union were able for the first time to speak the truth about their history and their lives. That meant that they could learn the truth and could acknowl-edge it to one another. The effect was cathartic, and the cathar-sis had a profound, indeed a revolutionary, impact on Soviet pol-itics. It began to undo the enduring effects of the terror that the Communist Party had routinely practiced during its first three decades in power. Of the first wave of that terror, imposed not by Stalin in the 1930s but by Lenin during the civil war, the his-torian Richard Pipes has written:

> The Red Terror gave the population to understand that under a regime that felt no hesitation in executing innocents, inno-cence was no guarantee of survival. The best hope of surviv-

ing lay in making oneself as inconspicuous as possible, which meant abandoning any thought of independent public activity, indeed any concern with public affairs, and withdrawing into one's private world. Once society disintegrated into an agglomeration of human atoms, each fearful of being noticed and concerned exclusively with physical survival, then it ceased to matter what society thought, for the government had the entire sphere of public activity to itself.

Glasnost enabled the people of the Soviet Union to lay claim to the public sphere after seven decades of exile from it. Through democratization they had the opportunity, for the first time, to act collectively in that sphere. Gorbachev's purpose in permitting elections, again, was to generate popular support for his program. Democratization was to be a political weapon in his battle against the Communist Party apparatus. That apparatus was deeply entrenched, wholly mistrustful of what he was trying to do and generally adept at frustrating his plans. The experiment in democracy that he launched did not demonstrate, as Gorbachev had hoped, that he enjoyed popular support. Rather it showed that two widely held beliefs about the political inclinations of the people of the Soviet Union were wrong.

Party Discredited

Elections discredited the official dictum that the Communist Party had earned public gratitude and support for the "noble far-sighted" leadership it had provided since 1917. They discredited, as well, the view held by many Western students of the Soviet Union that the party did have a measure of legitimacy in the eyes of the population. Its achievements in defeating fascism between 1941 and 1945 and providing a modestly rising living standard thereafter were thought to have earned it a measure of respect, which was reinforced by the political passivity, the resignation to things as they are, that was presumed to be the dominant Russian approach to public life. The elections of 1989 and 1990 showed the people of the Soviet Union to be neither respectful of nor resigned to communist rule.

Democratization also created the opportunity for the beginnings of an alternative to the communist political elite to emerge. In Russia its main orientation was anticommunism and Boris Yeltsin became its leading figure. Outside Russia the opportunity for political participation revealed that popular political allegiance was not to socialism, or the Soviet Union, or to Mikhail Gorbachev, but rather to nationalism, which was deeply anti-Soviet in character.

Glasnost and democratization were, for Gorbachev, means to an end. That end was the improvement of Soviet economic performance. Economic reform was the central feature of his program. When he came to power in 1985 the Soviet elite believed that the regime's principal task was to lift the country out of the economic stagnation into which it had lapsed at the end of the Brezhnev era. Without revived economic growth, they feared, the Soviet Union would fall ever further behind the West in economic and perhaps in military terms. Ultimately it risked being overtaken by China, where Deng Xiaoping's market reforms were producing a surge of growth.

Jac/Pourquoi Pas?/Brussels

Stagnation posed dangers at home as well. Without economic growth the regime would be unable to fulfill its part of the unofficial "social contract," under whose terms the public renounced any say over public affairs in return for a slowly rising standard of living. The revolt of the Polish workers in 1980-81 under the banner of Solidarity served as a cautionary example for the men in the Kremlin.

At first Gorbachev continued the approach that Yuri Andropov had begun in 1982: he tried to impose greater discipline on the work force. The centerpiece of his initial set of economic measures was a highly publicized and intrusive public campaign against the consumption of alcohol. It earned Gorbachev the title of "Mineral Water General Secretary," but did not noticeably reduce Russian drinking. Instead, by forcing people to make their own liquor rather than buying it from the state, the campaign caused shortages of sugar and deprived the government of a large chunk of its income.

This, in turn, contributed to Gorbachev's most enduring and destructive economic legacy: a severe fiscal imbalance. The center's obligations expanded as it poured more and more money into investment and tried to buy public support with generous wage increases. At the same time its income plummeted, as republican governments and enterprises, having gained more power, refused to send revenues to Moscow. In the months before the coup the republics were engaged in what was, in effect, one of the largest tax strikes in history. The fiscal policy of the Brezhnev regime had been relatively strict; Gorbachev's was extremely lax. To cover the widening gap between obligations and income the central government printed rubles at an accelerating pace. By August 1991 the economy was reeling.

A Basic Decency

In the great historical drama that is the collapse of the Soviet Union Mikhail Gorbachev was neither a villain nor a fool— although in retrospect some of the things he did came to seem foolish. He was not a Western-style democrat, but it is scarcely conceivable that someone committed to Western political principles could have risen to the top of the Communist Party of the Soviet Union. His view of socialism, however muddled and contradictory, was plainly more humane than the reality of the system for which he inherited responsibility. For most of his time in power, moreover, he had to fight against the conservatism of that system, which expressed itself mainly in inertia but occasionally in active opposition to his designs. If he came increasingly to seem a political maneuverer, it was because he had to maneuver—or believed that he had to maneuver—to survive in power and to protect the liberal measures already taken.

Finally, and most important, Mikhail Gorbachev's character, however flawed, was marked by a basic decency missing in every previous leader of the Soviet Union and indeed in every ruler of imperial Russia before that. He abjured one of the principal methods by which his predecessors had governed. He refused to shoot. He refused—with the exception of several episodes in the Baltics and the Caucasus in which civilians were killed—to countenance the use of violence against the citizens of his country and of eastern Europe, even when what they did dismayed, angered or appalled him. For this alone he deserved the Nobel Peace Prize he received in the fall of 1990 and deserves as well the place of honor he will occupy in the history of the twentieth century.

But after August 21, 1991 Gorbachev belonged to history, not to the ongoing political life of what had been the Soviet Union. Although he was rescued from enemies who had only recently been colleagues, the act of rescue swept away the institutional platform on which he had stood. He had made his career as a reformer of communism. In the aftermath of the coup there was nothing left to reform.

After the coup failed Russia's second city reverted to the name it had borne before the revolution. Leningrad once again became St. Petersburg. The change symbolized a larger development: everything communism had built since 1917 was now either repudiated or destroyed. It was as if all of the twentieth century had been suddenly repealed. The economic and political systems that had bound together the three hundred million people of what had once been the Soviet Union lay in ruins, leaving uncoordinated fragments. For these people 1991 was what the historian John Lukacs called 1945 for Europeans: Year Zero.

A Commonwealth Without Gorbachev

After several months of drift the two most important pieces of the former Union, Russia and Ukraine, undertook to build a new political structure in its place. On December 1 the people of Ukraine voted overwhelmingly in favor of independence and at the same time elected Leonid Kravchuk, former leader of the Ukrainian Communist Party, as their president. Armed with this mandate, Kravchuk met Yeltsin and Byelorussian President Stanislav Shushkevich at the Byelorussian town of Brest and on December 8 formed the Commonwealth of Independent States.

The signatories were at pains to distinguish their new creation from the old Soviet Union. It was not, they emphasized, a state but rather a grouping of sovereign states, like the British Commonwealth or the European Community. Its headquarters were to be located not in Moscow but in the Byelorussian capital, Minsk. The non-Slavic republics of the old union were not included in the Commonwealth's founding meeting, and Mikhail Gorbachev learned of it only after it had taken place.

Other republics protested, and two weeks later, on December 22, in the Kazakh capital, Alma-Ata, the Commonwealth was "refounded," this time including 11 of the former Soviet republics. Gorbachev also objected to the new association. Since August he had tried to assemble a new, looser union. Yeltsin had been content to let him try. In the wake of the Ukrainian referendum, however, it became clear that Ukrainian authorities would not join any entity headed by Gorbachev. Yeltsin therefore abandoned him. After December 8 Gorbachev launched a last flurry of meetings in an attempt to salvage a position for himself, issued apocalyptic warnings about the fate of the Commonwealth, then gave up. On Christmas Day, 1991, he resigned as president of a country that no longer existed.

6

"The disintegration of the Soviet state was due in significant part to autonomous changes in Soviet civil society."

Political Reforms Alone Did Not Cause the Collapse of the Soviet Union

Francis Fukuyama

Francis Fukuyama is a resident consultant in the Washington, D.C., office of the Rand Corporation, a nonprofit think tank, and the author of *The End of History and the Last Man*. He is well known for his controversial belief that the fall of communism marked the end of conflicts over political and economic ideologies. In the following viewpoint, he argues that the collapse of the Soviet Union was not simply the result of Mikhail Gorbachev's political reforms. According to Fukuyama, Soviet institutions had been decentralizing and communism had been losing its credibility in the minds of the populace for years before the system broke up. The collapse of the country, says Fukuyama, was the consequence of its evolution to a modern industrial economy and an educated urban population.

As you read, consider the following questions:

1. According to Fukuyama, in what ways did a proto-civil society prepare the republics for the transition to democracy?
2. How did the ending of terror contribute to the decentralization of power, according to the author?
3. According to Fukuyama, how did education influence the Soviet military?

From Francis Fukuyama, "The Modernizing Imperative: The USSR as an Ordinary Country," *The National Interest*, Spring 1993. Reprinted with permission.

The Gorbachev-era earthquake that led to the collapse of communism and the disintegration of the Soviet state was due in significant part to autonomous changes in Soviet civil society, changes that were in some respects no different from the type of social evolution going on in other regions and countries with no experience of totalitarianism. The failure of a large section of the Sovietological community to perceive these underlying changes accounts in some measure for their blindness in not being able to anticipate the coming revolution.

Before making the case that changes occurring in civil society were important factors both in the collapse and in our blindness about the collapse, let me state at the beginning a number of caveats and qualifications. It should be absolutely clear that the Gorbachev-era earthquake had fundamentally political causes, which were its *sine qua non*. Perestroika was in no way a revolution from below. Frederick Starr's assertion that Mikhail Gorbachev merely uncorked change rather than created it goes too far, and those like Jerry Hough who argue that the USSR had become a pluralistic, participatory society prior to the late 1980s understand neither pluralism nor participation. It is perfectly possible to imagine substantially different and quite plausible outcomes to the events of the 1980s, given changes in the personalities involved. If Yuri Andropov or Konstantin Chernenko had been younger and/or healthier men, perestroika most likely would never have happened. If Viktor Grishin had won the subsequent power struggle, if Gorbachev's personality had been different, if he had been less adroit in political maneuvering or Yegor Ligachev more so, the entire sequence of events leading to the collapse of the Soviet Union would have been derailed and might never have happened. Moreover, to say that civil society was a factor is not to deny the myriad of other causes that contributed to the collapse, including pressures from the international system, and the United States in particular. One can argue that a healthy Andropov would have put off the collapse only for a decade or so, but the importance of such purely political factors is undeniable, and perhaps even central in explaining these events.

From Below

On the other hand, political factors do not tell the whole story. For while the major mileposts of Soviet reform may have been initiated from above, they received crucial support, or at least acquiescence, from below. The Soviet intelligentsia did not react suspiciously to glasnost, but rather embraced it enthusiastically and proceeded to push the boundaries of the permissible in journalism and the arts. Soviet voters, when given a chance to express a preference, did not elect the old apparatus or neo-fascist

Russian nationalists; they voted in 1990-91 for candidates from Democratic Russia and for Boris Yeltsin. Elites in the different Union republics organized themselves quickly into nationalist groups once given the chance, despite the fact that many Western Sovietologists believed they had been successfully assimilated as "new Soviet men." And finally, perhaps the most important factor was not what happened in civil society, but what did not happen: the old system's entrenched interests, particularly the Party, the army, and the police, did not act decisively to end the reform process, as they were designed to do. Clearly, something had happened "from below" to make all this possible. . . .

What we must look for are not concrete civil institutions prior to Gorbachev, but a "proto-civil society" that laid the groundwork for what was to follow. This proto-civil society is evident in two respects. The first were changes in Soviet institutions that reduced their functionality as guardians of Soviet power, and became the basis for the emergence of a new, non-Soviet civil society after perestroika. The second were changes in consciousness—that is, in the way that elites and the population more broadly thought about their own system and its legitimacy, which in turn influenced how they would respond to revolutionary change when it was initiated from above.

A Diffusion of Power

In the first category, there was a clear diffusion of power within the Soviet Communist Party from the center to the periphery, on a republic, an *oblast* (regional government), and even a local party level. It was a truism of the classical model of totalitarianism that while the party rules called for democracy from below, the reality was always strictly dictatorship from above. But by the early 1970s there was growing evidence that the lower reaches of the party were acquiring a substantial degree of bargaining leverage against the center. This was evident in economic affairs, where powerful *oblast* first secretaries were in a position to stymie reforms and initiatives coming from Moscow, just as enterprise directors were in a position to resist orders from central and republican ministries. The various economic and political institutes of the USSR Academy of Sciences, many designed as propaganda instruments, quickly became sources of intellectual opposition to the old Soviet state. The decentralization of Soviet institutions was most clearly evident in certain of the Union republics, where the local party organization in effect became entities independent of the central committee apparatus back in Moscow. While Leonid Brezhnev played a critical role in placing his friend Sharaf Rashidov as first secretary of the Uzbek Communist Party, it was Rashidov and not the Central Committee personnel department who thereafter controlled most appointments in the Uzbek Party apparatus. Moscow may have tolerated the vast, corrupt cotton empire off which Rashidov got rich, but it did not create or control it.

The growth of official "mafias" within the Communist Party was paralleled by the growth of mafias outside it. To this day we do not have reliable statistics on the size of the informal economy during the Brezhnev period, but estimates for the size of its overall contribution to Soviet GNP [gross national product] range as high as 25 percent. Much of this economic activity outside the official plan was either the work of private entrepreneurs—mostly *kolkhozniks* raising fruits and vegetables in their garden plots—or was carried out by informal groups who performed arbitrage, middleman, and even manufacturing functions. Though these sorts of activities flourished most in the non-Slavic republics, even in Russia they constituted an important source of flexibility in the otherwise rigidly controlled economy.

The importance of this "proto-civil society" is evident from subsequent events. In many cases, it was the local party organization, like Algidas Brazauskas's Lithuanian Communist Party, that took up nationalist themes and propelled the republics toward independence. In other cases, rather than form independent political parties, reformers were able to hijack parts of the old CPSU [Communist Party of the Soviet Union] and government structures, and use them to advance reformist aims. This is essentially what Yeltsin did with the Russian Federation's structures in 1990-91. Indeed, without the concept of a proto-civil society, it would be impossible to account for the great differences in post-communist political development in Eastern Europe. Those countries with more developed proto-civil societies, like Poland and Hungary, were much better able to make a transition to genuine democratic structures later. . . .

The Realm of Consciousness

It was in the realm of consciousness, however, that totalitarianism failed most completely. Gorbachev did not force the Soviet intelligentsia to take up the cause of reform. Brezhnev-era academic institutes were staffed with several echelons of economists who were familiar with "bourgeois" Western economic theory and ready to implement it. From the late Brezhnev period on, the Soviet intelligentsia had almost complete access to contemporary Western materials, regardless of ideological content. Within the party itself the corrective mechanisms that were supposed to keep the totalitarian machine on course failed, largely because critical people in its apparatus came quickly to see the old system as illegitimate. Not only could Gorbachev tap the Yakovlevs, Shevardnadzes, and Yeltsins for top posts, but custodians of the old system throughout the party, army, and police of the kind who in 1964 conspired to remove Khrushchev from power did not have the competence or the drive to do so in the late 1980s. (Yegor Ligachev has told Western audiences that no one in the Politburo even considered the possibility of intervention during the emigration crisis in East Germany in mid-1989.)

Chuck Asay, by permission of the *Colorado Springs Gazette Telegraph.*

As a measure of the broader Soviet population's ability to think for itself, the various elections that were held beginning in 1990 could serve as a limited but revealing measure. In the local elections held in the spring of 1990, candidates from the liberal Democratic Russia movement won fifty-seven of sixty-five seats in Moscow; while seventy "patriotic" nationalist or neo-Bolshevik candidates ran, only two were elected. The percentages of votes for "democrats" were lower in provincial cities and in the countryside, but this kind of voting pattern is absolutely typical for non-communist democratizing countries at a comparable level of social development. The Party apparatus put its weight behind electing Nikolai Ryzhkov in the election for Russian president in June 1991, and there were plenty of other unsavory authoritarian candidates who could have been elected. But it was for Boris Yeltsin that Russians voted.

If we want to explain why the political system began to diffuse power, and why there emerged a broad crisis in the Soviet belief system, we can look to two sorts of explanations, one particular to totalitarian systems, the other a more general one applicable to all societies. The first concerned the inability of totalitarianism to perpetuate itself in a pure form. The crucial event in this respect was the ending of the terror. For once it became clear that the state would not kill or incarcerate large numbers of people to enforce its rule, the balance of power between the state and society began to shift. From now on, failure of a ministry, region, or enterprise to meet its plan targets would not be punishable by death or imprisonment. Coercion took many other forms than outright terror, of course, and kept the nature of autonomous social action within strict limits. Still, the cessation of terror meant that the state-Party apparatus would increasingly have to bribe or cajole economic actors to get them to do its bidding.

Totalitarianism Outgrown

But the more important types of long-term social changes leading to the breakdown of the Soviet system were characteristic of non-communist societies as well. They had to do with the political effects of the transition from an agricultural economy to a modern industrial one. In this respect, Soviet society developed much like other non-communist ones; totalitarianism delayed but did not derail the political development process in the USSR. The imperatives of industrial maturity eventually forced a breakdown of the political system because truly modern technological societies cannot flourish except in an atmosphere permitting a certain degree of freedom.

The reasons for this are most evident in the economic sphere. Centrally planned socialism was a perfectly adequate engine of economic growth through the stage of industrialization represented by Europe or America in the year 1940, and characterized by heavy industries like steel, chemicals, and automobiles that populated the American Midwestern rust belt. But in the subsequent half century of economic development, modern economies have become vastly more complex, information- and communications-intensive, service oriented, dependent on constant technological innovation, and requiring increasingly high skill levels in the labor force. Under these circumstances economic decision-making has to become decentralized to be efficient. *Goskomtsen*, the former Soviet state committee on prices, reviewed some 200,000 prices per year, which represented 42 percent of all price decisions in the Soviet Union. This represents only a tiny fraction of the number of prices determined by markets in an advanced industrial economy like Japan or the United States, where a single airliner can consist of over a million different parts, each with its own price. The economic aspects of socialism clashed head-on, therefore, with the broad direction of modern industrial development.

Beyond economics, industrial maturity has a major impact on social and political attitudes as well. In Raymond Aron's phrase, "technological complexity will strengthen the managerial class at the expense of the ideologists and militants." It is very hard to keep the elites of modern industrial societies isolated from larger trends in the world given the rapid proliferation of communications technologies. The populations of complex, modern urban societies, increasingly well-educated and cosmopolitan, begin demanding more than simple security and food on the table. Above all, they begin to demand recognition of themselves and their social status, expressed as a demand for individual rights and political participation. While illiterate peasants in an agricultural society may defer to the authority of a landlord, warlord, or commissar, it is much less likely that a college-educated manager, scientist, or journalist will do so. In this respect, the Soviet Union was no different from Spain, Portugal, Taiwan, South Korea, or any other country that has made the transition from an agricultural to an urban-industrial society in the past couple of generations.

Technology, Education, Awareness

The view that technocrats would be the "gravediggers of communism" has been much ridiculed over the years, because the technological imperative could be violated by political authorities for so long. (One notorious example of this was the aircraft designer Andrei Tupolev, who did some of his most innovative work while a prisoner in Stalin's gulag.) But while the Party could delay the technological imperative, they could not put it off forever if they were to remain militarily and economically competitive with the West. The scientific elite had increasing contact with their Western counterparts over the years; the industrial/managerial elite had less, but promotion within it was nonetheless based on performance, not ideology. (A typical example of this generation was Gorbachev's second-to-last prime minister, Nikolai Ryzhkov, a technocrat and former head of a giant manufacturing conglomerate, Uralmash, who complacently supported perestroika until some time in 1990, when it had already become too late to turn back the clock.)

Part of the reason that the political effects of economic modernization were slow to be felt had to do with its forced nature. Between 1926 and 1960, the Soviet population went from 18 percent urban to approximately 49 percent. Such figures overstate the real degree of modernization that took place, however: a Soviet factory worker in the late 1950s was still a displaced peasant working on a deliberately simplified assembly line. This population had a much lower level of literacy, much less formal education, than their counterparts in Western Europe or the United States. Moreover, as Moshe Lewin has pointed out, much of the statistical urbanization that took place in this period was in fact the simple transplanting of entire peasant villages into urban areas, where the mores and social relationships of the countryside still prevailed. But in the generation following Khrushchev, a broader and deeper social modernization process occurred. The urban population grew to 65 percent of the total by 1985. As late as 1959, 91 percent of workers and 98 percent of peasants had no more than a four year elementary school education, while by 1985 the figure for manual workers was only 18 percent. By Gorbachev's time, fifteen million Soviet citizens had received a higher education.

The importance of this kind of broad socio-economic modernization is evident if one looks at the role of the military. In China, Deng Xiaoping and his conservative allies were able to call in a peasant army from the provinces to put down the student protesters in Tiananmen Square in 1989. In the former Soviet Union, by contrast, the military units called into Moscow by the State Committee for the State of Emergency on August 19, 1991, proved to be very unreliable counterrevolutionaries. The officers and soldiers were not peasant boys, unfamiliar with and distrustful of city ways; many appeared to be as politically aware as the Muscovite population they were intended to suppress. The Red Army of the 1950s, by contrast, would have consisted largely of politically inert peasants, who would not have felt any squeamishness about killing unruly civilians. . . .

Another Troubled State

Now that everyone admits the Cold War is over, it is time for Sovietology to come out of its conceptual ghetto. Russia is today just another troubled state, trying to make a difficult simultaneous transition to both democracy and markets. If it relapses into authoritarianism of either a Russian nationalist or neo-Bolshevik form, it is unlikely that the new rulers would attempt to revive the totalitarian experiment, and even less likely that they would succeed even if they were to try. The skills that students of the Soviet successor states will have to bring to bear will not be different in essence from those of students of other regions: they will have to become familiar with problems of democratization and economic modernization in Asia and Latin America, and apply broader developmental models to their part of the world. And those seeking a retrospective account of the collapse of communist systems will have to open their eyes as well to the forms of proto-civil society that existed in the former communist world.

Periodical Bibliography

The following articles have been selected to supplement the diverse views presented in this chapter.

Bob Abernethy   "Pilgrims at the Barricade," *Sojourners*, November 1991.

Peter J. Boettke   "Why Perestroika Failed," *The Freeman*, March 1992. Available from The Foundation for Economic Education, Irvington-on-Hudson, NY 10533.

George Bush   "A New Crusade to Reap the Rewards of Our Global Victory," *Vital Speeches of the Day*, September 15, 1992.

Anthony R. Dolan   "Premeditated Prose: Reagan's Evil Empire," *The American Enterprise*, March/April 1993.

Theodore Draper   "Who Killed Soviet Communism?" *The New York Review of Books*, June 11, 1992.

Charles H. Fairbanks Jr. "The Nature of the Beast," *The National Interest*, Spring 1993. Available from PO Box 3000, Denville, NJ 07834.

Martin Malia   "Leninist Endgame," *Daedalus*, Spring 1992.

Adam Meyerson   "Ronald Reagan: Terminator," *Policy Review*, Winter 1992.

Stephen Miller   "The Soviet Coup and the Benefits of Breakdown," *Orbis*, Winter 1992.

Peter Reddaway   "The Role of Popular Discontent," *The National Interest*, Spring 1993.

Phyllis Schlafly   "Setting the Record Straight," *The Phyllis Schlafly Report*, December 1992. Available from PO Box 618, Alton, IL 62002.

Serge Schmemann   "A Russian Is Swept Aside by Forces He Unleashed," *The New York Times*, December 15, 1991.

Stephen Sestanovich   "Did the West Undo the East?" *The National Interest*, Spring 1993.

Ronald Suny   "Incomplete Revolution: National Movements and the Collapse of the Soviet Empire," *New Left Review*, September/October 1991.

How Will the Breakup of the Soviet Union Affect the World?

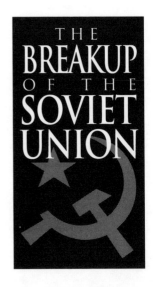

Chapter Preface

The collapse of the Soviet Union marked the end of the cold war era and heralded a new, possibly more peaceful time in world history. As political science professor Ted Hopf states, "One could easily believe that the collapse of the Soviet Union is all to the good. The military threat that emanated from Moscow throughout the cold war has been all but eliminated. Peoples whose identities were suppressed for three-quarters of a century under Communist rule, and as long as 250 years under Russian rule, can now exercise their right to national self-determination. Socialist economic practices are being consigned to the dustbin of history."

Not all of the hopes for a tranquil new era, however, have come to pass. The positive changes cited by Hopf have been accompanied by what he calls a "dark and dangerous side" marked by an increased risk of nuclear proliferation, nationalism and ethnic conflict, and other threats to peace and stability. The vacuum left by the collapse of the totalitarian Soviet empire has already opened the door to long-repressed, deep-seated ethnic hatreds in Yugoslavia, for example.

Clearly, few observers of international affairs would wish for a return to the cold war era. But the negative consequences of the collapse of the Soviet Union make some wonder if the collapse was a mixed blessing. The authors in the following chapter evaluate how the demise of the Soviet empire has affected the world.

"The collapse of centralized authority over the territory of the former Soviet Union . . . has increased the danger of nuclear proliferation."

The Breakup Increases the Threat of Nuclear Proliferation

Daniel Ellsberg, interviewed by Jerry Sanders and Richard Caplan

Daniel Ellsberg is a senior research associate at the Center for Psychological Studies in the Nuclear Age at Harvard Medical School in Cambridge, Massachusetts. He is perhaps best known for disclosing the Pentagon Papers in 1971, thereby revealing the U.S. government's cover-up concerning the extent of American involvement in Vietnam. In the following viewpoint, Ellsberg explains that the former Soviet Union is now an unstable region with an extensive stockpile of nuclear weapons. This fact poses a threat to the world, Ellsberg maintains, for the emerging republics may be tempted to use or sell the weapons, thereby increasing the risk of nuclear proliferation. Ellsberg is interviewed by Jerry Sanders, a professor at University of California, Berkeley, and Richard Caplan, editor of *World Policy Journal*, a quarterly journal of social and political thought.

As you read, consider the following questions:

1. In what two ways could the collapse of the Soviet Union encourage proliferation, according to Ellsberg?
2. Why does the author believe central control over the republics' nuclear weapons may not necessarily reduce the nuclear threat?

From Daniel Ellsberg, interviewed by Jerry Sanders and Richard Caplan, "Nuclear Security and the Soviet Collapse," *World Policy Journal*, Winter 1992-93. Reprinted with permission.

World Policy: How real are the dangers posed by the break-down of Soviet central control over nuclear weapons—the possibility that they will be used in a civil conflict between former Soviet republics, the prospect of diversion of fissionable materials and nuclear-weapons technology, and so forth?

Ellsberg: I think all of these concerns are valid and a basis for real anxiety over the long run. With the creation of the new commonwealth, it appears that the danger of conflict involving nuclear-armed forces on the territory of the former Soviet Union has been alleviated, at least in the short run. But the first real test of the stability of the commonwealth and the republican regimes lies just ahead, with harsh economic reforms in the dead of winter.

We can't rule out the possibility that economic problems and ethnic unrest will produce civil conflict sometime down the road, raising the horrible possibility of what former Secretary James Baker has called, "Yugoslavia with nukes." And even in the absence of internal conflict, the collapse of centralized authority over the territory of the former Soviet Union and the general erosion of social discipline has increased the danger of nuclear proliferation in a variety of ways, both in the immediate future and in the long run.

This is an urgent situation. Unless we can bring about a drastic change in the postures of the United States and other nuclear states toward policies of minimum deterrence and no first use, proliferation brings with it an increased likelihood in the long run that nuclear weapons, at least in limited numbers, will be exploded somewhere. This danger exists even though—and in part because—the ending of the Cold War has sharply reduced the risk that a crisis or limited war might escalate to all-out nuclear war.

No Central Control Increases Threat

World Policy: How, exactly, could the disintegration of the Soviet empire encourage proliferation?

Ellsberg: In two ways. First, the mere fact that the number of nuclear powers has been expanded almost overnight by four or more nuclear states is a setback to the nonproliferation regime, and could encourage other countries that might be on the verge of going nuclear to do so. More importantly, there is the potential for a hemorrhaging of fissionable material from the stockpiles of plutonium in the Soviet nuclear complex, as well as for the diversion of weapons components and even finished weapons. The breakdown of central authority and military discipline in the Soviet Union has created a situation in which practical control over the Soviets' 27,000 warheads—and especially the 17,000 tactical warheads—is very much in question. And the increased number of nuclear states makes it more likely that some of them will deviate from the nonproliferation aims they all profess to share.

World Policy: What about the formation of a new commonwealth and Russian President Yeltsin's statements during Baker's December 1991 trip to Moscow that all nuclear weapons will be under centralized command? Aren't these encouraging developments?

Ellsberg: Yes, but I think such assurances are premature and overstated. No simple assurances by any set of political authorities—or military commanders, for that matter—can eliminate the uncertainties surrounding nuclear weapons. Even under the new commonwealth, we are still facing an uncertain period in which various parts of the system controlling those weapons—in other words, the various former republics where these weapons were deployed—may well have differing objectives and even be in conflict with each other.

And for all the talk of a unified military command, it is unclear how that will be translated into physical safeguarding and control of the actual weapons, especially the tactical weapons. Tactical weapons, after all, were never under the same kind of tight, hierarchic, centralized control as strategic weapons, but were linked with individual military units. These units answer increasingly to republican, rather than central, authorities. And no one even seems to know precisely how many tactical weapons there are—or where they are located.

The *New York Times* reported the statements of U.S. officials that there were no tactical weapons outside the four republics that had strategic weapons, namely Kazakhstan, Byelorussia, Russia, and Ukraine. Well, that was a reassuring assertion, except that it was contradicted the very same day by stories in *Time*, *Newsweek*, and the *Los Angeles Times*, all of which maintained that there were still weapons outside those republics. The fact is, Soviet officials have said for years they have had tactical weapons in virtually all of the republics. Although at least some of those were apparently withdrawn from Azerbaijan and Armenia and the Baltic states, at this moment there seems to be a good deal of uncertainty as to just how many republics have such weapons and how many they have. Even in Moscow they may not know for sure, let alone in the republics themselves. There is great need for international cooperation on these matters—at Western expense, if necessary—and it can't come too quickly.

CIS Might Share Expertise

World Policy: If central control over nuclear weapons is consolidated, will we then be able to breathe easy?

Ellsberg: Not necessarily. Even that would not guarantee that there will be no leakage of nuclear technology. Because of the changes in the world environment and the economic difficulties it faces, the new commonwealth may not be as restrained about supporting other countries' nuclear efforts as the Soviet Union was in the past. The commonwealth could choose to follow in the footsteps of France or China, both of which have given significant aid in terms of expertise, testing, and perhaps even nuclear materials to other countries.

Tom Meyer. Reprinted with permission.

World Policy: What incentives would the commonwealth have for sharing nuclear expertise and technology?

Ellsberg: The same kinds of incentives that influence France and China—a need for hard cash, and a desire to enhance its diplomatic influence and strengthen its relationships with other countries by providing them with something they value highly. In the case of the former Soviets, of course, one has to emphasize cash above all. In the absence of massive Western aid, their need for hard currency is desperate, and nuclear weapons are, pound for pound, the greatest conceivable hard currency-earning export. For example, as Arjun Makhijani has pointed out, some 25 tons of plutonium were produced for the Soviets' breeder reactor program, which was then cancelled. This plutonium is just sitting there, not being used for anything. The incentive for the central government to sell some of it clandestinely is very large. By way of comparison, consider the challenge to police departments of storing as evidence huge caches of confiscated cocaine or heroin. It has a tendency to melt away—part of it, sometimes, to finance departmental programs like buying informants.

World Policy: Is there also the danger that individuals acting on their own initiative will contribute to nuclear proliferation?

Ellsberg: Yes. According to Chris Paine of NRDC [Natural Resources Defense Council] there are some 3,000 to 5,000 individuals with top security clearance out of perhaps 10,000 who work in the Soviet nuclear complex. Their incomes have been drastically cut now both by inflation and by the reduction in production. So they are individually subject to the same pressures as the commonwealth as a whole and the individual republics, and may seek to improve their incomes by yielding to the blandishments of "headhunters" from states with prospective nuclear programs. . . .

Confusing Reports

World Policy: What is your view of the statements of some major republics in the former Soviet Union that they want to be nuclear-free zones?

Ellsberg: Obviously, that is always a very welcome statement, whenever it is made. It was the position that the leaders of Ukraine, Kazakhstan and Byelorussia took prior to the August 1991 coup attempt, when they all were, in effect, provinces of the empire. And it is what Ukraine and Byelorussia reiterated to Secretary Baker. But in between, reports of each of their positions have varied so frequently that it is hard to be entirely confident of what their policies will be in the future. That applies not only to these three republics but to some others that may now have tactical weapons.

Russia has indicated all along that it means to keep strategic nuclear weapons as long as the United States does. Kazakhstan recently said it plans to keep nuclear weapons so long as Russia has any. Ukraine and Byelorussia now say that they want to become nuclear-free zones as soon as possible, even if Russia retains some nuclear missiles. But if civil strife erupts, leading to the prospect of conflict between republics, I wouldn't be surprised to see Ukraine's President Leonid Kravchuk or a successor revert to a position similar to Kazakhstan's. . . .

Kravchuk's reiteration of the intention to make Ukraine a nuclear-free area was apparently motivated by an urgent desire for U.S. recognition and aid. It indicates that the Ukrainians are now more concerned about their relations with the United

States than about their relations with a nuclear-armed Russia. Their willingness to forgo nuclear weapons is welcome, but it seems too soon to be sure that their position will not shift back again, before the weapons are gone. The point of this observation is not be be pessimistic, but to recognize the urgency of cooperating with Ukraine's latest commitment to become nuclear-free quickly, acting in every way to support it, and encouraging others to follow the same path.

Almost surely that means acting in a variety of ways to encourage Russia, too, to make the maximum reduction of its strategic forces, to eliminate tactical weapons, and meanwhile to reaffirm the Soviet commitment to forgo the threat or implementation of first-use of nuclear weapons under any circumstances.

First-Use Nuclear Threat

What I found during my visit to Moscow was that this last commitment on the part of the Russians can no longer be taken for granted. . . . I was told by Andrei Kortunov, a leading strategic analyst at the USA and Canada Institute—he is known as the author of a radical proposal for the Soviet Union's unilateral adoption of a minimum deterrence posture of 500 mobile warheads—that for cost reasons there was likely to be "a resuscitation of nuclear weapons" in the states of the former Soviet Union, including Russia. Because of budget constraints, he said, there was a growing conviction that "we cannot afford to defend our far-flung frontiers—against the Chinese or Central Asians—with conventional means alone."

I was appalled. He was, of course, referring not to deterrence of nuclear attack but to a supposed need for first-use nuclear threats. If such views were coming to prevail, it meant that the Soviet commitment to no first-use, our aspirations for a nuclear-free world, and even hopes for the abolition of tactical weapons were all moribund.

What I was hearing was the very reasoning, based on costs and budgets, that had led to the Eisenhower "new look" policy in 1953 of primary reliance on nuclear weapons: "more bang for the buck." The belief that nuclear weapons were a relatively cheap and effective—and adequately prudent and legitimate— substitute for conventional defenses had led, over the course of 30 years, to the seeding of Western and Eastern Europe with tens of thousands of tactical weapons and to their backup by 25,000 strategic weapons on hair-trigger alert.

The same belief could keep thousands of these same warheads in Russia and half a dozen other republics indefinitely, and encourage thousands of new ones in other countries around the world. Under these circumstances, I couldn't believe that another 40 years of limited wars and nuclear threats would pass without any of those weapons exploding on people.

It was precisely because this proposed Russian policy was, as Kortunov pointed out in a later conversation, "just what NATO had done, after all," that I was so dismayed. He was projecting a replay, in post-Soviet Russia in the post-Cold War era, of the most irresponsibly dangerous policy choices that had ever been made in human history. . . .

How Nuclear Weapons Are Used

World Policy: What exactly do these new states see as the advantages of possessing nuclear weapons?

Ellsberg: There is a common notion that nuclear weapons have never been used and have never proven useful since Hiroshima. I have argued for some years that this is false. Even if they are never actually detonated in combat, officials of nuclear states have perceived a number of uses for these weapons.

It is precisely this range of purposes that the Ukraine, Kazakhstan, and others began discovering as soon as they started thinking of themselves potentially as independent, sovereign possessors of these weapons. Not to my surprise, they very quickly began to think of a number of reasons to retain these weapons, especially when they noticed that they were next door to a large, overbearing neighbor with an aggressive, expansionist history, which not only was armed to the teeth with nuclear weapons but also had an enormous conventional superiority.

Nuclear weapons are useful, for instance, for acquiring international prestige and influence, and for gaining access to international councils. They are also useful for attracting attention, causing concern, and ensuring that a country is taken seriously. Ukraine has recently experienced all these benefits, as have the other nuclear republics.

A more esoteric objective in possessing nuclear weapons is to have what Seymour Hersh, in the title of his book, has called the "Samson option." Under the Samson option, a country threatens to use nuclear weapons, even in a potentially self-destructive way, in order to convince an ally or patron to rally to its side in order to forestall the need to carry out this threat. According to Hersh, Israel's nuclear program was primarily intended for the purpose of influencing the United States in this manner. If the Israelis needed and did not get full U.S. support in a crisis, they would threaten or warn that they had no choice but to use nuclear weapons, with potentially uncontrollable results. In particular, they were prepared to target the Soviet Union, so that the United States would face the possibility of escalation to an all-out nuclear war. According to Hersh, Israel used its nuclear weapons in precisely this way in the 1973 war, with precisely the desired effect of convincing a reluctant

United States to resupply the Israeli military. The French, too, always privately believed that what they were buying with their independent nuclear force was the ability to compel the United States to support them in a crisis.

World Policy: Would that same logic be applicable, say, to Kazakhstan today?

Ellsberg: Of course. And maybe Ukraine again tomorrow. If Russia ever began to make heavy moves to "protect" the Russian population across its Kazakh border, a Kazakhstan armed with nuclear weapons could count on getting much more attention for its point of view from the international community, and more helpful pressure on Russia to back off, than a Kazakhstan that had surrendered a nuclear monopoly to Russia, as Ukraine has been persuaded to do, at least for now. And that is true even if the implied threat of Kazakh first use looked suicidal or relied on a possible loss of control by leaders in Alma Ata to be credible. . . .

A Nuclear-Free World

World Policy: Do you have a wish for the new year?

Ellsberg: That the nuclear era would end with the Cold War. Of course, that's not what is happening. The superpower arms race is over (though in terms of strategic arsenals it has not gone into reverse, at least in any serious way), but the era of nuclear proliferation may be about to begin.

Whether we avert disaster will depend on a lot of things, including the activities of those of us inside and outside of government who believe that the nuclear era should end now. The problem is that a long, drawn out, piecemeal approach is unlikely to have much impact on the proliferation problem the world is facing. What's needed is a dramatic and comprehensive package of coordinated changes in policies and programs—an effort of the highest priority that expresses the desire of our society and our government to make a decisive shift in our relation to nuclear weapons.

"Besides Russia, each republic has declared its intention of getting rid of its nuclear inheritance."

The Breakup May Not Increase the Threat of Nuclear Proliferation

William Walker

"Who is controlling the region's nuclear weapons?" was one of the first concerns expressed by defense experts after the fall of the Soviet Union. These experts worry that extremists might gain control over the weapons, or that the new republics will sell their nuclear stockpile for much-needed hard currency. In the following viewpoint, William Walker agrees that these are concerns, but argues that the collapse of the Soviet Union may actually reduce proliferation. The republics, he states, have pledged to disarm. In addition, international attempts to decrease proliferation should also help reduce the threat posed by the region's nuclear weapons. Walker is senior fellow at the Science Policy Research Unit at the University of Sussex in England.

As you read, consider the following questions:

1. What four main dangers are posed by the collapse of the Soviet Union, according to Walker?
2. What does the author mean when he refers to the "lack of transparency" as a problem?
3. What are the "opportunities" that might decrease nuclear proliferation, in Walker's opinion?

From William Walker, "Nuclear Weapons and the Former Soviet Republics," *International Affairs*, April 1992, © 1992, Royal Institute of International Affairs. Reprinted with permission.

The Soviet Union has fallen apart. While empires come and go, the disintegration of this empire confronts the international community with a unique problem: how to cope with the arsenals of nuclear weapons which are dispersed across the former imperial territories. How many weapons are there, and where are they? Who will control them and the production facilities which gave rise to them? Will the new republics be bound by international treaties and agreements? How will nuclear relations between one republic and another, and between the republics and the external nuclear weapon states, be stabilized? How can the dismantling of the republics' nuclear arsenals be managed and financed?

At present, there are few clear answers to these questions. There is concern, however, that the issues should be addressed urgently in case the political situation worsens. There are four main dangers. The first is that the republics will not only take possession of the weapons on their territories, but will begin to re-target them on each other and on other countries. The second is that nuclear weapons will become embroiled in civil wars or other conflicts within and between the republics. A loss of central control raises the spectre of nuclear terrorism, and of serious risk to health and the environment. The third is that nuclear weapons, or more likely the materials, technologies and human expertise involved in their manufacture, will spill over into other countries seeking to acquire weapon capabilities. A disintegrating Soviet Union could thus lead to weapon proliferation inside *and* outside its territories. The fourth is that the emergence of several nuclear weapon states in the Soviet territories would increase the incentives for countries in Asia and the Middle East to acquire nuclear arms. Moreover, it would seriously damage the Nuclear Non-Proliferation Treaty (NPT) in the approach to the 1995 extension conference.

An Intent to Disarm

These are the dangers. It needs stressing, however, that the situation is by no means beyond remedy. Although three republics besides Russia—Ukraine, Kazakhstan and Belarus (formerly Byelorussia)—now hold large numbers of nuclear weapons, they seem to be regarding them mainly as bargaining chips. Besides Russia, each republic has declared its intention of getting rid of its nuclear inheritance. The main question has been how this can be managed, by whom, and on which and whose terms; and whether it can be achieved in time to prevent the kinds of horrors mentioned above.

There is also a positive side to the breakdown of the massive Soviet commitment to nuclear weapons. The bulk of US and Soviet nuclear weaponry has already been withdrawn from Cen-

71

tral Europe. If the new republics, including Russia, press ahead with destroying all or the great majority of their nuclear weapons, a large part of the Eurasian land mass will become free of them. Together with an intensified effort to stem the spread of weapons in the Middle East, Asia and Latin America, nuclear disarmament could become a realistic goal rather than the empty pledge it has been these past 50 years, leaving the NPT strengthened rather than weakened. . . .

Strategic Nuclear Weapons in the Soviet Territories

Republic	Sites or Bases	Launchers	Warheads	(%)
Russia				
ICBM	24	1,064	4,278	
HB	4	122	367	
SLBM	2	940	2,804	
Sub-total: warheads in Russia			7,449	(72)
Ukraine				
ICBM	2	176	1,240	
HB	2	101	168	
Sub-total: warheads in Ukraine			1,408	(14)
Kazakhstan				
ICBM	2	104	1,040	
HB	1	40	320	
Sub-total: warheads in Kazakhstan			1,360	
Belarus				
ICBM	2	54	54	(<1)
Total ICBM	28	1,398	6,612	
Total HB	7	263	855	
Total SLBM	2	940	2,804	
Total warheads			10,271	(100)

Key: ICBM: intercontinental ballistic missile; SLBM: submarine launched ballistic missile; HB: heavy bomber.

Source: Evidence accompanying the START Treaty.

Following so closely upon the revelations about Iraq's clandestine nuclear weapon programme, the disintegration of the Soviet Union has brought a wave of pessimism about nuclear proliferation. It has been an extraordinarily unsettling event. Not only has it raised the spectre of further countries becoming nuclear powers, it has revealed serious flaws in the structures and institutions underpinning the regimes developed to regulate nuclear weaponry. It has also punctured the myth that nuclear weapons are 'safe' in the hands of the nuclear weapon states.

Among the problems arising out of the Soviet Union's dissolution, six stand out:

1. *The lack of transparency.* There are no clear, verifiable inventories of warheads and tactical weapons in the Soviet territories. Moreover, information is scarce on several aspects of the productive infrastructure, such as the amount of fissile material that has been produced, and the capacity for dismantling nuclear warheads. This lack of transparency is not just a feature of the Soviet Union: it is a privilege extended to all nuclear weapon states.

2. *The huge redundancy of capabilities and their potential mobility.* For years to come, there will be many unemployed assets—weapons, skilled labour and technologies—which could fetch good prices on the international black market. Dismantling weapons, re-employing people and stemming technology flows will require new investments and new institutions, and considerable foreign assistance.

3. *Maintaining control amid disarray.* Due to its large scale and complexity, and its many hazards, nuclear technology requires exceptional organizational cohesion and honesty if it is to be operated safely. This is true of nuclear weaponry and its production system as it is of nuclear power. The question is whether adequate control can be maintained when people are suffering hardship and institutions are under stress.

4. *Risks of military conflict.* It will be difficult to maintain unified control over nuclear weaponry, or to manage nuclear disarmament, or to keep pledges, if deteriorating relations between the republics make it difficult to conduct affairs. Disarmament requires considerable political stability and trust.

5. *The insufficiency of disarmament mechanisms.* The techniques and procedures for handling nuclear disarmament are not well developed. The INF and START treaties were only beginnings, and were primarily bilateral between the US and USSR. The Nuclear Non-Proliferation Treaty provides a framework for regulating (to a limited extent) the behaviour of those who are already armed, and for preventing the armament of those that are not. But it is not a disarmament treaty, even if several of its provisions are helpful to disarmament.

6. *Loss of the Soviet 'pillar'.* The non-proliferation regime was in many respects jointly managed by the US and USSR. The USSR's successor, Russia, will have neither the resources nor the influence to continue performing this leading role.

Republics Have Cooperated to Reduce Weapons

Taken together, these problems are daunting. But they are *not* insuperable. Given the speed of events, and the dislocations attending them, it is remarkable how much has already been achieved. It is a case of 'so far so good'. At the time of writing the unified control over nuclear weapons has held, and the military institutions responsible for nuclear weaponry seem robust to the changes happening elsewhere. The non-Russian republics appear to be sticking to their pledges to disarm and to join the NPT as non-nuclear weapon states. Nuclear weapons are being withdrawn to Russia, and the task of disabling and dismantling them is being set in motion. And despite their differences, the larger republics seem intent on settling their disputes by peaceful means. At this stage in their relations, it can even be argued that the need to find common solutions to the control over nuclear weapons has helped them manage the transition to independent statehood without being drawn into serious conflict.

"Problem Countries"

The non-proliferation regime's flexibility and capacity for development should also not be underestimated. Although the circumstances were very different, we should remember that the crisis besetting nuclear relations in the mid- and late-1970s seemed every bit as severe. The regime emerged strengthened by the experience. Moreover, there has never been a time when there has not been a clutch of 'problem countries'. They have always been a small if significant minority (their numbers are smaller today than they were in the 1970s), and what has held the regime together has been the determination of the great majority to continue fighting against proliferation. The concern being voiced today suggests that sentiment against nuclear proliferation remains as strong as ever.

While we cannot afford complacency, some of today's pessimism therefore seems overdone. It also carries its own dangers. We have to recognize that some powerful institutions stand to benefit from this pessimism. In particular, it provides an argument, which has recently been much in evidence in Britain, France and the US, for modernizing and re-orienting nuclear forces whose legitimacy has been weakened by the end of the Cold War. The spectre of proliferation is becoming the nuclear planner's best friend. Equally serious, playing up the risks of proliferation refreshes the mystique of nuclear weapons, while creating an atmosphere of mutual distrust. It encourages countries in unstable regions to regard their neighbours with even greater suspicion, and to develop at least contingency plans for arming themselves.

It is therefore important to emphasize the opportunities in the present situation, because they are substantial, and because nuclear proliferation feeds on a sense of hopelessness. Three deserve emphasis.

First, the removal of nuclear weapons from Central and Eastern Europe, including the Baltic states, Belarus and Ukraine, and from the former USSR's southern republics would be the most significant act of denuclearization in history. This is what is in prospect. Along with South Africa's accession to the NPT, and the submission by Argentina, Brazil and North Korea of all their nuclear facilities to international inspection, nuclear proliferation would become localized and a problem mainly affecting parts of Asia—the arc of countries from Israel through the Middle East into southern Asia.

Second, the trend towards much lower levels of armament by the remaining nuclear 'superpowers', the US and Russia, seems irreversible. The dangers and irrationality of deploying so many weapons stand revealed. Moreover, neither country can afford the expense of maintaining such large arsenals, and the production facilities which support them are beset with safety and environmental problems. What is at issue is the depth and pace of reductions, and the means by which they are achieved. There is a potential virtuous circle here: arms reductions will increase allegiance to the non-proliferation regime and reassure countries like Kazakhstan and Ukraine that the nuclear weapon states are not getting something for nothing; while the denuclearization alluded to above will increase US and Russian confidence in making deep cuts, and weaken the influence of institutions which have interests in maintaining the status quo.

Third, the dissolution of the Soviet Union has demonstrated that nuclear weapons cannot act as guarantors of the long-term influence and security of states. On the contrary, the security of the Soviet state, in its deepest sense, was mortally wounded by its obsession with nuclear and other military hardware, and with the styles of production and illusions of grandeur associated with them. The great shifts in power in the international system over the past 20 years have derived from relative economic performance, and the dynamism of economic institutions, and not the possession of weapons of mass destruction.

Nuclear Weapons Impede Economic Progress

The NPT has often been portrayed by the 'rejectionists', such as India, as an instrument for preserving the sway of the nuclear weapon states over the international system. This can be turned on its head. The NPT has been one of the institutions ensuring that power has ebbed away from the nuclear weapon states. Its main beneficiaries have been its non-nuclear weapon state parties, which through their abstinence have channelled their ambitions and resources into economic advance. As economic development is now the supreme priority, Russia should be concerned that it, alone among the Soviet republics, is inheriting the burden of nuclear weaponry.

"Soviet communism has been removed, and America is unquestionably the world's greatest military power."

The Breakup Makes America the Leader of the World

Elliott Abrams

The collapse of the Soviet Union leaves the United States the world's sole superpower, Elliott Abrams states in the following viewpoint. As such, America must lead the world and not withdraw. Abrams maintains that although the cold war is over, worldwide conflict continues, and the United States must play the leading role in reducing this conflict. Abrams is a senior fellow at the Hudson Institute, a conservative think tank in Washington, D.C. He was assistant secretary of state for Inter-American affairs in the Reagan administration, and is the author of several books, including *Undue Process*, his memoir of the Iran-Contra affair.

As you read, consider the following questions:

1. Some experts believed that a multipolar world would be more stable than the bipolar world that existed during the Cold War. How does Abrams refute this belief?
2. Why does the author believe Japan and Germany are unable to lead the world?
3. How have advances in military technology affected the United States, according to Abrams?

The struggle for mastery in Europe engaged the United States for nearly three-quarters of a century. It was a struggle that exacted enormous sacrifices. In the two world wars over half a million Americans lost their lives, and another 100,000 were killed in a global Cold War that was not always cold. The question arises: With the Cold War won, should the American definition of security now begin to contract? Are the great tasks and sacrifices of the last seventy-five years finally behind us?

The temptation to withdraw from leadership in international politics is great. A variety of sophisticated and plausible arguments is an offer to justify such a course. As the year 2000 approaches, some take a millenarian position that non-violence and democracy have already triumphed, leaving little reason for American activity. Some argue that the collapse of communism and Soviet power has eliminated any serious physical or ideological threats to American interests. Others maintain that while threats remain, a collective security system will emerge to protect us. Perhaps most important is the assertion that, however real the need for American leadership, our own social and economic weaknesses are so deep as to prevent us, now or in the near future, from continuing to carry the burdens involved.

Whether reflecting optimism about the international system or pessimism about America, these views have a common thread: they manifest a desire to declare an end not only to the Cold War but also to the period of American leadership. Arguments that the world's problems are solved, or irrelevant to U. S. security, or likely to regulate themselves in a new and interdependent world political system, or beyond the range of current American influence, all excuse (and often celebrate) the reduction of American activity, influence, and power. But before accepting such arguments and joining in the celebration, we should subject them to close scrutiny; and when we do, they appear seriously flawed. . . .

A Self-Regulating System?

The sense of relief at the end of the Cold War was both enormous and understandable. Understandable, too, was the initial, euphoric belief that, with its conclusion, international stability was almost assured. If the danger to us and our allies, and more generally to world peace, had come from immensely powerful and aggressive dictatorships and their totalitarian ideology, it seemed reasonable to conclude that the demise of those regimes and their ideology would deliver us from problems of security and stability. The new interdependent, multipolar world would surely lend itself to a stable balance of power, replacing the prolonged superpower confrontation.

This view, however attractive, lacks both logical and historical foundation. Two centuries ago, Rousseau observed of the states of Europe that they "touch each other at so many points that no one of them can move without giving a jar to the rest; their variances are all the more deadly, as their ties are more closely woven." More recently Robert W. Tucker pointed out in the Fall 1991 *Foreign Affairs* that "interdependence itself is not constitutive of order . . . [but] creates the need for greater order because it is as much a source of conflict as of consensus."

Peace is not the normal state of affairs. Equilibrium in the international system is not a natural or automatically realized phenomenon. History establishes that the international system can be peaceful only if determined, sustained, and intelligent efforts are made to keep it so.

The Victor Must Lead

America has won the cold war—almost without trying. America's aim, at least since 1956 when the stark exigencies of the Hungarian uprising disabused Americans of the illusions of a Communist rollback, has been not to win this conflict but to negotiate a truce. It won nonetheless, not on the strength of its arms or the skill of its diplomats, but by virtue of the power of the democratic ideas on which the American system is based and the failure of the Communist idea. . . .

The various totalitarian systems now all seem to be ending in failure, but while they lived, they called the action. America emerged victorious over them all, but each of those victories came in defense. If, however, we can advance the spread of democracy, perhaps not everywhere but at least to the majority of mankind, then the twenty-first will be the true American century. This will come about not by the spread of American power or by the exact imitation of American institutions but by the spread of those profound and humane ideals on which America was founded.

Joshua Muravchik, *Exporting Democracy: Fulfilling America's Destiny*, 1991.

The replacement of the historically rare bipolar system with a new but more familiar multipolar system serves to underline this point. It was characteristic of the Cold War that *everything* counted, at least briefly; in a twist on Andy Warhol's dictum, during the last four decades it seemed that every locale, no matter how small, remote, barren, poor, and obscure, had its fifteen minutes of fame: Quemoy and Matsu, Vientiane and Pnomh Penh, Leopoldville and Addis Ababa, Managua and even St. Georges, Grenada. Everything mattered, and every win and every loss imparted a sense of historical momentum.

From this it followed that little was done by any country without taking the interests of the superpowers into consideration. Their boundless concerns constrained not only one another but also every other actor in the international system. True, the superpowers could occasionally be defied; but they could never be ignored, and defiance required careful calculation. Intermittently, one superpower or the other would give a sharp pull on the leash, as a reminder of who really ran the show: thus Eisenhower forced the British, French, and Israelis to withdraw in humiliation from Suez in 1956; and thus the Soviets removed their missiles from Cuba in 1962 without consulting Castro.

The Pitfalls of a Multipolar World

This way of carrying on, which has characterized a good portion of our lifetime, is a historical rarity. What preceded it, from the Congress of Vienna to the Second World War, represents the more usual pattern. Typically, no single power or pair of powers predominated. Instead, nations formed and broke alliances in a multipolar system with a facility dubbed Metternichian after its master practitioner.

While a bipolar system is "managed" by the two powers that dominate it, or is constrained by their rivalry, a multipolar system is freer, more fluid. This obviously has much to recommend it, but there are pitfalls as well. For the balance of power is the product of human endeavor. The most powerful members of a multipolar system must be willing to act resolutely when the rules of the game are broken; without that willingness the system becomes less stable and more prone to violence. The Pax Britannica of the nineteenth century was remarkably peaceful because there was a leading (though not dominant) power actively enforcing the rules and willing to intervene, if necessary with force, to maintain the system's stability.

Determinism is the enemy of resolution. As Robert W. Tucker and David Hendrickson observe in *Empire of Liberty*, the balance of power "may be most endangered precisely when men persuade themselves that the tendency toward equilibrium is an iron law, for in this way they free themselves from the onus of maintaining it." In Hans Morgenthau's terms, some nation must act as "holder of the balance" or "arbiter" of the system, bestowing "restraint and pacification" upon it. Many of the conditions prevailing in the European state system during the eighteenth and nineteenth centuries no longer exist. The system has expanded to embrace the world. Communication, transport, weaponry, and many other things have been revolutionized. But if the terms have changed, the basic requirement remains: one nation, deeply committed to the rules of international conduct and strong enough to enforce them, must assume the role of "holder of the balance." The only country capable of this in today's world is the United States.

The role is particularly important when circumstances call for coalition-building. The participation of the most powerful nation helps other, weaker states to reach agreements or to undertake actions that they might otherwise be reluctant to. The latter are aware that the absence of the most powerful nation can render their decision tentative and frustrate their efforts. They can be undone by its opposition. The American-led coalition against Iraq could not have been assembled by the Soviet Union, or Japan, or France, or Great Britain, without the engagement of the United States. Why should states with fewer resources risk committing them if the greater nation hangs back? Its reluctance to act will reduce the chance that a coalition will be formed at all, let alone succeed, and it will raise the cost enormously for those who proceed without it.

The Weaknesses of Collective Security

The most critical role for the arbiter lies in its capacity to enforce the rules of international behavior. The invoking of collective security mechanisms all too often fails to achieve this, for collective security is little more than a system of mutual promises among peacefully inclined states. "A system of general collective security," Henry Kissinger observes, "has historically proved useless against the biggest threat to peace—a major rogue country. How would the 'peace-loving' states respond? What sanctions would be at their disposal?" (*Washington Post,* March 15, 1990). With the disappearance of Cold War constraints on rule-breaking, some other form of enforcement—and its crux, military force—must be found if rogue countries are to be restrained.

Neither Germany nor Japan is a convincing candidate to succeed the United States as world leader. Within living memory, both these countries made unsuccessful efforts to achieve dominance and, as a result, suffered the trauma of utter defeat, disgrace, and occupation. In both cases the experience has left deep scars that make it difficult for the two countries to carry their full weight as major powers. Both are inhibited about possessing or projecting military force. Both are aware that they are viewed with suspicion by other countries in their regions. Even more important, behavior in which timidity and assertiveness tend to alternate in an unpredictable manner suggests that, even in their own eyes, the two countries lack legitimacy as world leaders. In the case of Japan, in particular, its attempt to accumulate and exert political influence has been purposely circumscribed by the Japanese themselves, precisely to protect them from involvement in divisive and dangerous crises.

In addition to all this, Japan and Germany are not quite today the economic superpowers they appeared to be yesterday. Japan's export of capital is slowing markedly, and Germany is both suffering under the great economic burden of absorbing the East and showing signs of entering a period of political turmoil. Moreover, they are among the most rapidly aging countries in the world. The impact of an aging population is evident in a contracting labor force, a rising dependency ratio (defined as population aged sixty-five and over as a percentage of population aged fifteen to sixty-five), a decline in the savings rate, and an ever-larger welfare bill. These are not historical and economic conditions conducive to strong international leadership. Except in rare and usually minor regional crises, the central actor in the enforcement of standards of international behavior must remain the United States. . . .

Is America Invulnerable?

It is comforting to believe that whatever the world's troubles, their salience for the United States has dropped dramatically now that the bipolar struggle has ended. The physical and ideological threat of Soviet communism has been removed, and America is unquestionably the world's greatest military power. While the fate of Nicaragua, Cuba, or Vietnam is of surpassing interest to their citizens and perhaps their neighbors, it is of little import to Americans. The United States no longer needs to dedicate nearly so much time, personnel, and money to safeguarding European security. Instability in the Balkans is unfortunate, fighting between Armenians and Azeris is tragic, but these are not matters seriously affecting the security of the United States.

All true. But if many issues have faded in importance, others continue to grow. The argument that if during the Cold War everything mattered, after it nothing does, cannot be sustained. Even at its height, the Cold War did not define the sum of American interests in the world. Indeed, the disintegration of the Soviet Union and the end of its control of the countries of Eastern Europe, combined with advances in military technology, have created a new peril for the United States: the ready availability of weapons of mass destruction to dozens of states and terrorist organizations, along with the incentive to acquire them.

A more fluid international order, even as it leaves some nations safer, will leave others feeling more vulnerable. As security guarantees by superpowers to friends and client states weaken or end, these states are most likely to seek security not in new alliances or new superpower guarantees, but in new weaponry.

The spread of sophisticated military technology has given

many lesser nations, including terrorist states, unprecedented capabilities and potential in chemical, biological, and nuclear warfare, as well as delivery systems for their new arsenals. Long-range missile technology is already available in some of the world's most volatile regions, and the number of countries with ballistic missiles has doubled to eighteen in the last decade. Efforts to limit proliferation have failed in part because purchasers have been able to modify short-range missiles to reach longer-range targets and to adapt space-launch vehicles for military use; in part because the most advanced nations no longer maintain a monopoly on production. Many countries hostile to the U.S., including Iran, Iraq, and North Korea, are developing biological or chemical weapons. Many developing countries are also investing heavily in conventional forces (India, for example, now has the world's third-largest army and seventh-largest navy).

Only One Certainty

There is a painful irony for the United States in all this. After seventy-five years of costly conflicts, we are now finally at peace with all of the most powerful nations, only to find that developments in, and the dissemination of, military technology threaten to make America vulnerable once again.

The end of the Cold War, then, has produced a number of perceptions which, although superficially plausible, are mistaken. It is a mistake to believe that democracy's triumph worldwide is assured; that the international system will regulate itself in the absence of a leading power; that violence will wane; and that the United States is now militarily invulnerable.

The post-Cold War order is characterized not only by opportunity but by uncertainty. One thing, however, is certain: American leadership, far from being a casualty of the peace, remains a precondition for a peaceful world.

"Not only is the 'evil empire' not there to kick around anymore, but U.S. paramountcy is threatened by competition from the new European and East Asian superpowers."

The Breakup Signals the End of America's World Leadership

Zoltán Grossman

Military overspending, ethnic conflict, and the other forces that caused the demise of the Soviet Union will also lead to the demise of the United States, Zoltán Grossman asserts in the following viewpoint. Grossman argues that the cold war enabled the United States to maintain its status as one of the world's two superpowers. Now that the cold war is over, Grossman concludes, America has no leadership role in the world. It will decline and Europe and Asia will replace it as the world's leading regions. Grossman, a cartographer and writer in Madison, Wisconsin, is an activist for anti-war and native American causes.

As you read, consider the following questions:

1. Why does Grossman believe Europe will become a world superpower?
2. Why would it be difficult for Japan to lead the world, and how could a Japanese-Chinese partnership be effective, according to the author?
3. How will the United States attempt to retain its place as a world superpower, in the author's opinion?

From Zoltán Grossman, "The Geopolitics of the New Superpowers: Not the 'New World Order' He Had in Mind," *Forward Motion*, March 1992. Revised by the author for inclusion in the present volume. Reprinted with permission.

Historically speaking, the break-up of the Soviet Union is not that big a deal. To us cartographers, the fall of empires and their replacement by new empires is old news. On a history textbook project, a cartographer usually compiles a new empire map each day—from the Romans and the Mongols to the Austrians and Ottomans. The disintegration of the old Russian Empire is just one part of a much larger picture—the musical chairs of empires, the shift of superpowers.

Since the Mercantile Revolution began 500 years ago, the world stage has generally been dominated by two superpowers at a time; by Spain and Portugal until the mid-1700s, by Britain and France until the early 1900s, by Germany and Japan until 1945, and by the U.S. and USSR until today. In each instance, the pursuit of empire tallied up such high political and socio-economic costs that it not only ended, but dragged down the imperial power with it.

The Demise of Nations

The current shift of superpowers is combined with a profound revolution in communication that is dismantling the very concept of the nation-state. The new superpowers are likely to be economically based regional alliances, containing autonomous or even independent ethnic nations. New definitions of sovereignty, whether in the Commonwealth of Independent States, or in plans for European political unity, will make it harder to even make maps. The world is getting both smaller and larger at the same time—breaking up nation-states into ethnic enclaves, but then in turn uniting those ethnic enclaves in larger economic associations.

The two best candidates for superpower status by the 21st century are a European alliance, with Germany at its hub, and an East Asian alliance, with Japan at the economic center. Having emphasized economic growth over military prowess, and integration of national economies over internal trade wars, Europe and East Asia are replacing the U.S. and USSR as the two preeminent world powers. The process will be marked by inconsistencies, setbacks, and the periodic reassertion of the old order. But the overall trend is unmistakable.

While the U.S. may maintain status as a third superpower for a short interim period, it is folly to think it immune from the forces that brought down the USSR—military overspending, a crumbling civilian infrastructure, ethnic conflict, ecological destruction, a sense of popular powerlessness, and the loss of satellite states. When the current shift is completed, the U.S. may end up looking like Britain after the loss of its empire a strong but second-rate power, licking its domestic wounds. . . .

The unification of Germany, the break-up of Yugoslavia and the

USSR, the attacks on foreigners, the resignation of Margaret Thatcher, the adoption of a single currency, the opening of the Channel tunnel, and the lowering of trade barriers—all fit into a larger picture: the elimination of obstacles to European unity. The integration of Europe is now an irreversible process, with NATO bound to go the way of the Warsaw Pact. Its replacement would be a core alliance of nations in Western and Central Europe, with cooperative economic, political and military structures. They will be coupled with a periphery in Eastern and Southeastern Europe that will provide a ready labor pool. By the end of the decade, Europe will be seen as a single entity, as a superpower.

This trend was predicted by the late Trinidadian activist C.L.R. James, when he said in 1985:

> Already the whole of Western Europe is ready for one society, one army, one government . . . Marx and Engels foresaw that with the development of the economy, means of communications, regularity and similarity in ways of life, there will be an increasing community. And that's what's taking place . . . The objection to Europe forming a community is Moscow...There used to be the town, the town-cities. Later there were town-cities brought into the country and formed the country . . . The whole tendency of modern society in its basic structure is the unification of large areas.

A united Europe would have four component parts: first, the nations of the European Community (EC), which eliminated trade barriers on January 1, 1993; second, the "neutral" nations of the European Free Trade Association (EFTA) planning to join the EC; third, the former Communist nations of Central Europe; and fourth, the Eastern Orthodox and Muslim regions of Europe. At least in the short term, the nations in the first three groups would retain their sovereignty, but turn more and more power over to a united parliament, a central bank, and an integrated military structure. The future has already been prefigured in the recently formed Franco-German military force, the EC-EFTA formation of the new European Economic Area, and the Maastricht treaty on currency and political union.

"Europe" has always been a political definition. Geographically, it exists only as a peninsula on the huge Eurasian land mass. The 19th century geographers who delimited Europe generally used a racial definition, drawing what they saw as the borders of the white race and "Western civilization." Yet Europe includes peoples outside the mainstream of that civilization, whose technical and cultural level is not judged adequate by Western European elites.

Western Europe is showing increased acceptance of the Catholic and Protestant regions of Central Europe, which were once part of its economic and political domain, and is letting them into the new Europe. Poland, the Baltic states, and the states formerly under Austrian rule (The Czech Republic, Slovakia, Hungary, Slovenia, and Croatia) are again fulfilling their traditional role as a halfway house between Western and Eastern Europe. . . .

The East Asian Superpower

While most world attention has centered on European integration, a similar process is taking place in East Asia. Though less defined than the process in Europe, it is potentially more dramatic in its global implications. Japan's emergence as an economic superpower—much like Germany's—cannot be viewed in isolation from its growing interrelationship with neighboring nations. Just as European integration led to the reunification of Germany, East Asian integration will almost certainly lead to the reunification of Korea, and possibly the reunification of China and Taiwan. It could also lead to tensions along the former Sino-Soviet frontier, where the two new superpowers would meet head-to-head, and in the Middle East, the main supplier of oil to both Europe and Japan.

Japan, like Germany, launched World War II to achieve dominance over surrounding resources, markets, and labor supplies. The Japanese put forth their "Co-Prosperity Sphere" as a mutually beneficial system for East Asians, but it turned out to be another exploitative imperial system with Japan at the center. As a militaristic formula, it failed to win substantial support among the conquered peoples, and came into fatal conflict with U.S. and British interests in the region. The current trends in East Asia point toward a new "Co-Prosperity Sphere," but based on economics and politics instead of Japanese military power. In other words, though Japan would play the pivotal role, this alliance would be more genuinely "co-prosperous." The two centerpieces would remain Japan and China.

While both Japan and China openly aspire to be superpowers, neither is capable of going it alone. China has what Japan needs, and Japan has what China needs. Japan has the capital reserves, high technology, and refined technical and managerial skills—precisely the formula that modernizing China is looking for. China has a gargantuan, cheap labor supply, a huge standing army, and natural resources—precisely what energy-poor and partly demilitarized Japan lacks. The developing Sino-Japanese partnership, based more on trade than investment at this point, could blossom to joint superpower status. Japan is already the largest aid donor to China, a status cemented by Prime Minister Kaifu's 1991 visit to Beijing and the 1993 visit of the Japanese Emperor.

The incorporation of the other East Asian industrial economies in the formula could further strengthen a regional alliance. Hong Kong is already due to become part of China in 1997. Regional integration would speed up the reincorporation of Taiwan, since it would no longer be forced to mold itself into a Chinese province, but into an integral part of a larger region. Similarly, bringing both Koreas into a regional alliance would render their political division moot. Largely ethnic Chinese Singapore would also lend technical expertise. The formation of the Asia-Pacific Economic Forum (APEF) prefigures the future of the region, though for the moment it includes the United States. Malaysia has advocated an Asian alliance that excludes Washington, but this may be slow in coming. By 2000, projections show that the level of U.S. trade across the Pacific will be twice that of U.S. trade across the Atlantic.

KAL/Cartoonists & Writers Syndicate. Reprinted with permission.

The East Asian regional alliance would be divided into three sections. The first would be the capitalist industrial economies—Japan, southern Korea, Taiwan, Hong Kong, Singapore, and certain Chinese provinces such as Guangdong and Fujian. The second would contain the state-controlled labor and military pool in the other Chinese provinces, northern Korea and perhaps Indochina. The third would be the presently Western-aligned nations such as the Philippines and Indonesia, which would continue to provide resources and labor to the industrial centers. . . .

Like in Europe, the process of integration can be uneven and sporadic. It can even at times resemble intense Sino-Japanese competition, as Tokyo and Beijing jockey for position, and the Japanese economy fluctuates. These changes take place as International Monetary Fund releases new 1993 data showing China as the world's 3rd strongest economy—behind the U.S. and Japan, but ahead of Germany and Russia. The East Asian superpower could potentially dwarf anything Europe or North America have to offer.

The United States

With such momentous changes around the world, it is laughable that the leadership of the United States assumes that it will remain unscathed, that the U.S. is an island of calm in the middle of the storm. The "euphoria" of a military victory over Iraq and a political victory over the USSR can only be short-lived. The crushing debt load from years of military deficit spending, the two-tiered educational system leading to a two-class society, the spontaneous uprisings in Los Angeles and other cities, are only a few of the early warning signs of what lies ahead. As Boris Kagarlitsky has said, "If one superpower collapsed, why not try to change things in the other hemisphere?"

For the past four decades, the projection of U.S. power around the world has depended on the Soviet bogeyman, the alter ego to the land of democracy. Now, simultaneously, not only is the "evil empire" not there to kick around anymore, but U.S. paramountcy is threatened by competition from the new European and East Asian superpowers. Washington is trying to stave off the inevitable by mimicking their regional integration plans, negotiating the North American Free Trade Alliance (NAFTA) pact with Canada, Mexico, and other nations in the hemisphere. But the effort is crippled by the lack of powerful partners, and inadequate resources in technical research and development. You heard it here first: no Americans will be shouting "We're Number One!" at the 2000 Olympic Games. Already, the German auto giant BMW is building a plant in South Carolina to take advantage of cheap labor.

Former CIA officer John Stockwell has detailed the use of U.S. foreign policy as a method of controlling the population of the U.S. itself. He asserts that the federal government not only opportunistically uses foreign crises to distract attention from domestic problems, but actually searches for and in some cases creates new enemies in order to reinforce its legitimacy. A long string of demonized scapegoats—Khomeini, Qaddafi, Noriega, Saddam—attests to this strategy. But in the absence of a looming threat from a major power, can such a "search for enemies" pacify enough U.S. citizens? The new rallying cries against Middle Eastern dictators and Latin American drug lords are hardly enough to sustain a superpower through times like these.

The decline of the U.S. is already proving more violent for the rest of the world—from Panama to Iraq—than the decline of the USSR. War abroad also provides the perfect framework for the militarization of domestic life. The police-state conditions in neighborhoods of Los Angeles and other cities, increased FBI political harassment, the use of 4,500 Canadian troops against the Mohawks, and U.S. contingency plans for martial law—all are extreme versions of an overall trend.

U.S. Colonies

Unlike Russia, the United States did not manage to annex most of its sphere of influence in the 19th and 20th centuries. It did annex many Indian nations and northern Mexico to establish a territorial base. It made colonies out of Puerto Rico, the Virgin Islands, Hawaii, the Philippines, and five other Pacific island groups. It also hoisted protectorate status on Panama, Nicaragua, Honduras, Cuba, Haiti, the Dominican Republic, and Liberia, guaranteeing those countries a special instability that persists to the present day. Its economic sphere of influence was also extended over nearly all of the Americas and parts of Asia, including South Korea and Israel.

Also unlike Russia, the U.S. is not about to withdraw its investments and troops without a fight. Quite the contrary: Washington is returning in force to its former colonies and protectorates. Since 1988, it has directly used military force in Nicaragua, Honduras, Panama, the Virgin Islands, the Philippines, and Liberia. It has virtually extended protectorate status over six oil-rich Persian Gulf states, especially Kuwait and the nearby strategic outpost of Somalia. . . .

Just as Hiroshima was intended more as a message to the Soviets than to the Japanese, any new U.S. intervention is carefully calculated to impress Washington's emerging competitors. Former conservative French Premier Jacques Chirac correctly viewed the U.S. role in the Gulf War as securing control over the energy supply of Western Europe and Japan. Placing U.S. troops in the middle of Kurdish uprisings in Iraq and Turkey guarantees a U.S. role in the carving of new borders in the entire oil-rich Transcaucasian region. A foray into South America, such as Peru or Colombia, would assert the Monroe Doctrine against new economic competition. And a second Korean War would project U.S. power right between Japan, China, and Russia, just at the time it's most needed. . . .

As R.P. Lester wrote in his book *Genghis Khan*, "When a man has achieved great power, what is there left for him to achieve but more power? When he has overcome all his enemies, what does he find but more enemies?"

"Communism died in 1991."

The Breakup Marks the End of Communism

George Bush

George Bush was president of the United States from 1988 to 1992. Prior to becoming president, Bush held numerous public offices, including head of the Central Intelligence Agency, chairman of the Republican party, and U.S. ambassador to China. In the following viewpoint, Bush proclaims the death of communism and America's victory in the cold war. He concludes that the United States is the sole remaining power and the primary advocate of freedom.

As you read, consider the following questions:

1. Who does Bush credit for winning the cold war?
2. What role did the American taxpayer play in defeating communism, according to the author?
3. Why does Bush believe the world trusts the United States?

From George Bush's state of the union address, Washington, D.C., January 28, 1992.

Since December 1991, the world has known changes of almost biblical proportions. And even now . . . I am not sure we've absorbed the full impact, the full import of what happened.

But Communism died in 1991. And even as President, with the most fascinating possible vantage point, there were times when I was so busy helping to manage progress and helping to lead change that I didn't always show the joy that was in my heart.

But the biggest thing that has happened in the world in my life, in our lives, is this: By the grace of God, America won the cold war. . . .

The Cost of Winning the Cold War

Let me tell you something I've been thinking these past few months. It's a kind of roll-call of honor. For the cold war didn't "end"—it was won.

And I think of those who won it, in places like Korea and Vietnam. And some of them didn't come back. Back then, they were heroes, but this year they were victors. The long roll-call, all the G.I. Joes and Janes, all the ones who fought faithfully for freedom, who hit the ground and sucked the dust and knew their share of horror.

This may seem frivolous, and I don't mean it so. But it's moving to me how the world saw them.

The world saw not only their special valor but their special style, their rambunctious, optimistic bravery, their do-or-die unity unhampered by class or race or region. What a group we've put forth, for generations now, from the ones who wrote "Kilroy was here" on the walls of the German stalags to those who left signs in the Iraqi desert that said, "I saw Elvis." What a group of kids we've sent out into the world.

And there's another to be singled out, though it may seem inelegant. And I mean a mass of people called the American taxpayer. No one ever thinks to thank the people who pay a country's bill or an alliance's bill. But for half a century now, the American people have shouldered the burden and paid taxes that were higher than they would have been to support a defense that was bigger than it would have been if imperial Communism had never existed.

But it did.

It doesn't anymore.

And here is a fact I wouldn't mind the world acknowledging: The American taxpayer bore the brunt of the burden, and deserves a hunk of the glory.

No More Fear

And so, now, for the first time in 35 years, our strategic bombers stand down. No longer are they on round-the-clock alert. Tomorrow our children will go to school and study history and how plants grow. And they won't have, as my children did, air-raid drills in which they crawl under their desks and cover their heads in case of nuclear war. My grandchildren don't have to do that, and won't have the bad dreams children had once in decades past. There are still threats. But the long drawn-out dread is over.

In January 1991 I spoke to you at a moment of high peril. American forces had just unleashed Operation Desert Storm. And after 40 days in the desert skies and 4 days on the ground, the men and women of America's armed forces and our allies accomplished the goals that I declared, and that you endorsed: We liberated Kuwait.

And soon after, the Arab world and Israel sat down to talk seriously, and comprehensively, about peace, an historic first. And soon after that, the last American hostages came home. Our policies were vindicated.

Reprinted by permission: Tribune Media Services.

Much good can come from the prudent use of power. And much good can come of this: A world once divided into two armed camps now recognizes one sole and preeminent power, the United States of America.

And they regard this with no dread. For the world trusts us

with power, and the world is right. They trust us to be fair, and restrained. They trust us to be on the side of decency. They trust us to do what's right.

And I use those words advisedly. A few days after the war began, I received a telegram from Joanne Speicher, the wife of the first pilot killed in the gulf, Lieut. Comdr. Scott Speicher. Even in her grief, she wanted me to know that someday, when her children were old enough, she would tell them

> that their father went away to war because it was the right thing to do.

She said it all. It was the right thing to do. . . .

America's World Role

There are those who say that now we can turn away from the world, that we have no special role, no special place. But we are the United States of America, the leader of the West that has become the leader of the world. . . .

We are still and ever the freest nation on earth, the kindest nation on earth, the strongest nation on earth.

And we have always risen to the occasion.

"'Former' communists continue to dominate most of the former Soviet republics."

The Breakup Does Not Mark the End of Communism

Robert W. Lee

Throughout the world, people perceived the collapse of the Soviet Union as the death of communism. In the following viewpoint, Robert W. Lee warns that communism is not dead. Many of the new republics, he states, are being led by politicians who, although they claim to be democrats, are still communists. Lee concludes that the United States must be wary of the new republics and their leaders. Lee is the author of the book *United Nations Conspiracy* and a frequent contributor to the conservative periodical *The New American*.

As you read, consider the following questions:

1. The author cites several examples of former Soviet republics that have been overtaken by communists. Name three of these examples.
2. What policies of Uzbekistan's president Islam A. Karimov does the author believe are communist?
3. Why is Lee concerned that Ukraine is being led by communists?

From Robert W. Lee, "Dubious Reforms in Former USSR," *The New American*, January 25, 1993. Reprinted with permission.

In February of 1992, the *Dallas Morning News* profiled the John Birch Society in an article that began, somewhat derisively: "The Soviet Union is dead. The Iron Curtain is gone. The Cold War is over. But for the bastion of anti-communism, the John Birch Society, this is no time to rest, let alone gloat. How can they rest, say society members, when the world is simply further along on the same disastrous course?"

It's a good question. Consider the former Soviet Union.

A few weeks earlier, the elected anticommunist president of the republic of Georgia had been deposed in a violent military coup, and would later be supplanted by the country's erstwhile Communist Party boss who had once had him jailed for speaking out against Soviet oppression. By the end of November 1992, Associated Press reporter Deborah Seward would write: "Nearly a year after the Soviet Union collapsed, voters in two of its republics have returned former communist leaders to office. In most of the others, they never left." The supposedly "former" communists managed to stay in power, Seward continued, "by dropping Marxist rhetoric and embracing popular demands for independence. When the Soviet Union finally collapsed, they preached reform while keeping control of the security police and judiciary."

Events in the Baltics

In Lithuania, "voters have thrown out the Sajudis movement that led the Baltic nation to independence, in favor of Algirdas Brazauskas, the former Communist Party leader." Taking note of the "Communist longevity in some republics, such as Georgia, Kazakhstan and Ukraine," Seward also observed that "heavy-handed methods have kept career communist bosses in office in some remote republics, such as Uzbekistan and Turkmenistan." In Ukraine, "President Leonid Kravchuk, a career communist accused of embracing the independence movement only to stay in power, cracked down on student protesters and has threatened to imprison opponents," and instead of embracing market reforms "has openly praised the [Red] Chinese model of economic reform with tight political controls."

In Estonia, it was a close call when "former communist Arnold Ruutel got more votes than non-communist Lennart Meri in September 1992, but fell short of a majority. Parliament chose Meri as president." In Latvia, "President Anatolijs Gorbunovs, the former deputy Communist Party leader, has not faced election since Latvia won independence in 1991." And in Russia, Seward stated, President Boris Yeltsin "has emerged as one of the staunchest anti-communist leaders in the former Soviet Union, although he spent three decades as a party apparatchik."

Yeltsin joined the Communist Party in 1961, rose to its central committee in 1981, and became a member of the policy-making Politburo in 1985. He formally quit the party in July 1990, a ploy which positioned him to assume power in Russia as an allegedly "reformed" communist, a guise that has been exploited to, among other things, justify the continuing massive transfer of aid to Russia from the West in general and U.S. taxpayers in particular. It is truly dazzling disinformation to portray Boris Yeltsin as a staunch "anti-communist."

Soviets Should Still Be Viewed Skeptically

Many of the same old comrades are running today's bureaucracy in the Commonwealth of Independent States. As a Polish-American, I have a deep distrust of the people who imposed communism on Eastern Europe and the Baltic states for two generations. . . .

I cannot forget the history of the past 75 years. I urge my colleagues to continue to regard the former Soviets with caution and skepticism.

Barbara A. Mikulski, before the U.S. Senate, July 2, 1992.

Our government continues to hunt down the few remaining, aging Nazis suspected of assisting Hitler's holocaust during World War II, even as it (and much of our media) accepts at face value the imagined "repentance" of thugs who were active participants in the even more oppressive and deadly Marxist-Leninist movement, with no thought of holding them accountable for their crimes against humanity. . . .

Lithuanian Communists

In March 1990, Vytautas Landsbergis, who had an impressive record of opposition to communism, became the first non-communist to head one of the Soviet republics when he was elected president of Lithuania's *Sejm* (national parliament). He defeated Communist Party chief Algirdas Brazauskas by a margin of more than two-to-one. Subsequently, Lithuania became the first republic to break ties with Moscow, after which Mikhail Gorbachev sent Soviet troops and police on a rampage throughout the republic and imposed an economic embargo on key products, including oil and natural gas.

Brazauskas had been trained as an engineer and had worked in construction before becoming a state economic planner in 1966. In 1977 he was appointed secretary of the Communist Party in charge of economic affairs, and in 1988 became the party boss.

In 1990, he and a group of fellow communists who had allegedly broken with the Soviet Communist Party because they supported Lithuania's independence drive, formed the Democratic Labor Party (DLP). In the country's first post-Soviet parliamentary elections in October and November of 1992, the DLP and its coterie of "former" communists, led by Brazauskas, won a working majority and with it the authority to form a government and oust Landsbergis. The DLP presently holds around 80 seats in the 141-member Sejm, while Landsbergis' Sajudis national movement retains only about 40 seats. On November 25th, the new parliament elected Brazauskas as its chairman and as acting head of state.

President Landsbergis lamented that Lithuania was headed back to the "one-party rule" of the openly communist era and accused Russia of "actively participating" in the election to assist the DLP. . . .

Uzbekistan

The *Times* of London reported on March 27, 1992, that one could still find "silver statues of Lenin" on the road leading to the Uzbekistani city of Samarkand, interspersed with such slogans as, "The final victory of Communism," and, "Lenin is more alive today than anyone living." Nevertheless, The *Times* contended, "the death of communism has reached Uzbekistan as it has other parts of the former Soviet Union."

On August 31, 1991, the republic's communist-dominated parliament approved an independence declaration which was widely heralded as the first step by a Central Asian republic "toward leaving the Soviet Union." Critics of the heavy-handed rule of President (and Communist Party chief) Islam A. Karimov viewed the declaration, instead, as a cynical effort on his part to preserve his authoritarian rule. A leading opposition figure stated at the time that, in the wake of the attempted "coup" in the Soviet Union earlier in the month, "the government decided the best way to save itself was to declare independence. The party will change its name, but it won't matter. Here is an island of communism."

President Karimov, who had been appointed to the Soviet Politburo in 1990, had been a communist since 1964. Three days prior to the Soviet "coup" he had declared that Uzbekistan was not ready for either "democracy" or a market economy. He endorsed instead the Red Chinese economic strategy toward which Russian president Boris Yeltsin now appears to be moving. . . .

On December 8, 1992, parliament approved a new constitution promising freedom of thought and travel and a multi-party "democracy." It granted Karimov even more personal power. Two days later, the Red lawmakers demonstrated their commitment to "democracy" by voting 383 to 7 to ban the opposition nationalist Birlik (Unity) Popular Front movement which, according to Reuters news service, advocates "Western-style democracy." Other parties large enough to pose a potential problem for the ruling Reds have also been banned. . . .

Such is the "death of Communism" in Uzbekistan. . . .

Business as Usual

"Former" communists continue to dominate most of the former Soviet republics. For instance:

Kazakhstan: In Kazakhstan, as in most of the former Soviet republics, "former" communists continue to control the workings of government. President Nursultan A. Nazarbayev was a Gorbachev ally who joined the Communist Party in 1962 and only resigned from its central committee, and the central committee of the Politburo, in the wake of the 1991 "coup."

Kyrgystan: When President Askar Akayev was elected in 1991, he was lauded as the "first freely elected" president of the republic. Actually, he was the only candidate, receiving some 95 percent of the vote. He joined the Communist Party in 1981. Parliament remains top-heavy with Akayev's fellow "formers.". . .

Moldova: President Mircea Snegur, another "former" Communist Party official, resigned as chairman of the national legislature in February 1991, claiming that the party was intent on smearing him. But he quickly agreed to stay on as caretaker pending a direct presidential election. As luck would have it, he was the sole candidate when the election was held on December 8, 1991.

Tajikistan: On September 23,1991, the communist-dominated legislature declared a state of emergency, fired Tajikistan's noncommunist acting president, and replaced him with Rakhman Nabiyev, a former Communist Party first secretary. In November of that year Nabiyev was elected president in what was widely perceived to be a rigged plebiscite. . . .

Ukraine: The second most populous of the former Soviet republics continues to be ruled by President Leonid M. Kravchuk, the country's former Communist Party chief for ideology. Prior to becoming Ukraine's first directly elected president in December 1991, he chaired the Supreme Soviet (parliament). . . .

On August 26th, 1992, Kravchuk's controlled newspapers announced that emigres who "openly call for opposition to the government, Supreme Soviet and the president's policies . . . will be expelled beyond the borders of the Ukraine without the right ever to visit it."

So communism has collapsed, Boris Yeltsin is a staunch anticommunist, and the John Birch Society is chasing a nonexistent threat. Better take a closer look.

Periodical Bibliography

The following articles have been selected to supplement the diverse views presented in this chapter.

Shlomo Avineri — "The Return to History," *The Brookings Review*, Spring 1992. Available from 1775 Massachusetts Ave. NW, Washington, DC 20036.

Roger Burbach — "Russia's Upheaval," *Monthly Review*, February 1993.

Francis Fukuyama — "The Beginning of Foreign Policy," *The New Republic*, August 17 & 24, 1992.

Colin S. Gray — "Back to the Future: Russia and the Balance of Power," *Global Affairs*, Summer 1992. Available from 2401 Pennsylvania Ave. NW, Washington, DC 20037.

Thomas Hazlett — "The Morning After," *Reason*, March 1992.

Susan V. Lawrence — "Profit in Moscow's Losses," *U.S. News & World Report*, July 6, 1992.

Ellen Poteet and David Finkel — "Dialogue: On the Soviet Upheaval," *Against the Current*, January/February 1992.

William C. Potter — "Nuclear Exports from the Former Soviet Union: What's New, What's True," *Arms Control Today*, January/February 1993. Available from 11 Dupont Circle, Suite 250, Washington, DC 20036.

Carla Anne Robbins — "Caught in the Middle," *U.S. News & World Report*, May 11, 1992.

Sergei Rogov — "International Security and the Collapse of the Soviet Union," *The Washington Quarterly*, Spring 1992. Available from 113 E. Centre St., Nutley, NJ 07110.

Alvin Z. Rubinstein — "In Search of a Foreign Policy," *Society*, October 1992.

Jennifer Scarlott — "Nuclear Genie Redux," *Peace & Democracy News*, Winter 1992.

Ronald Steel — "Losing an Empire, Finding a Role," *New Perspectives Quarterly*, Summer 1992.

How Should the U.S. Respond to the Breakup of the Soviet Union?

Chapter Preface

The collapse of the Soviet Union in December 1991 marked the end of an antagonistic relationship between the United States and the Soviet Union that had existed since the end of World War II. Instead of one nation, which was clearly defined as "the enemy," the United States is now faced with fifteen separate countries with diverse identities and unique problems. The new situation has forced America to rethink its policies toward its former antagonist. One of the issues facing the United States is what to do about the huge arsenals of nuclear weapons built up by both sides during the cold war.

Some commentators, such as former arms negotiator Paul C. Warnke, believe the United States should lead the world toward nuclear disarmament by greatly reducing its own nuclear arsenal. The Soviet threat no longer exists, Warnke and others assert, so the United States no longer has a need for a huge nuclear arsenal. As former U.S. president George Bush states, "The threat of a nuclear nightmare is more distant now than at any time since the dawn of the nuclear age." Former secretary of state Dick Cheney concedes that "the shadow of global nuclear war that darkened half of the 20th century is lifting. Our children," he adds, "aren't growing up learning duck-and-cover drills in school."

Some argue, however, that a nuclear threat remains, and has perhaps increased. The former Soviet nuclear arsenal is scattered throughout several republics. Although most of the republics have agreed to turn their weapons over to Russia, Senators Sam Nunn and Richard Lugar note that the presence of nuclear arms in areas experiencing ethnic tensions and political struggles is perilous. Furthermore, the collapse of the superpower could increase the risk of nuclear proliferation if the economically strapped republics sell their nuclear weapons and technology to countries in the Middle East and the Third World. According to former ambassador Richard Burt, "Nuclear know-how, technology and perhaps even arms are spreading into a world that is increasingly fragmented and chaotic." In light of these threats, some argue that the United States should maintain a strong defense, including a substantial nuclear deterrent force. "The United States," says arms control advisor Paul H. Nitze, "must continue to rely on nuclear weapons as an insurance policy."

Although the breakup of the Soviet Union and the end of the cold war raise hopes for a safer world, dangers still exist. The U.S. policies discussed in the following chapter could profoundly influence the shape and stability of the region and the world for years to come.

"There is no escape from acknowledging the centrality of Russia to American interests."

U.S. Foreign Policy Should Focus on Russia

Dimitri K. Simes

Since the collapse of the Soviet Union, U.S. foreign relations have been complicated by the emergence of fifteen independent countries with unique problems and varied forms of government. In the following viewpoint, Dimitri K. Simes argues that in its dealings with the former Soviet republics, the United States should focus its attention on the Russian Federation. According to Simes, Russia is important to the United States because it controls the ex-Soviet nuclear arsenal and influences the political stability of all the former Soviet republics. The United States should encourage democracy in Russia, says Simes, because if it fails in Russia, it will fail in all the other republics as well. Simes is a senior associate at the Carnegie Endowment for International Peace in Washington, D.C.

As you read, consider the following questions:

1. According to Simes, why is Ukraine hesitating to give up its nuclear weapons? Why does he believe it will eventually give them up?
2. Why is Russia capable of rapid development, according to the author?
3. According to Simes, why should the United States encourage stability in the republics outside Russia?

From Dimitri K. Simes, "America and the Post-Soviet Republics." Reprinted by permission of *Foreign Affairs*, Summer 1992. Copyright 1992 by the Council on Foreign Relations, Inc.

For the second time since World War II the United States must make historic choices about dealing with the Soviet/Russian challenge. This time the issue arises from the collapse of the former enemy, and the new geopolitical situation is a mix of enormous opportunity and tremendous danger. As before Russia may well be central to the future of world politics and, as before, in this realm there is no substitute for American leadership. . . .

Although American policy should be oriented toward the individual post-Soviet states, differentiation among them is a necessity. The fact that all of them once belonged to the same now defunct communist superpower is surely not reason enough to pretend that they are of equal importance to the United States, or that they have similar commitments to political and economic reforms, identically agreeable foreign policies or comparable human rights standards.

Russia Is Central

There is no escape from acknowledging the centrality of Russia to American interests. Russia will be the only major nuclear power in the region. Kazakh President Nursultan Nazarbaev has stated that, although he is willing to transfer tactical nuclear weapons to Russia for destruction, strategic missiles should be eliminated only in the context of a comprehensive disarmament package involving Russia and the other nuclear states. Yet it is likely that his primary motive is to use nuclear weapons as a bargaining chip to draw more attention to his country and to obtain political and economic concessions from Moscow and Washington alike. In the end his record of pragmatism suggests that he will find some face-saving formula and give up nuclear weapons deployed in Kazakhstan rather than risk alienating both Russia and the West.

The Ukrainian situation is more complex. Unlike Nazarbaev, who is exposed to relatively few internal pressures to take an uncompromising stand against Moscow, [Ukranian] President Leonid Kravchuk has to cope with the radical, nationalist Rukh movement. Because of the Ukrainian leader's background as a Communist Party functionary and his current lack of economic accomplishments, standing tall against Russia is his main claim to legitimacy. That, coupled with the hope that nuclear status can bring Ukraine additional prestige and benefits from the West, explains Kravchuk's zigzagging on the issue of delivering Ukrainian tactical nuclear weapons for destruction in Russia. Still Kiev is eager to build bridges to the West and does not want its interests to be neglected in favor of Russia's. This desire for a Western connection puts pressure on the Ukrainian leadership not to overplay its nuclear card.

Neither Ukraine nor Kazakhstan is known to have operational

control over the nuclear weapons on its territory—this control apparently remains in Moscow's hands. Moreover, without Russian know-how, technicians and spare parts, neither Ukraine nor Kazakhstan is in a position to maintain a major nuclear capability. Of course if North Korea or Iraq can develop nuclear weapons, so can Ukraine. Yet the United States and the West in general have considerable leverage to prevent this from happening. Any possible Ukrainian or Kazakh nuclear arsenal, however, would pale dramatically in comparison with Russian nuclear forces.

Russia: The Decisive Republic

The basic course of events in the former Soviet Union depends overwhelmingly on what will happen within the Russian Federation.

This is not to suggest that the other republics, particularly the other major republics, beginning with the Ukraine, are not also important. . . . They are indeed deserving of our attention and resources, but I am prepared to argue that what happens in the Russian Federation is of such a scale, the risk of its spillover is so vast in the other republics and so inescapable, that, for me, it becomes the decisive consideration.

Robert Legvold, statement before the Subcommittee on Europe and the Middle East, House of Representatives, January 21, 1992.

Moreover, among all 15 former Soviet republics, Russia is the only state capable of being more than a regional power. Its territory is twice as large as that of all the other republics combined. More than half the former Soviet population, about 150 million people, lives there. There are also 25 million Russians living outside Russia's borders, many of whom maintain strong ties, if not outright loyalty, to Russia. A large number of them are likely to move back if the CIS disintegrates or if they are subjected to discrimination in their states of present residence. Even more important, Russia is far ahead in terms of the two factors that give the post-Soviet states the best chance for rapid development: abundant natural resources and a cheap but highly skilled labor force. Russia controls 90 percent of the oil, nearly 80 percent of the natural gas, 70 percent of gold production and 62 percent of electricity output of the former Soviet Union.

The highly centralized nature of the Soviet Union assured that the best universities, research centers and think tanks were located disproportionately in Moscow, St. Petersburg, Novosibirsk and a few other major Russian cities. It was common practice for the most able and dynamic representatives of the other republics to come to Russia for their education and settle there for life. Due to Russia's multiethnic composition and the imperial tradition of welcoming minorities into the elite, they are less likely to encounter discrimination there than in the other republics. Chances are that the majority of these people will not go back to their native lands, where they would encounter housing shortages, difficulties in finding new professional jobs and in many cases a more primitive and parochial way of life than that to which they have grown accustomed.

The Future Hangs on Russia

The last and most crucial point is that if democracy fails in Russia the chances are slim that it will survive in the other post-Soviet states. Success of the Russian experiment with political pluralism and a market economy does not guarantee that all other republics will automatically follow suit. But if a nationalist, revanchist and authoritarian regime comes to power in Moscow—one that starts to destabilize and bully its neighbors—it is hard to imagine how, with the possible exception of the Baltic states, the fragile democracies in the region could survive. Even if they managed to maintain their independence with Western security assistance, neo-imperialist Russian pressures would trigger strong nationalist backlash and demands for emergency rule incompatible with the patient introduction of freedom and tolerance.

After all, if it had not been for actions taken by Russia the Soviet communist empire would still be in place. Its collapse was not the result of a military defeat, as was the case with the Austro-Hungarian and Ottoman empires. Nor did Russia reluctantly abandon a costly struggle against pro-independence resistance movements, unlike the colonial empires of Britain, France, Portugal and Spain. Mikhail Gorbachev's government would have had little difficulty keeping the Baltic republics under control if Yeltsin, then chairman of the Russian Supreme Soviet, had not come to their defense: first through expressions of solidarity, then in January 1991 by appealing to Russian soldiers and officers not to take part in a military crackdown and ultimately in February 1991 by calling for Gorbachev's resignation because of his embrace of reactionary policies.

Similarly, during the fateful days of the failed August 1991 putsch, it was the Russian government and parliament that organized the defeat of the conspiracy. With the notable exception of the Baltic states and Armenia, which despite their courage were hardly in a position to influence the coup's outcome, the leaders of the other republics either endorsed the junta or failed to resist it.

Russia was the central force in the destruction of the Soviet totalitarian state, and Russia's continuing commitment to democracy and to a non-imperial foreign policy is a precondition for the freedom and prosperity of the other Commonwealth members. . . .

The American focus on Russia, of course, should not mean neglect of the other newly independent states or license for Russia to get away with aggressive behavior in its policies toward them or any other country. Instead the American approach should reflect an appreciation that Russian developments are central to shaping the entire region's political character. Any sensible U.S. policy would use this as its point of departure.

This comprehensive approach should include security, economic and moral dimensions. . . . The United States has an interest in making sure the newly independent states are stable and secure, if for no other reason than to eliminate any neo-imperial temptation on Russia's part to meddle in their affairs. At the same time America should be careful not to give the impression that it is siding with these states against Russia in order to create a new *cordon sanitaire* to exclude Russia from Europe. That approach would only provide ammunition to those in Russia who charge that the West is inherently hostile to their country. . . .

Of course the ultimate outcome of the historical drama unfolding in the former Soviet Union will not be determined by foreigners. There is the real possibility that, no matter what the West does, democracy in these lands will prove only a brief interlude. But there is the virtual certainty that without a major constructive engagement by the West—and, realistically, this can only be arranged by the United States—the Russian democratic experiment will go up in smoke, taking the rest of the region with it.

On the one hand is the prospect that Russia will reestablish itself as a great power. If it does so without abandoning its commitment to democracy—due to the fact that its economy is relatively underdeveloped and its exports are mainly commodities—then it would have less reason than Germany or Japan to be at odds with the United States. Russia's revival thus has the potential of making a positive contribution to the global economic and geopolitical equilibrium that is beginning to drift against U.S. interests.

On the other hand one does not need excessive imagination to conjure up disasters of an apocalyptic magnitude if the Russian empire is reborn and attempts to strike back. The stakes are high for the United States, and they require an immediate, purposeful and comprehensive effort.

"The United States . . . needs to focus immediately on the precise nature of the problems of the 15 successor states."

U.S. Foreign Policy Should Focus on All of the Republics

Paul A. Goble

Paul A. Goble is a senior associate of the Carnegie Endowment for International Peace, a Washington, D.C., organization that conducts research in foreign policy and foreign affairs. In the following viewpoint, he argues that the United States has increased instability in the former Soviet Union by refusing to recognize the emergence of fifteen separate countries. By focusing diplomatic attention on Russia and failing to establish strong ties to the other republics, says Goble, the United States has sent disruptive messages and alienated important states. Goble concludes that the United States must deal with the new republics as separate nations, rather than as one empire.

As you read, consider the following questions:

1. Why is Ukraine the first republic the United States should address, according to Goble?
2. According to the author, why are the Baltic states important to the United States?
3. The United States has sent the message that possessing nuclear weapons can draw Western attention, according to Goble. Why might this be dangerous?

From Paul A. Goble, "Forget the Soviet Union: Talk About the Independent States," *Foreign Policy* 86 (Spring 1992). Reprinted with permission.

The sometimes comic, sometimes pathetic efforts to come up with a new name for what used to be the Soviet Union conceal a far deeper problem: Policymakers in practice are unwilling to acknowledge that the USSR no longer exists, that it has been replaced by 15 independent states, and that this change profoundly affects the global standing of the United States. Given the personal and national investments in the old status quo, this reluctance is entirely understandable. Nevertheless, it is extremely damaging to U.S. interests. Without an intellectual and emotional shift among both the American public and policymakers, the United States will not be in a good position to promote American values, encourage stability on one-seventh of the earth's land surface, and gain access to what is surely the largest new market and source of raw materials to open to the West in this generation. . . .

The West's . . . continued use of the Russian government in Moscow as an interlocutor on most questions virtually guarantees that the other republics will move away from Russia even faster than would otherwise be the case. The possibility that any of them will move closer is extremely unlikely, at least in the short term. The United States therefore needs to focus immediately on the precise nature of the problems of the 15 successor states, because those are the issues it will have to choose to address or ignore in the future.

In addition to maintaining an affection for some kind of single state, U.S. policymakers have thus far been constrained by a failure to distinguish carefully among the very different kinds of problems the new countries face. Analytically and practically, the problems fall into three large categories: those facing all successor states by virtue of their common experience within the former Soviet system, regional problems among the new states, and the specific problems of specific countries. To date, most Western attention has focused on the first and second of these categories; the third has been largely ignored. . . .

The Individual Republics

In focusing almost exclusively on the difficulties common to all of the new states and on the emerging interstate challenges, the West has largely ignored the more numerous and complex problems confronting the former republics: those at the level of the individual republics. Most of the West's attention should be fixed on these problems. Unfortunately, the United States, like other Western countries, has very little expertise with the republics; officials tend to extrapolate from the more familiar areas to the unfamiliar ones. In doing so, they increasingly resemble the blind men and the elephant. Observers of events in Georgia, for example, are likely to expect the coming of the apocalypse. Those who focus on Ukraine, on the other hand, are likely to conclude just the reverse. The United States must take particular care to acknowledge this problem, or misplaced assumptions will lead to inappropriate policies, such as the misdirection of aid or even more serious missteps. Obviously many of the problems of the individual republics will and perhaps even should remain outside the U.S. government's radar scope. Others, however, can only be ignored at great peril.

Reprinted by permission: Tribune Media Services.

First among the problems that should concern the United States are those of Ukraine. Ukraine is, after Russia, the largest country in Europe and very much hopes to play a major role in the ever-expanding Eastern Europe. A major immediate issue is whether Ukraine will try to become a nuclear power. At the moment, it has no such intentions. Because of the 1986 Chernobyl disaster, antinuclear sentiments run strong in Ukraine. But the official policy can change if Ukraine comes to believe that it is insufficiently protected by European institutions against Russian power, that the West wants Ukraine to simply hand over weapons on its territory to its most likely foreign adversary (Russia), and that the West will pay attention to it only because it possesses nuclear weapons. A minority in Kiev has already drawn these conclusions; should other officials do so, the Ukrainian government will undoubtedly seek to gain actual control over the nuclear weapons on its territory. (For now it does not have such control and is thus a nuclear "power" in much the same sense that West Germany was during the Cold War.) Ukrainian success in gaining that control could prompt Germany to reexamine its nonnuclear status, raising a host of new security questions for Europe.

Second, although the three Baltic states received a disproportionate amount of Western attention in the past, unfortunately they are now receiving less and less attention in the United States. As a glance at any map of Europe will show, there are only six major deepwater, ice-free ports on the European edge of the former Soviet Union. Four of them are either located in the Baltic countries themselves or controlled by the Balts by virtue of their control over transportation between Kaliningrad and the Russian Federation proper. The Germans and the Japanese appear to have a far better conceptual understanding of developments in the Baltic region: There is now a Japanese school in Riga and a major contingent of German government and economic officials in all three Baltic capitals. In the short term, the Germans and Japanese may achieve little. But through their actions in the Baltic countries, these two governments have positioned themselves to gain access to what in a few years will be the largest new market—Russia—to open this decade, as well as the largest new source of raw materials in the postwar period.

Developments in Russia

Third, the United States must be attentive to certain developments in Russia. By virtue of its size and likely control of all nuclear weapons, Russia will remain the West's leading interlocutor—even if it must not become the only one. But Russia faces certain problems that are likely to affect America's ability to conduct business as desired with Moscow. Russia faces a major challenge by the independence-seeking Kazan Tatars, who sit across most of the major east-west transportation arteries between European Russia and Siberia and who politically dominate the region in which the West Siberian oil field is located. While that leading Soviet oil field is declining in productivity, its importance is likely to increase dramatically in the short run, as Azerbaijan shifts to sell its oil abroad for hard currency rather than north for increasingly worthless rubles or barter. Boris Yeltsin . . . will have to move carefully to avoid undercutting his democratic reforms and alienating the Muslim republics to the south. . . .

Given these and other complexities, it should come as no surprise that there is a kind of nostalgia for the older and simpler days and a tendency to preserve old methods of conducting relations. Unfortunately, both can contribute to serious problems, the first by diminishing our appreciation for the achievements of Yeltsin and others, and the second by creating some unintended and regrettable consequences. To date, the U.S. approach to the republics has been grudging and slow: The Baltic countries will not soon forget that Washington recognized them after Mongolia did, thus coming in 36th overall.

More seriously, the initial American failure to establish diplomatic ties with all the remaining 12 republics at once has sent unintended and possibly dangerous messages. While the United States has been explicit that it wants only one nuclear successor state, U.S. policy has demonstrated that possessing nuclear weapons can draw Western attention—a lesson not lost in Kiev, Minsk, or Alma Ata, not to mention other capitals. This impression will only be shaken when the United States moves to exchange diplomats with all the successor states.

Likewise, by extending diplomatic relations to Armenia but not to Azerbaijan, the United States has further alienated Baku from the West and increased the likelihood of violence in the Caucasus in the short run. . . . In Central Asia, as in Azerbaijan, the United States unwittingly gave aid and comfort not to the more secular elites now in power but to Islamic radicals, who have one more argument that the West is no friend to the Muslims.

None of these problems are beyond correction, though reversing course will not be easy. The problems highlight a need that has not yet been widely recognized. In the past, Soviet specialists who spoke Russian could keep up with events in each of the republics. Now, to understand in Kiev or Alma Ata, an analyst must know the local language and history. In the case of most of the new countries, there are very few if any in the U.S. government who possess these capabilities, and there are often no students of these languages in U.S. universities. This trend will have to change if the United States is to avoid making more mistakes.

Only a few years ago, most policymakers viewed any interest in the Soviet nationalities as an exoticism—an image that few in the field did much to counter. Now the problem is serious because it involves interests critical to the United States: economic growth, access to markets and raw materials, and political power. The demise of the USSR has transformed not only the region, but America's role in the world as well. The comfortable bipolar world is gone; and while the United States remains a superpower, it must now compete with Europe, Japan, and other increasingly important countries on a basis and in a region offering few advantages to the United States. In that new world, there will be far less order—and the tasks of promoting stability and extending American values will be far more difficult.

111

"Bringing Russia . . . into the family of peaceful nations will serve our highest security, economic, and moral interests. "

Western Aid to the Republics Will Ensure U.S. Security

Warren M. Christopher

Warren M. Christopher was appointed U.S. secretary of state under President Bill Clinton in January 1993. Previously, he served as deputy secretary of state under President Jimmy Carter. He is best remembered for his implementation of Carter's human rights policies and for his role in the release of the U.S. hostages from Iran in January 1981. In the following viewpoint, Christopher expresses his support for American economic, technical, and educational aid to Russia in its transition to democracy and a free-market economy. Without Western help, Christopher argues, Russia and the other former Soviet republics could revert to anarchy or despotism, renewing the military threat and thereby forcing the United States to increase defense spending.

As you read, consider the following questions:

1. What does Christopher mean when he says the United States needs to harness its diplomacy to serve its economic goals?
2. Why should the United States help Russia repair its oil wells, according to the author?
3. According to Christopher, why would exchange programs help Russia?

From Warren M. Christopher, "Securing U.S. Interests While Supporting Russian Reform," *U.S. Department of State Dispatch* 4, no. 13 (March 29, 1993): 173-77.

Our world has changed fundamentally in recent years. Walls have come down. Empires have collapsed. Most important, the Cold War is over, and the Soviet Union is no more. Soviet communism is dead. But with it so is the reference point that guided our policies for over 40 years. It was easy when we could simply point to the Soviet Union and say that what we had to do was to contain Soviet expansion. That reference point explained why our international leadership was so necessary, why our defense burden was so heavy, and why assistance to other countries was so critical.

Today, we face a vastly more complicated world. It is a world of breathtaking opportunities to expand democracy and free markets. But it is also a world of grave new perils. Long-simmering ethnic conflicts have flared up anew in the former Yugoslavia and elsewhere. Weapons of mass destruction are falling into the hands of very dangerous dictators. And new global challenges cry out for attention around our entire world—challenges like the environment, overpopulation, drug-trafficking, and AIDS.

Like the last generation's great leaders who met the challenges of the Cold War, we need a new strategy for protecting and promoting American interests in this new era. We need a strategy that will face the questions that Americans are asking, and most understandably asking: Why, they say, with the threat of Soviet expansionism gone, do we need to be active on the international front? Why must America continue to carry the heavy burdens of leadership? Why, when we so urgently need renewal here at home, should we continue to dedicate large resources abroad?

The Three Pillars of U.S. Policy

President Clinton has responded to these challenges by laying out an American foreign policy based upon three pillars:

First, building American prosperity;

Second, modernizing America's armed services; and

Third, promoting democracy and human rights abroad.

This policy's fundamental premise is that in today's world foreign and domestic policy are inseparable. If we fail to maintain our strength at home, we will be, certainly, unable to lead abroad. If we retreat into isolationism, it will be impossible to revitalize our domestic strength. America cannot thrive in a world of economic recession or violent conflicts or a world which is riven with dictatorships.

It is no accident that President Clinton has identified promotion of America's economic security as the *first* pillar of our foreign policy. We've entered an era where economic competitiveness is vital to our ability to succeed abroad. . . .

But steps at home cannot ensure America's prosperity. Today, we are irreversibly linked to the global economy. Our lives are constantly touched by huge flows of trade and finance that cross many borders. To take another example, over 7 million Americans are now employed in export-related jobs. . . .

Our ability to prosper in this global economy depends upon our ability to compete. That means harnessing our diplomacy to serve our economic goals. We must ensure that foreign markets are open to US goods and US investments. We must fight unfair competition against US business and labor. And we must press the world's other financial powers to enact responsible policies that foster growth.

Keeping Peace and Promoting Democracy

The *second* pillar of our foreign policy will be to modernize our armed forces to meet new needs around the world and to meet continuing threats. The collapse of the Soviet Union enables us to significantly scale back our military establishment. But, nevertheless, our power must always be sufficient to counter any threat to our vital interests. We must be able to deter and, when necessary, to defeat any potential foe. That's why we are taking steps to make our military more agile, mobile, flexible, and smart. Let me emphasize that President Clinton is determined to have the best-equipped and best-fighting force in America to defend America.

As we talk about our armed forces, I think it's important for me to say that America cannot be the world's policeman. We cannot be responsible for settling every dispute or answering every alarm. We are indispensable, but we certainly must not be indiscriminate. America's leadership will require that we wisely marshal the West's collective strength.

Ethnic conflicts—and the humanitarian disasters they generate—deeply offend our conscience. In many cases, they also pose a serious risk to international peace. And they produce thousands of refugees, so often, that strain the political and economic stability of an entire region. Our imperative is to develop international means to contain and, more important, to prevent these conflicts before they erupt. Here, it is critical that we use the United Nations in the manner its founders intended, and there is high, new hope that this may take place. UN peacekeeping capabilities must be strengthened so as to allow prompt, preventive action. Our other instruments of collective security, such as our NATO alliance, must be adapted in this new era to support the UN efforts. . . .

Let me now turn to the *third* pillar of this Administration's foreign policy: encouraging the global revolution for democracy and human rights that is transforming the world. By helping promote democracy, we do more than honor our deepest values. We are also making a strategic investment in our nation's security. History has shown that a world of more democracies is a safer world. It is a world that will devote more to human development and less to human destruction. And it is a world that will promote what all people have in common rather than what tears them apart.

These three pillars of American foreign policy—building America's prosperity, modernizing America's armed forces, and promoting democratic values—form the core of the Clinton Administration's new diplomacy. Now I would like to tell you how these three pillars converge and form the basis for one of our highest foreign policy priorities—and that is helping the Russian people to build a free society and a market economy. This, in my judgment, is the greatest strategic challenge of our time. Bringing Russia—one of history's most powerful nations—into the family of peaceful nations will serve our highest security, economic, and moral interests.

Russia a Great Security Challenge

We need to respond forcefully to one of the greatest security challenges of our time, to help the people of the former Soviet bloc demilitarize their societies and build free political and economic institutions. We have a chance to engage the Russian people in the West for the first time in their history. . . .

I know it isn't popular to call for foreign assistance of any kind. It's harder when Americans are hurting, as millions are. But I believe it is deeply irresponsible to forgo this short term investment in our long term security. Being penny wise and pound foolish will cost us more in the long run in higher defense budgets and lost economic opportunities.

Bill Clinton, speech delivered to the Foreign Policy Association, April 1, 1992.

For America and the world, the stakes are just monumental. If we succeed, we will have established the foundation for our lasting security into the next century. But if Russia falls into anarchy or lurches back to despotism, the price that we pay could be frightening. Nothing less is involved than the possibility of renewed nuclear threat, higher defense budgets, spreading instability, the loss of new markets, and a devastating setback for the worldwide democratic movement. This circumstance deserves the attention of each and every American. . . .

My intention is not to announce a detailed program of new initiatives; rather, what I would like to do is to try to provide a strategic context for the approach that we will follow. I want to explain the tremendous interest we have in doing everything we can to help Russia's democracy succeed.

Let me stress that by focusing on Russia, I do not mean to neglect the other new independent states. The well-being of Ukraine, of Kazakhstan, of Belarus, of Armenia, and, indeed, of each of the former republics, is a matter of utmost importance to America. We are committed to developing strong bilateral relations with each of these countries. We will support their independence and do everything we can to assist in their integration into the world community. Indeed, it is partly out of concern for their welfare that I want to concentrate on Russia today. For the fact is that the future security of each of these neighbors of Russia depends so heavily on Russia's own democratic revolution.

Breathtaking Benefits

Let me step back for just a moment and analyze with you the breathtaking benefits that the end of the Cold War has brought to the United States and the world. To mention just a few of the results:

• Historic agreements have been reached to slash the nuclear arsenals that threatened our country with annihilation.

• The nations of the former Warsaw Pact are now free of Soviet domination and of the burden of communism.

• The possibility of a superpower conflict on the European continent has now all but vanished, allowing us to bring home thousands of troops and to reduce our defense budgets.

• Around the globe, totalitarian regimes that looked to the Soviet Union for help and support are now isolated and on the defensive.

• And from Vilnius on the Baltic to Vladivostok on the Pacific, vast new markets are opening—opening slowly but nonetheless opening—to Western business.

With a reforming Russia, all of these historic achievements were possible. But without it, many will not be sustainable.

So we stand again at a historic crossroads. It is very reminiscent of the crossroads that we faced in 1918 and 1945. Then, we were summoned after conflicts to lead the world by building a new peace. After World War I, we chose to retreat, and the consequences were disastrous. However, after World War II, our leaders had the wisdom to answer the call. We fostered institutions that rebuilt the free world's prosperity. And we helped to lead a democratic alliance that contained and, ultimately, drained Soviet communism.

A Historic Opportunity

Today, for the third time this century, we have a historic opportunity to build a more secure world. We must redouble our efforts to help the Russian people as they struggle in an effort that has no historical precedent. With great courage, they are attempting to carry out three simultaneous revolutions: first, transforming a totalitarian system into a democracy; second, transforming a command economy into one based upon free markets; and third, transforming an aggressive, expansionist empire into a peaceful, modern nation-state. If they succeed in this tremendous experiment, we all will succeed. . . .

The United States has strongly supported Russia's efforts to build a democracy. Under President Boris Yeltsin's leadership, historic progress has been made toward a free society. We urge that this progress continue and that the Russian people be allowed to determine their future through peaceful means and with full respect for civil liberties. On that basis, Russia can be assured of our full support in the days ahead.

Now, today's crisis in Russia results from one indisputable fact: The pain of building a new system virtually from scratch is exacting a tremendous toll. The patience of the Russian people is wearing thin. . . . Nevertheless, we should notice that President Yeltsin and Russia's other democrats have demonstrated their commitment to reform in many ways. Civil liberties have been dramatically expanded. The military budget has been significantly cut. Prices have been freed in most sectors, and the result has been [that] the once-long lines that formed outside Russia's stores have come to an end. Tens of thousands of shops, restaurants, and other firms have been put into private hands, and a real start has been made on the most difficult process of even privatizing the large enterprises. As a result of these steps, the share of the work force engaged in private commerce has more than doubled since 1991.

I'm glad to say that President Yeltsin [has] recommitted his government to economic reform. He [has] laid out in clear and strong language the key elements of such a program: continued privatization of firms, selling land to farmers, stopping inflation, and stabilizing the ruble. If this program is implemented, our capacity to help will be greatly enhanced.

In U.S. Interests

Russia's reformers are now looking to the West for support at this moment of extreme difficulty. The United States has a deep self-interest in responding to this historic challenge. We should extend to the Russian people not a hand of pity but a hand of partnership. We must lead a long-term Western strategy of engagement for democracy.

Here in America, it is very important that we not create a false choice between what is required to renew our economy at home and what is necessary to protect our interests abroad. We can and must do both. During the long struggle of the Cold War, we kept the American dream alive for all people here at home. At the same time, we made great sacrifices to protect our national security, and today we can and must meet the same challenge. To succeed, we must first change our mindsets. We must understand that helping consolidate democracy in Russia is not a matter of charity but a security concern of the highest order. It is no less important to our well-being than the need to contain a hostile Soviet Union was at an earlier day. . . .

Targets of Aid

My task is not to spell out specific initiatives. Nevertheless, I would like to offer just a few thoughts on the central issue of Western aid to Russia in general terms. Clearly, our assistance must be better targeted and better coordinated than it's been in the past. It must focus on areas and constituencies in Russia that have the greatest impact on their long-term reform. It must not and cannot be limited solely to public funds. Rather, it must catalyze our private sectors to take a leading role in Russia's transformation through trade, investment, and training. And our aid must be felt at the grassroots, to ease the pain of the Russian children, workers, and senior citizens who are suffering through this transformation.

Despite all of its current economic difficulties, it is worth remembering that Russia is inherently a rich country. Its people are well-educated. Its natural resource base exceeds that of any other country in the world. For example, Russia's oil reserves are huge and, if properly exploited, could probably finance much of Russia's economic reform. But thousands of aging oil wells and pipelines in Russia stand idle, decaying and desperately in need of critical spare parts. If Russia could find the means to repair them, perhaps with our help, the oil sold would be a lucrative source of foreign exchange that could do a great deal to stabilize their economy.

One area of possible assistance where America's vital interests are directly engaged is our effort to dismantle the nuclear weapons of the former Soviet Union. The $800-million program established through the leadership of Senators Sam Nunn and Richard Lugar to destroy these weapons is a direct investment in our own security. Unfortunately, some bottlenecks, both here and in Russia, have allowed only a small fraction of the $800 million to be spent. Part of it has been caused by bureaucratic delays in Washington, and we are fully determined to remove these obstacles. We want to see these weapons dismantled in the very shortest possible time.

Another important goal we should have is strengthening the groups in Russia that will form the bulwark of a thriving democracy. There are public opinion polls in Russia, too, as you know, and time after time they show one thing: By large margins, it's the younger generation that expresses the greatest sympathy for democracy. The younger people are the ones who are pushing for more economic freedom and closer contacts with the West. Ultimately, whatever the result of today's political turmoil, this is the group that will carry the day for Russia's successful transition to democracy.

Through exchange programs, many young Russians can be brought to the West and exposed to the workings of democracy and our free market. Russian students, public officials, scientists, and businessmen are hungry for such experiences. Upon their return home, they can adapt their knowledge to best suit Russia's conditions. And, perhaps most important of all, we can win long-term friends and partners for freedom.

The existence, to take another example, of a strong, independent media is also essential for a democratic society. While Russia's free press has experienced tremendous growth in recent years, there is still a real need for professional training of reporters, editors, and news managers. Here, technical assistance can make a real difference.

Another area that deserves strong support is Russia's privatization effort, which, as I said, has made some progress. This process has continued across many of Russia's regions despite the political problems in Moscow. Putting private property into the hands of the Russian people is a critical step in building a free market economy. It will create millions of property owners and private entrepreneurs—a genuine middle class with a powerful stake in continued reform.

Of course, at the end of the day, Russia's progress toward the market and democracy cannot occur without an overhaul of the general ground rules of the Russian economy. It will be vital to reduce their budget deficit, control the money supply, stabilize the ruble, and close down inefficient factories. Unfortunately, these are also steps that will cause the greatest pain and political risk. Here again, Russia needs our help. The West must find a way to respond, and the response can't be limited to big promises and little delivery. We are now engaged in intensive consultations with our partners from the leading industrial democracies to develop a program of joint assistance to Russia in these areas.

For the Duration

We must have no illusions about the situation in Russia. Even with our help, the road ahead is rocky. Setbacks will be inevitable. Russia's transformation will take a great deal of hard work—probably a generation to complete. . . . It's important that we maintain a long-term perspective. Just as our vigilance in the Cold War took more than 4 decades to pay off, our commitment to Russia's democracy must be for the duration. Our engagement with the reformers must be for the long haul—whether they're "out" as well as when they're "in," whether they're "down" as well as when they're "up." However difficult things may be in the short run, we should have faith that the strategic course we have set—supporting democracy's triumph—is the correct one.

We should know that any realistic program to assist Russia won't be cheap. But there's no question that our nation can afford its fair share of the international effort. We can't afford, indeed, to do otherwise. Together with President Clinton, I am determined to work with the Congress to find the funding. I am confident that the necessary resources can be found as we restructure our defense budget. But it will require bipartisanship, leadership, and vision, and, vitally, it will take a Russian partner committed to democratic values and to market reform.

At a time of great domestic challenge, some would say that we should delay bold action in the foreign realm. But history will not wait. As Abraham Lincoln advised his countrymen, "We cannot escape history. We . . . will be remembered in spite of ourselves." Today, history is calling again for our nation to decide whether we will lead or defer, whether we will shape this new era or be shaped by it. How will history remember us? I, for one, am confident that we will make the right choice—that we will be bold and brave in revitalizing our nation here at home, while continuing to promote our interests and ideals abroad.

"Economic assistance cannot serve as a surrogate for a potent national defense."

Western Aid to the Republics Will Not Ensure U.S. Security

Steven Rosefielde

Many commentators assume that Western economic aid to Russia in support of democratic economic reforms would indirectly ensure U.S. security by establishing in Russia a pro-American democracy. Steven Rosefielde, the author of the following viewpoint, disagrees. The West is wrong, says Rosefielde, to assume that the economic reforms under way in Russia are democratic. Rather, Rosefielde believes that they constitute a corrupt form of socialism. He concludes that American aid would only encourage a socialistic system which might pose a threat to U.S. security. Rosefielde is a professor of economics at the University of North Carolina in Chapel Hill.

As you read, consider the following questions:

1. According to Rosefielde, why is the West employing a "minimalist approach" toward Russia?
2. How is the Russian definition of "market economy" different from that of the West, according to the author?
3. How does Rosefielde define "kleptocratic socialism"?

Steven Rosefielde, "Russian Aid and Western Security," *Global Affairs*, Fall 1992. Reprinted by permission of the International Security Council.

Western advocates of massive foreign assistance to the former Soviet Union have long argued that aid would increase international stability, promote democracy and nudge the region toward market capitalism. These ideas took a variety of forms. Sometimes they were expressed as support for key political figures like Mikhail Gorbachev and Boris Yeltsin; sometimes as inducements for specific reforms. Although neither approach was likely to succeed, they were never given a decisive empirical test. Events kept overwhelming them. The twists and turns of regional politics, and the manifest failure of domestic economic reforms always seemed to stay in the G-7's hand at the critical moment.

The resulting frustration increasingly encouraged advocates to deny the fundamental chaos besetting the Soviet Union and the C.I.S [Commonwealth of Independent States], and to search for a rationale that justified massive financial assistance regardless of the circumstances. The rallying cry, "Save Russia!" coined by former President Richard Nixon, appears to serve this purpose. It encompasses most of the old objectives; the stabilization of Russia, the strengthening of Yeltsin, the pursuit of democracy, market capitalism and peace, but goes beyond these by setting aside all concerns about the merit, feasibility and cost of this neo-Wilsonian crusade.

The impact of the formula has been immediate and profound. Although the substance of Nixon's proposed program is trivial, the concept was widely hailed, and within a matter of weeks President George Bush felt impelled to join German chancellor Helmut Kohl in announcing a seemingly munificent assistance program with few, if any, significant reservations. So long as Yeltsin reiterates his commitment to democracy, market reform, and peace, the spigot purportedly will be opened wide, unless he is deposed, or becomes embroiled in a hot war with one of the successor states over the fate of its Russian minority or its resources.

The Kohl-Bush Initiative

The centerpiece of the West's "Save Russia!" campaign is the Kohl-Bush initiative which has the virtue of consolidating dispersed pledges by the G-7 industrial powers into a unified assistance package with an explicit price tag: $24 billion for the year 1992. This figure was arrived at by the International Monetary Fund which estimated that Russian import needs will exceed export receipts by $18 billion. The IMF contends that these excess imports are vital for the success of Russia's economic transition program, and therefore proposes that the G-7 provide financial assistance in the form of diverse import credits, even though NATO economists contend that Russia could cover most of the deficit with its $11 billion gold reserve.

The remaining $6 billion in assistance will serve another purpose. These monies are not intended to augment the transfer of goods and services to Russia; they are supposed to support foreign exchange rates when the ruble becomes partially convertible. When short-term foreign demand for rubles declines, the G-7 agrees to buy them with dollars, thereby helping to maintain exchange parities. Assuming that the exchange rates initially fixed by the authorities are consistent with balance of payments equilibrium, and the Russians do not import more than the IMF plans, no monies may be needed. However, if they are, the cash will be borrowed from the IMF's General Arrangements to Borrow, intended for use in the West, which presently holds $23 billion. This permits the G-7 to intervene in defense of the ruble without having to create a new facility. . . .

Ramirez/Copley News Service. Reprinted with permission.

The disparity between the content of Kohl-Bush initiative and its lofty political rhetoric reflects the triumph of political imagination over economic problem solving. The G-7 has embraced the mission of saving Russia without committing itself to providing the aid and know-how to get the job done. Its plan amounts to little more than a decision to allow Russia to join the IMF, World Bank and EBRD [European Bank for Reconstruction and Development]. Statements to the contrary notwithstanding, it is this decision, not the much publicized $12 billion American "replenishment" contribution to the IMF which provided all $4.5 billion of new credit assistance to Russia.

This minimalist approach insofar as it is anything more than an expedient attempt to seize the moral high ground, while allowing matters to sort themselves out, is predicated on the dubious premise that vast sums are not needed because Russia has embarked on a series of reforms which will enable the private sector to transform the economy with the guidance and assistance of the IMF. The G-7 apparently is content to operate on the supposition that if Western trade barriers are removed, joint ventures encouraged, and the Russian government is fiscally responsible, $18 billion of grants, credits, loan guarantees and debt deferral will provide the kick-start the market requires to generate self-perpetuating prosperity.

This theory of course is hardly novel. It is the same sort of thinking that governed Western assistance to Gorbachev's Russia. IMF officials acknowledge this, but assert that this time things are different because Yeltsin's reforms are genuine.

The Market Reform Plan

This assertion does not imply that the reforms instituted by Yegor Gaidar, the Russian deputy prime minister and former finance minister, differ fundamentally in concept from those of his predecessors. Gaidar's policies are precisely those elaborated in Stanislav Shatalin's "500 Days" plan and partly adopted by Gorbachev. The G-7 merely takes the position that Yeltsin is actually doing what the Soviets only contemplated. The essence of Gaidar's program is to bring about a rapid transition to the market *perekhod krynku* through a strategy of forced state-sector budgetary self-sufficiency, financed by Western foreign aid. The domestic aspect of this policy, as in the Shatalin plan, is to be accomplished by partially privatizing the state sector, abolishing state planning, curtailing the administrative powers of the regulatory bureaucracy, substituting inter-enterprise contracting for state directives, eliminating price controls, abolishing subsidies and making the ruble convertible.

Western financing, as Shatalin urged in August 1990, is to be sought in the forms of humanitarian assistance, loan guarantees and credit provided by the IMF, World Bank and EBRD. Shatalin's initial target, which was explicitly likened to a new Marshall Plan, was $10-20 billion. Gaidar's inventory of domestic reforms has the resonance of capitalism: Surely if the Russian economy is based on private property which can be used entrepreneurially in pursuit of personal gain by competitively contracting at negotiated prices, the end result must be free enterprise.

This is a logical inference, but it overlooks the reality of "Soviet-speak." Russian market rhetoric bears very little correspondence to Western practice. The goal of Shatalin and Gaidar is the creation of a marketized form of state socialism, efficient enough to compete with the West. Their commitment to socialism is abiding and decisive.

Privatization as they use the term means maintaining "the commanding heights of the economy" in state hands for the foreseeable future, both with respect to formal ownership and centralized control. Curtailing the bureaucracy means reducing administrative meddling in the daily affairs of state enterprises, not foreswearing comprehensive regulation. Competitive contracting means that state enterprises can negotiate with state purchasers about the terms of state orders, not that firms vie with each other to satisfy private consumer demand. Eliminating price controls, including wage levels, means that prices for state enterprises, wholesale distributors and retail outlets are fixed behind the scenes by ministerial price boards, instead of by the State Price Committee. Abolishing subsidies means that firms will often be forced into bankruptcy due to systemic irrationalities beyond their control, whenever compensatory bank credit is unavailable. And ruble convertibility means foreigners can acquire Russian currency at more or less competitive rates, but cannot put it to constructive use because of pervasive export controls.

In short, the state is prepared to adopt all the trappings of markets, so long as they do not infringe on its monopoly of administrative power.

This of course, as Gorbachev discovered the hard way, is a recipe for disaster. The strategy gives the illusion of creating a free enterprise economy governed by the laws of supply and demand. The system in fact would be a degenerate controlled economy where enterprises are forced to fend for themselves in an environment dominated by state orders, capricious frugality, fiscal irresponsibility and runaway inflation.

The empirical proof is readily at hand for all who want to see. Although Russian statistics for the 1990s are especially suspect, real GNP since 1989 has fallen at least 30 percent, and more likely by half, under the shock therapy of Shatalin, Gorbachev, and Gaidar. This behavior manifestly contradicts all the tenets of neoclassical market theory, and belies the assumptions of the G-7's assistance strategy.

Kleptocratic Socialism

Sophisticated advocates of saving Russia are usually prepared to admit that the transition to market capitalism has not gone as smoothly as they might have imagined. But they attribute this lapse to other factors, such as political disunion and incipient civil war. They acknowledge that command planning still holds considerable sway, but counter that the market is making headway, and will soon emerge triumphant. In doing so they point to several significant developments: The relaxation of price and wage controls (including the exchange rate), the creation of private commodity exchanges, an explosion of part-time entrepreneurship as budget cuts drive professionals out of the institutes into the market, and most important of all, the sudden outbreak of spontaneous privatization.

Instead of waiting patiently for the Russian Congress of Peoples Deputies to devise a comprehensive privatization program, institutions, bureaucrats, politicians and managers are asserting ownership rights to assets under their control. These properties, which may be held privately, cooperatively, collectively, or in mixed labor-management forms, include office buildings, institutes and factories. They, conceivably, could lead to the swift emergence of a capitalist class. It is easy to see, therefore, why some specialists might be hopeful that market capitalism is self-generating, and will soon be ascendant despite considerable internal opposition.

The blithe equation of bureaucratic thievery with capitalist entrepreneurship however is fundamentally misleading. Spontaneous privatization in Russia is not creating capitalism; it is the basis for kleptocratic socialism, where the ruling state elites acquire legal title to key properties they administer. These kleptocrats are primarily interested in passive wealth, and are only prepared to tolerate privatization for other purposes if would-be entrepreneurs subordinate themselves to the political authorities and pay the requisite tribute.

As a consequence they assiduously promote the illusion of change to open Western purse strings, while opposing reforms that would transfer power to would-be capitalist rivals. Again, if matters were otherwise, the economy would not be in free fall.

Dim Prospects for Democracy

It can be safely concluded that insofar as the G-7's wager on Gaidar's "market capitalist" reforms is sincere, it is a sucker's bet. Russia has yet to extricate itself from the thrall of socialism, and has embarked on still another futile quest to build an economy that is both prosperous and subservient to the state's will. The experiment cannot have a happy ending for Russia, the G-7, Western taxpayers and joint venturers who are going to be stuck with the bill. But even if the G-7 were to partly succeed by stabilizing kleptocratic socialism, what precisely would be accomplished to warrant the expense?

Yeltsin came to power as a result of a failed coup d'etat, and rules like an autocrat despite his euphemistic title as president.

126

In this regard his claim to legitimacy differs little from that of Peruvian president Alberto Fujimori. Prospects for democracy and social justice are dim, and evidence of imperial domination both internally, and over the other members of the commonwealth, are unmistakable.

Perhaps an argument can still be made for the G-7's initiative to "Save Russia!" on other grounds. But if the case has merit, it should be defended as such in the professional literature, and not under the much abused banner of freedom, democracy and capitalism.

Aid Is No Defense

The "Save Russia!" crusade has been marketed by the G-7 to its publics as a cost-effective strategy for securing the peace. In doing so an impression has been created that foreign assistance is a workable substitute for military prowess and deterrence. It has become almost axiomatic that America should drastically reduce its defense expenditures and relinquish its superpower capabilities, despite direct testimony from ranking Russian military authorities that weapons procurement continues at high levels, and that it intends to devote no less than 10 percent of GNP to defense *ad infinitum*.

A thorough discussion of post-Soviet international security policy lies beyond the scope of this essay. But it is essential to observe that insofar as the G-7's "Save Russia!" strategy is technically misguided, the West cannot capriciously assume that economic assistance is a remotely viable alternative to a robust national defense.

The leaders of the G-7 industrial states have found it politically expedient to mount a campaign to "Save Russia!" without making a corresponding commitment to provide the colossal resources such an effort entails. In doing so, they have taken the position that the financial assistance required is less than might be supposed, because the reforms fashioned by Gaidar have already initiated a self-generating economic transition from administrative command planning to the market. But the reforms Russia has undertaken will foster kleptocratic socialism, not democratic, market capitalism. This degenerate system is not only ethically repugnant, but has thrown the economy into a free fall from which it will not soon emerge.

As a consequence, it must be concluded that the G-7 initiative cannot "Save Russia!" even if rescuing kleptocratic socialism were a worthy cause. This suggests that economic assistance cannot serve as a surrogate for a potent national defense, and that students of international security affairs should be alert to this reality.

"Nuclear weapons are of decreasing importance."

The U.S. Should Greatly Reduce Its Nuclear Arsenal

Center for Defense Information

Most commentators agree that the breakup of the Soviet Union reduces the need for the huge stockpiles of nuclear weapons built up during the cold war. The question is not whether nuclear arms should be cut, but how much they should be cut. In the following viewpoint, the Center for Defense Information argues that the United States has failed to adjust its policies to the post-cold war world. By trying to retain an obsolete level of nuclear force, the United States has alienated the former Soviet republics and encouraged proliferation. The authors argue that greater reductions would reduce U.S. defense spending, discourage proliferation, and promote national security. The Center for Defense Information is a nonprofit organization that gathers and publishes information regarding U.S. defense policies.

As you read, consider the following questions:

1. According to the authors, how does U.S. policy encourage nuclear proliferation?
2. What is the purpose of the U.S. nuclear triad, according to the authors, and why is it obsolete?
3. Why has no one used nuclear weapons since 1945, according to the authors?

From Center for Defense Information, "Nuclear Weapons After the Cold War: Too Many, Too Costly, Too Dangerous," *The Defense Monitor* 22, no. 1 (1993): 1-7. Reprinted with permission.

The end of the Cold War and the demise of the Soviet Union have allowed the world to move back from the brink of destruction. Treaties to reduce nuclear weapons and other confidence building measures have reduced tensions and the threat of nuclear war.

Nevertheless, thousands of nuclear weapons remain ready for war. Reductions in long-range nuclear weapons are scheduled to take 10 years. Russian proposals for deeper cuts have been rebuffed by the U.S. In the Pentagon, the Cold War lives on in its nuclear programs.

The Pentagon will spend $38 billion in 1993 and $350 billion over the next 10 years to prepare for nuclear war. The U.S. continues to buy missiles and bombers designed to fight a nuclear war with the Soviet Union. The Department of Energy [DOE] is busy designing new nuclear warheads.

Although steps have been taken to reduce the risk of nuclear war, greater opportunities are ignored. Until the U.S. recognizes the changed environment and adapts its nuclear strategy, forces, and spending accordingly, the nuclear catastrophes of which Einstein wrote will remain a disturbing possibility.

Too Many Bombs

Fewer than 50 years ago there were only two nuclear weapons in the world. Today, they number more than 48,000. Collectively they have the explosive power of 11,700 megatons of TNT—2.2 tons for each person on the planet.

A one-megaton bomb is 75 times more powerful than the bomb that leveled Hiroshima, killing an estimated 140,000 people by the end of 1945. The world's nuclear arsenal today has explosive power equal to 900,000 Hiroshima bombs.

The START [Strategic Arms Reduction Talks] Treaty, the Bush-Yeltsin (START II) accord, and the independent initiatives of Presidents George Bush, Mikhail Gorbachev, and Boris Yeltsin could, if implemented, reduce the U.S. nuclear arsenal over the next century from 20,000 to 8,500 warheads and the former Soviet arsenal from 27,000 to 7,000 warheads.

No cuts are expected in the arsenals of the three other declared nuclear powers: Britain, France, and China. In the year 2003, the world will still have as many as 20,000 nuclear warheads containing the explosive power of more than 200,000 Hiroshima bombs.

U.S. Creates Demand

India, Pakistan, and Israel are generally suspected of having nuclear weapons. South Africa, Iran, Iraq, Algeria, Libya, and North Korea are also believed to have sought nuclear weapons. These nations do not pose a threat to the U.S., nor do their actions justify large U.S. nuclear forces. On the contrary, their interest in nuclear weapons is unlikely to change as long as the nuclear powers cling to thousands of their own nuclear weapons. . . .

U.S. actions have not eased the demand for nuclear weapons. The U.S. insisted that no warheads be dismantled under START I or II and also insisted on keeping a minimum of 3,500 strategic nuclear warheads. In addition, the U.S. has consistently foiled international efforts to obtain a Comprehensive Test Ban (CTB) treaty. All of these actions promote the belief that nuclear weapons are valuable and prestigious additions to military power. . . .

In the Republics

All tactical nuclear weapons have reportedly been returned to Russia for safekeeping. President Yeltsin reaffirmed former President Gorbachev's commitment to destroy roughly 10,000 of these weapons, to deploy 2,000, and to store the remaining 5,000.

Three former republics besides Russia have strategic nuclear weapons: Belarus, Kazakhstan, and Ukraine. It is hoped that they will comply with the treaties signed and initiatives taken by the former Soviet Union. Unfortunately, the wish that the end of the Cold War will result in blissful harmony with the U.S. is far from being realized. Tensions remain and economic hardship is sure to afflict these new nations for years.

Noting the economic crisis plaguing his nation, Ukrainian First Deputy Prime Minister Igor Yukhnovsky warned that, although Ukraine was still committed to becoming a nuclear-free state, "perhaps that will not apply if somebody doesn't want to buy this wretched stuff (nuclear weapons materials)...The United States and Russia are rich, they must help Ukraine in this terrible situation. We know that what we have is a treasure, and on this we will insist.". . .

Counterproductive Policies

Tension over reductions in nuclear weapons is not confined to Ukraine. Russian military officials claim that START II is unfair because it requires Russia to eliminate the core of its nuclear forces (i.e. multiple warhead land-based missiles), but only makes a dent in the heart of the U.S. nuclear force (i.e. multiple warhead submarine-based missiles).

Disagreement over targeting each other with nuclear weapons was recently aired by Russian Marshal Yevgeny Shaposhnikov. In September 1992, he announced that Russian land-based missiles had not been retargeted away from the U.S., as was promised several months earlier, because the U.S. did not reciprocate. The Pentagon resisted retargeting because it claimed it was impossible to verify if Russia should stop targeting the U.S.

Although the former Soviet republics have been eager for further progress, the U.S. is neglecting opportunities for two main reasons. First, U.S. officials believe that plans for serious reductions have already been accomplished making further cuts unnecessary. Second, Pentagon officials resist deeper cuts in the nuclear arsenal which they feel could force them to abandon a portion of the nuclear triad of land-based missiles, submarine-based missiles, and bombers.

© Frank Cotham. Reprinted with permission.

U.S. hesitancy to rethink Cold War nuclear policies and weapons may help undermine evolving democracy in Russia and the other former republics. U.S. reluctance may also interfere with agreements to reduce nuclear weapons.

Russian eagerness for further progress is fading fast. Perceptions of inequity with the U.S. and economic chaos contribute to anti-Western sentiments as was reflected in a recent article in the Russian Defense Ministry's newspaper, *Red Star*. Mikhail Rebrov wrote, "As for the Americans, they have such a plot in mind: to buy for pennies our unique technologies and erase from the people's memory Russia's glory, the glory of a great nuclear and space power.". . .

While strategic nuclear weapons have been cut on paper, little else has changed. Many U.S. officials have failed to reexamine the basic foundation of U.S. nuclear policy: the strategic nuclear triad of land-based missiles, submarine-based missiles, and bombers. The argument follows that if one of these legs is destroyed by a first strike, the U.S. could still use the remaining two legs to demolish the enemy.

Protecting the nuclear triad was the primary reason why the U.S. bargained the Russians up from their proposal of a 2,000 warhead cap to 3,500. The Pentagon argued that if U.S. strategic nuclear weapons were capped at any level below 3,500 warheads, it would hinder U.S. retaliatory capabilities and make maintaining all three legs of the triad economically impractical.

There is no military need to maintain these three separate strategic nuclear forces. The Russians have reduced the alert status of many of their long-range missiles along with all of their strategic bombers, providing the Pentagon with ample warning time of any nuclear strike preparations. . . .

The end of the Cold War, closer relationships with the nations of the former Soviet Union, and the proven effectiveness of U.S. conventional weapons have eliminated any need for new nuclear weapons. As a Presidential candidate, Bill Clinton agreed that the U.S. did not need any new nuclear weapons, but then only argued for a "moderate reduction" in DOE's nuclear budget.

U.S. officials acknowledge that the Cold War is over. Nevertheless, the fact that Cold War military spending, weapons programs, and strategies continue indicates that officials are not responding to the new circumstances.

The enemy is no more. World War II, the Cold War, and the arms race are over. Targets vanished with the demise of the Warsaw Pact. Troops of the former Soviet Union are retreating, leaving bases in Eastern Europe as fast as housing in Russia can be provided. . . .

Nuclear Weapons Reconsidered

The role of nuclear weapons must be rethought in order to respond appropriately to the dramatic changes in the world and ensure the security of the U.S. and its people.

Nuclear weapons are basically useless militarily. Although they did draw World War II to a close, they did not prevent the Korean conflict, Vietnam war, or Iraq's invasion of Kuwait. Nuclear weapons could not help win in Korea or Vietnam and their use was never considered in the war against Iraq.

Nuclear weapons and the age-old role of deterring attacks was a product of a world in which the U.S. had a designated enemy and the possessors of nuclear weapons were known. That world has passed away. Targeting to intimidate and therefore prevent war does not work against nuclear weapons delivered in a clandestine way. If the perpetrator of a nuclear attack is unknown or the attack is the work of a terrorist group without a geographic home, it is impossible to target and retaliate with nuclear weapons.

Today, in this increasingly interdependent world, nuclear and conventional weapons do far less than economic, political, and personal ties to discourage attacks on the U.S. and its allies. Nuclear weapons are of decreasing importance, especially given demonstrated U.S. superiority in conventional weapons.

Nuclear weapons by their very nature are self-inhibiting. The absolute deadliness of nuclear weapons makes them an unlikely warfighting tool. In addition, any use of nuclear weapons will undoubtedly incur widespread public outcry. This is probably why no one has used nuclear weapons since 1945.

Conventional Weapons Preferable

General Colin Powell, Chairman of the Joint Chiefs of Staff, expressed the military's doubts about the value of nuclear weapons: "I think there is far less utility to these [nuclear] weapons than some Third World countries think there is, and they are wasting a lot of money, because what they hope to do militarily with weapons of mass destruction of the kind we are talking about, I can increasingly do with conventional weapons, and far more effectively. . . . There are better ways to spend your monies if you are looking for means by which to undertake military aggression."

The U.S.-led war against Iraq provided a stage to demonstrate the weapons to which General Powell referred. Conventional Tomahawk Sea-Launched Cruise Missiles (SLCMs) proved their ability to compete with their nuclear SLCM siblings without the public outcry. Laser-guided bombs and numerous standoff missiles displayed U.S. conventional might.

While General Powell aptly questions the utility of nuclear weapons, he demonstrates the increasing likelihood of conventional war. Concerns about the morality of nuclear weapons, plus fear of retaliation, contribute to restraining their use. The absence of public wariness about the use of U.S. conventional weapons, compounded by the sense that these weapons are unfailingly precise, does nothing to discourage the military from using them.

1,000 Is Enough

While some level of nuclear weapons may be justifiable, the 3,500 strategic and 5,000 tactical nuclear weapons the U.S. will likely have in the year 2003 are far too many. This would translate into an explosive force equal to 80,000 Hiroshimas. Clearly the U.S. would be hard-pressed to find 1,000 genuine military targets today, given the dissolution of the Soviet Union and Warsaw Pact.

Moreover, the U.S. need not threaten every Russian military target with nuclear weapons. As John Kennedy's Secretary of Defense Robert McNamara claimed, "The lessons of the (Cuban) missile crisis are simple. . . . It takes very, very few (weapons to deter)."

Careful analysis by the Center for Defense Information indicates that 1,000 strategic nuclear weapons deployed solely on submarines would more than adequately cover all potential targets. Under this plan the U.S. would give up its obsolescent nuclear triad strategy. It would eliminate all land-based missiles and either eliminate all strategic bombers or convert them to conventional roles.

Additionally, tactical nuclear weapons are of dubious military utility. Complete and verifiable dismantlement of all battlefield nuclear weapons would encourage others to do likewise.

Significant Changes

This reduction to 1,000 warheads is possible today irrespective of the actions of Russia, China, or any other current or aspiring nuclear powers. There is no need to hang on to the excesses of the Cold War.

A force of 1,000 warheads ensures a potent retaliatory force and better serves U.S. nonproliferation goals by devaluing nuclear weapons and increasing world confidence that U.S. nuclear intentions are solely defensive. This will also save taxpayers $150 billion from now until 2003.

Once the U.S. has reduced to a level of 1,000 warheads, it would be advisable to seek even deeper reductions, provided that relations among nuclear powers continue to improve.

Significant changes in the world since 1990 give nations the opportunity and impetus to stop preparations for nuclear war. Some of these steps have been taken, such as planned reductions in the nuclear arsenals of the U.S. and former Soviet Union and declared nuclear testing moratoria. Nevertheless, there is still much to accomplish.

Only by recognizing the dramatic changes in the world, redesigning U.S. nuclear strategy, cutting nuclear spending, quickly reducing nuclear arsenals further, and reaching other agreements such as a Comprehensive Test Ban, extension of the Nonproliferation Treaty, and a ban on the production of fissile materials will the people of the world emerge from under the shadow of the mushroom cloud.

"We must be careful not to press on with further reductions too quickly."

The U.S. Should Retain a Significant Nuclear Arsenal

American Defense Institute

The American Defense Institute is a nonprofit educational organization that studies national and international issues. In the following viewpoint, the authors argue that while the breakup of the Soviet Union and the end of the cold war warrant nuclear arsenal reductions, the United States should not reduce its levels too quickly. In light of the unstable political situations in Russia and Ukraine, as well as the danger of nuclear proliferation, the authors advocate a ceiling of 3,500 warheads, which is consistent with the levels prescribed by START (Strategic Arms Reduction Treaty) I and II. To further reduce America's arsenal would be too costly to the United States both financially and strategically.

As you read, consider the following questions:

1. According to the authors, why is it significant that the START treaties have not begun to be implemented?
2. Why do the authors believe it is unlikely that the United States will give Ukraine the money it wants?
3. According to the authors, will U.S. nuclear arms reductions stem proliferation?

American Defense Institute, "United States Strategic Policy," a position paper written expressly for inclusion in the present volume.

Events over the last four years have forced the United States to reevaluate its strategic nuclear weapons strategy for the first time in over forty years. The collapse of the Warsaw Pact, and then the Soviet Union, effectively ended the Cold War and paved the way for a truly startling series of arms control agreements. In short order, the ten-year START [Strategic Arms Reduction Treaty] negotiations ended, soon followed by the far more ambitious START II treaty. Whereas START reduced the number of warheads and delivery systems by almost 30% (to roughly 8-9,000), START II reduces the number of ceilings all the way to 3,000-3,500. . . . Furthermore, the alert status of the heavy bombers has been scaled back dramatically, targeting has changed, and both sides have removed their tactical nuclear weapons from both the Army and the Navy. The U.S. now finds itself financially aiding countries it had recently regarded as the enemy.

Not Too Quickly

With Russian President Boris Yeltsin receiving a vote of confidence in the April 25, 1993, referendum, it appears that START I and II are back on track. This new ceiling is indeed a major reduction worthy of rethinking our nuclear strategy. However, we must be careful not to press on with further reductions too quickly simply because of harmonious relations with Russia. To begin with, the START treaties have not yet entered into force. This means that the 7- and 9-year implementation periods for the respective treaties have not yet begun. Though some long-scheduled dismantlements have occurred in the U.S., the thousands of necessary warhead removals are awaiting formal ratification by all parties. As a result, it is futile to discuss additional reductions while we are still seven years from being close to the new ceiling.

Though this 3,500 number may seem rather arbitrary, it corresponds quite nicely to the construct of the strategic triad. This limit leaves America with exactly half its projected SLBM [Submarine-Launched Ballistic Missile] force, a mere 500 single-RV [warhead] Minuteman III ICBMs [Intercontinental Ballistic Missile] and a drastically reduced bomber force (all 95 B-1Bs will be reoriented to strictly conventional roles). Still, this is a radical reduction, especially considering the negligible true arms reductions as a result of previous arms control agreements. U.S. strategic forces have remained at similarly high numbers for many years and the planned reductions must conform with our strategic doctrine. New targeting, deployment and budgetary plans must be created to help USSTRATCOM [U.S. Strategic Command] carry out its mission of protecting the United States from nuclear attack and providing it with sufficient warfighting capabilities, if necessary. The U.S. is in the process of foregoing any first strike capability and greatly reducing its retaliatory ability. Though these occurrences are welcome, they need to be handled judiciously to ensure the strategic force remains effective and flexible in times of crisis. With less than half its accustomed warheads, the planners will require time to reach this desired stage.

Beyond force structure, there are other compelling reasons to refrain from further reductions at this time. The end of the Cold War has brought about a new world that is anything but in order. First, the entry into force of START I is still far from guaranteed. Ukraine, now the world's 3rd largest nuclear power has voiced the desire to be non-nuclear but has yet to act in anything but a contradictory manner. There is little chance that Ukraine will receive either the amount of money or the security guarantees it is requesting from the West (i.e. America): the U.S. simply does not have the money and the West is loath to isolate the Russians (by embracing their antagonist, Ukraine) given the tenuous political position in which President Yeltsin finds himself today. Without Ukrainian ratification of START I, as well as the nuclear Nonproliferation Treaty (NPT), START II cannot proceed within Russia.

Nuclear Weapons: An Insurance Policy

Much as we might wish otherwise, nuclear weapons cannot be disinvented; their existence, or potential existence, will continue. Therefore, the primary role of U.S. nuclear arms should continue to be deterrence of nuclear use by others. For the immediate future, the chief U.S. concern is likely to remain the former Soviet Union's arsenal. . . . Whoever controls it or substantial portions of it will retain the ability to inflict catastrophic damage on the United States and its allies and friends worldwide.

Because the United States cannot be sure that control of ex-Soviet weapons will not some day revert to a leadership hostile to American interests, the United States must continue to rely on nuclear weapons as an insurance policy to deter any future leader who may control all, or a major portion, of the former Soviet arsenal and may contemplate using it.

Paul H. Nitze, *The Bulletin of the Atomic Scientists*, May 1992.

Russia itself is a ratification concern given the increasingly anti-Yeltsin tenor emanating from the rightward leaning Congress of People's Deputies which the treaty must pass. With START II inexorably tied to Yeltsin's fortunes, the [near future is] key to the treaty's future. In addition to the political turbulence throughout the former Soviet Union (FSU), nuclear proliferation is becoming a far more serious problem. Despite the heightened international awareness of the problem in the wake of the uncovering of Iraq's impressive nuclear program, the number of states pursuing these weapons, successfully in some cases, is growing. The hope fostered by South Africa's divesting itself of its 6 nuclear weapons has been countered by North Korea's withdrawal from the NPT and Iran's continuing arms buildup. Combined with the surplus of delivery systems on the international arms market (ballistic missiles and aircraft), the potential nuclear threat to the U.S. and its allies by states other than Russia will continue to grow. As one nuclear hopeful's defense minister stated clearly and coldly, the Gulf War illustrated that a nation must have a nuclear weapon if its interests diverge from those of the U.S. When potential enemies feel they absolutely must have nuclear weapons, no level of U.S. reductions will achieve the desired abandonment of their nuclear program.

A Mammoth Undertaking

Even if the political issues fall into place for START I and II to be fully ratified and enter into force, there is no guarantee that the mandated reduction schedules will be met. The dismantlements required for U.S. strategic forces under START I and II will certainly take several years, if not most of the allotted time. Still, the difficulty of this task pales in comparison to the mammoth undertaking necessary to bring Russia's force into compliance with the treaties. The Russians are already backlogged what with the continuing dismantling of almost 20,000 tactical nuclear warheads withdrawn as a result of the dueling initiatives instigated by Bush and Gorbachev in late 1991.

Furthermore, time is far from the only precious commodity in short supply in Russia. In fact, both Russia and Ukraine are demanding U.S. financial aid to continue the expensive process. So far, the U.S. has been magnanimous with its technical expertise but Congress has thus far withheld any large sums due to America's own economic problems. It is easy to guess Russia's budget allocation decisions between feeding and housing its people versus dismantling the very weapons that represent the proud country's last remnant of its superior status. Thus, even under the best circumstances, START II will not be fully implemented until after the turn of the century. For the U.S. to unilaterally go beyond these numbers would accomplish very little strategically or financially, given the high cost of dismantling U.S. weapons.

Little Return

The deep reductions currently scheduled to be completed by the early 21st century are universally hailed as long overdue given the dramatic end of the Cold War. However, the treaties face a tough battle before they are ratified by all parties. The political upheaval evident throughout the FSU indicates a grave potential for instability and greater proliferation. Even without their help, proliferants are gaining on the rest of the world. Thus, to reduce any further in the near future would provide very little in return for the U.S. and only serve to leave our strategic forces unnecessarily weaker and less capable.

Periodical Bibliography

The following articles have been selected to supplement the diverse views presented in this chapter.

Leon Aron — "The Battle for the Soul of Russian Foreign Policy," *The American Enterprise*, November/December 1992.

Jonas Bernstein — "Aid: The Best Way Up?" *Insight on the News*, March 9, 1992. Available from PO Box 91022, Washington, DC 20090-1022.

Stephen F. Cohen — "American Policy and Russia's Future," *The Nation*, April 12, 1993.

John M. Deutch — "The New Nuclear Threat," *Foreign Affairs*, Fall 1992.

Dennis M. Drew — "Recasting the Flawed Downsizing Debate," *Parameters*, Spring 1993. Available from U.S. Army War College, Carlisle Barracks, Carlisle, PA 17013-5050

Fred Charles Iklé — "Comrades in Arms: The Case for a Russian-American Defense Community," *The National Interest*, Winter 1991/92. Available from PO Box 3000, Denville, NJ 07834.

Dunbar Lockwood — "Strategic Nuclear Forces Under START II," *Arms Control Today*, December 1992. Available from the Arms Control Association, 11 Dupont Circle NW, Washington, DC 20036.

Vladimir P. Lukin — "Our Security Predicament," *Foreign Policy*, Fall 1992.

Nicolai N. Petro — "Russian-American Relations: Looking for a New Agenda," *Global Affairs*, Summer 1992.

Eugene V. Rostow — "Cold Shoulder," *The New Republic*, April 13, 1992.

Charles G. Stefan — "American Relations with the Former Soviet Union," *Mediterranean Quarterly*, Winter 1992. Available from Duke University Press, Box 6697, College Station, Durham, NC 27708.

4 CHAPTER

What Policies Would Strengthen the Republics' Economies?

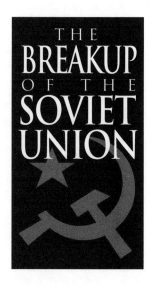

THE
BREAKUP
OF THE
SOVIET
UNION

Chapter Preface

Since the Soviet Union collapsed into fifteen separate republics, many commentators and officials have been urging the West to assist the new republics in the difficult transition to free-market economies. Humanitarian aid, educational and technological exchanges, and large sums of money to stabilize currencies are among the suggested forms of assistance. Without these kinds of aid, according to former CIA official Arthur Macy Cox, economic reforms might fail, leading the republics back to authoritarian governments, which would threaten United States security. In addition, many believe aid would also benefit the U.S. As former secretary of state James A. Baker III states: "The growth of democracy and free markets in Russia and Eurasia can be a new source of trade and investment for American businesses and companies."

Opponents of aid to the republics argue that giving the former Soviets aid may not foster democracy and consequently may not ensure U.S. security. Even with aid, says commentator Samuel Francis, "there is little in Russian . . . history to encourage Westerners to think democracy and free markets can survive." Aid might even do more harm than good, according to columnist Doug Bandow, by alleviating the economic hardships that might motivate the former Soviets to reform. Others assert that Western aid is motivated by greed and self-interest. The region is rich in natural resources, including vast oil fields, which some, like Russian historian Roy Medvedev, believe the United States seeks to exploit. Indeed, Medvedev asserts that "western aid is a myth! . . . Western countries have only been active in destroying the Soviet Union and Russia. There is a vast plundering of Russia underway, being carried out by western capital."

Whether or not the West successfully fosters free-market economies in the former Soviet republics, the collapse of Soviet socialism has initiated drastic change. Future economic choices made by the republics are likely to influence the quality of life in their new societies and in the rest of the world for years to come. The authors in the following chapter debate the economic decisions faced by the republics.

"Aid to a free-market economy in Russia is an investment in prosperity for the United States."

Western Aid Would Strengthen the Republics' Economies

Richard Nixon

Since the breakup of the Soviet Union in 1991, economic conditions in the new fifteen independent states have been chaotic. In the Russian Federation, for example, President Boris Yeltsin has initiated drastic economic reforms which include price liberalization and a movement toward privatization. Richard Nixon, the author of the following viewpoint, believes that democracy in the former Soviet Union—and consequently the prosperity and security of the West—hinges on the success of Yeltsin's economic reforms. He calls for U.S. economic aid to ensure Yeltsin's success. Nixon served as the thirty-seventh president of the United States from 1969 to 1974. He resigned to avoid impeachment for his involvement in the Watergate scandal. Since his resignation, he has written numerous books and advised several U.S. presidents on foreign policy issues.

As you read, consider the following questions:

1. What types of political developments does Nixon foresee if economic reforms fail in Russia?
2. How would aid to Russia ensure U.S. security, according to the author?
3. According to Nixon, how would the success of Russian reforms influence other countries?

From Richard Nixon, "Clinton's Greatest Challenge," *The New York Times*, March 5, 1993.
Copyright © 1993 by The New York Times Company. Reprinted by permission.

The major foreign policy issue of our time . . . is the survival and success of political and economic freedom in Russia.

That is not to say that the Mideast, Iraq and Bosnia are not also important, or that the nations of Eastern Europe and the other former Soviet states do not also deserve priority attention where they have democratically elected governments and have initiated serious free-market economic reform. But what happens in Russia will have an enormous effect on those nations, on our allies and on the United States.

Without a substantial increase in aid from the West, the Yeltsin Government will not survive. The U.S. must lead in providing it. It is a very tough sell for the President. The last Gallup poll showed that only 4 percent of voters considered foreign policy to be an important issue. In Mr. Clinton's nationally televised town meeting, there was only one question concerning foreign policy. It was about Bosnia. His political advisers understandably will tell him, as they did in the campaign, "It's the economy, stupid!"

But foreign and domestic policy are like Siamese twins—one cannot survive without the other. If Boris Yeltsin's democratic Government collapses and is replaced by an aggressive, hard-line nationalist government, this will have a far greater impact on the American economy than all the Clinton domestic programs combined. The peace dividend will be down the tubes. The defense budget will have to be increased by billions of dollars rather than cut. This would mean that the President's plan to cut the deficit would have to be taken off the table.

A Deadly Crisis

The Russian democracy is going through a deadly crisis. The negative factors are frightening. Russia has 31 republics and provinces that have declared their sovereignty and 132 nationalities. Before the peaceful revolution of December 1991, the Russian people had never known either political or economic freedom. What works in Poland, the Czech Republic and Hungary will not work in Russia.

Russia is going through an economic downturn worse than the Great Depression of the 1930's in the United States. In 1992 inflation was 25 percent a month, the gross national product [GNP] was down 20 percent, and living standards were down 50 percent. There has been an alarming increase in crime and corruption. Separatist tendencies and nationalistic conflicts which had been cooled by the cold war are getting hot again, ranging from bloody war in the Transcaucasus and Central Asia to confrontation over minority rights in the Baltic states.

But despite these overwhelming odds, the conventional wisdom of most of the American media that the Russian democracy

144

is doomed is off the mark. There is still strong support for re-form among political leaders and the Russian people. The real political battle today is not between reformers and reactionaries, but between different kinds of reforms.

Cannot Win Alone

A new day has dawned throughout the Commonwealth of Inde-pendent States, with hope for a fundamental transformation in the way people live and work and think. . . .

Let us help the people throughout the independent states to make the leap from communism to democracy, from command economies to free markets, from authoritarianism to liberty. Then, let us pull together to win the peace in this post-Cold War era.

We should not underestimate the enormity of this challenge and the difficulty of unraveling economic dislocations resulting from over 70 years of communist economics. Ultimate success or fail-ure rests squarely with the efforts and wisdom of the peoples of Russia and the Ukraine and the Caucasus [and] Central Asia. The battle is really theirs to win. But they cannot win it alone. These 12 new countries will need the hard work, creativity, and good-will of all of our countries from every continent.

George Bush, *U.S. Department of State Dispatch*, January 27, 1992.

There are those like Mr. Yeltsin who prefer to act swiftly and decisively, and those like the Civic Union which would rather move more gradually. The fact that all political leaders except for the extreme reactionaries pay at least lip service to a free market economy means there will be no turning back to Communism.

The Positive News

The negative news from Russia has completely obscured the positive news. Just as Washington is not America, Moscow is not Russia. While political infighting is big news in Moscow, privatization and growth are proceeding irreversibly in other parts of Russia. Twenty percent of the G.N.P. is now produced by private enterprise. More than 30 percent of Russian workers are in private enterprise. The press is free. Privatizing the econ-omy has helped to eliminate shortages. No one talks about the possibility of starvation. . . .

Most important, as experts like James Billington and Gerald Corrigan have pointed out, the caricature that Russian workers are not responding to economic incentives is false. In a meeting in St. Petersburg, private entrepreneurs unanimously agreed that, when given the opportunity to enjoy the benefits of a free society, Russian workers are among the best in the world. They are also among the best educated: Ninety percent have graduated from high school—a higher percentage than in the United States.

Can Boris Yeltsin survive? Some Western leaders I talked to question it. Some of his opponents in Russia doubt it. Most shocking, the State Department officer who was in charge of aid to Russia publicly predicted that he would not last. With friends like that, Mr. Yeltsin needs no enemies.

Yeltsin Deserves Help

His approval rating is down sharply because of the economic downturn. But he is still the most popular politician in Russia. He has made serious mistakes in dealing with the Parliament he inherited from Mikhail Gorbachev. But while revolutionary leaders are generally good at destroying old orders but not good at governing new ones, Mr. Yeltsin has surprised even his critics by his political skill in handling what must be the most difficult political position in the world.

To his credit, he is attempting to find a compromise with the Parliament rather than becoming authoritarian, as many predicted. Those who would count him out should bear in mind that he has remarkable recuperative powers. He is a fighter. When he seems to be down and out, he gets up and continues the battle.

Most important, President Yeltsin shares our values. Unlike Mr. Gorbachev, he has repudiated both socialism and Communism, believes in a free market and supports the private ownership of property. Mr. Yeltsin unequivocally supports a non-aggressive foreign policy. After meeting all the major leaders in Russia, I am convinced that our choice is not between him and somebody better, but between him and someone worse. He deserves our help, both to further our interests as well as his.

In addition to increasing aid, President Clinton should . . . take the lead in persuading our allies, particularly the Germans and Japanese, to join us in rescheduling for 15 years the $84 billion debt Mr. Yeltsin inherited from Mr. Gorbachev.

Shortsighted Western governments and bankers have to face up to the fact that if the debt is not rescheduled, they are likely to get nothing from any government which replaces Mr. Yeltsin's. We should demand that the bureaucrats running the International Monetary Fund not treat Russia like a third world country.

We should insist that the allies we helped recover from World War II now help Russia and the other independent nations in Eastern Europe and the former Soviet Union recover from the cold war. The Germans have their plate full with eastern Germany. But the Japanese participation in the multilateral aid program is shockingly inadequate. The Japanese should quit conditioning aid on Russia's return of four tiny northern islands. If Mr. Yeltsin fails, they will never get the islands back.

Why should we even consider aid to Russia in view of our problems at home? Because aid to a non-aggressive democratic Government in Russia is an investment in peace. Russia is the only nation which has the power to destroy the United States. Russian diplomatic support in hot spots like Iraq, the Mideast and Bosnia is indispensable.

During the cold war, many thought the Soviets were evil. None thought they were crazy. That can't be said for some of the smaller nations trying to acquire nuclear weapons. Russia and America, as the only two nuclear superpowers, must play the crucial role in preventing proliferation of nuclear weapons.

Aid to a free-market economy in Russia is an investment in prosperity for the United States. Consider these facts. Russian G.N.P. in 1992 was seven times as great as China's. China's trade with the U.S. was eight times as great as Russia's. Why? Because China's private enterprise produces over one-half of its G.N.P. Russia's private enterprise produces only one-fifth of its G.N.P. As Russia's private sector grows, this will mean thousands of jobs and billions in trade for the U.S.

High Stakes

Even greater stakes are involved. For 75 years, Communist Russia, as a major Soviet state, tried to export Communism to the rest of the world. Today, democratic Russia can serve as a powerful example of how political and economic freedom is the best choice for nations who want to progress. If political and economic freedom fails in Russia, this will encourage the reactionary leaders of other nations to resist reform. If it succeeds, this could have a major impact on a nation like China, which has significant economic reform but no political reform.

Above all, it is time to quit treating Russia like a defeated enemy. Russia did not lose the cold war. The Communists did. The U.S. and our allies deserve great credit for maintaining the military and economic power to resist and turn back the Soviet aggression. A democratic Russia deserves credit for delivering the knockout blow to Communism in its motherland. Russia should be treated as a proud struggling friend, not as a weak former enemy looking for a handout.

The demise of Soviet Communism was one of mankind's greatest victories. But the victory will not be complete until Russia and its neighbors can enjoy the benefits of political and economic freedom. It would be tragic if, at this critical point, the United States fails to provide the leadership only it can provide.

"Russia is not ours to win or to lose."

Western Aid Alone Would Not Strengthen the Republics' Economies

Henry A. Kissinger

Henry A. Kissinger, the author of the following viewpoint, disagrees with the argument that the fate of Russian democracy rests on Western aid to ensure the success of Boris Yeltsin's economic reforms. A successful market economy will not guarantee democracy, according to Kissinger; nor will capitalism's failure ensure a return to communism. Citing the dangers in favoring Russia, Kissinger calls for the West to develop a comprehensive policy of aid which insists on cooperation between all the former Soviet states. Kissinger is an American political scientist who served as U.S. secretary of state in the Nixon and Ford administrations.

As you read, consider the following questions:

1. According to the author, why is it unrealistic to call Russia "democratic"?
2. Why does Kissinger insist on a "dialogue" between Russia and the other former Soviet states?
3. How might aid to Russia backfire on the United States, according to Kissinger?

Henry A. Kissinger, "Proposals, Like Nixon's, to Send Money to Save Democracy in Russia Won't Work" *Los Angeles Times*, March 29, 1992. Reprinted with permission.

After being told that it would take a five-year program of $30 billion annually to save Mikhail S. Gorbachev and the future of democracy in the Soviet Union, we now hear that a similar program of $20 billion a year is needed to save Boris N. Yeltsin and democracy in the former Soviet Union. Having great faith in redemption by conversion, Americans are impressed by the proposition that U.S. aid is needed to sustain democracy, and that democracy, coupled with market economics, will sustain the peace.

But is it true? Russia is not ours to win or to lose. We do Russian leaders no favor and ourselves a considerable disservice by creating the impression that outside help can avoid years of the most painful austerity; at best, it can somewhat ease the pain of the transition to market economics. The future of democracy in a country that has never known it is bound to depend on factors far more complex than how to make the ruble convertible.

The key issue is not whether aid should be given. Everybody agrees that some assistance is necessary, at a minimum for humanitarian reasons. Nor is there much debate about the resources available and that even the upper range falls short of what is needed. The issue is the excessive claims made by some of the aid proponents. Nostalgia for the Marshall Plan overlooks that it was implemented in societies with long traditions of democratic government, well-established civil services and managers experienced in market economics. None of these conditions applies to the former Soviet Union.

Democracy at Point Zero

The presidents of the successor states, including Yeltsin, are all former communist cadre—with the exception of Belarus President Stanislav Shushkevich. They are elected, and that is a great step forward; most are ostensibly anti-communist, but they represent a unique political system: without established political parties, effective parliaments or constitutions. Calling these former apparatchiks governing by decree "democratic" is a courtesy and a hope, not a description of reality.

The process of democratization in the former Soviet Union starts practically from point zero. None of the elements that produced democracy in the West has ever been significant in Russia. The Western church, even when it was run in an authoritarian manner, established the premise of limited government by insisting on a spiritual sphere beyond the state's reach. By contrast, the Russian church was generally the voice of militant state nationalism. Russia never experienced the Reformation, with its appeal to individual conscience, the Enlightenment, with its invocation of the power of reason, or capitalism, with its encouragement of individual initiative. Iso-

149

lated pockets of all these trends existed, but they never permeated Russian society.

A new political upheaval, rather than bringing about a qualitative change, would most likely deepen the various shades of gray. Yeltsinism will almost certainly not be replaced by central

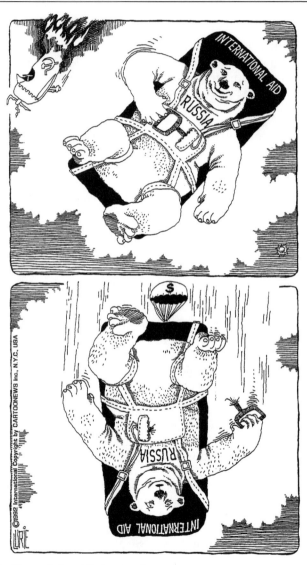

planning and adventurous foreign policy. The existing cadre have witnessed the failings of Stalinist central planning too closely to be tempted by it; their economic convictions are more anti-communist than their political ones. The so-called new despots, if they change the system at all, are likely to be tempted by *perestroika* without *glasnost*. They will still need help from the market economies, hence foreign policy might not change much.

Possible Backlash

Given the barren democratic soil, we must avoid the temptation of overselling—to the Western public and to the Russian people—the likelihood that such aid will produce democracy. For when it becomes clear that it won't, the consequences could be unfortunate. The West could become the scapegoat for Russian and other nationalists who would blame their economic failures on it. The Western public, its high hopes disappointed, may turn away and, in its disillusionment, could be tempted to use sanctions and other pressures. By causing Russian and other nationalism to boil over, these could generate the aggressiveness their sponsors seek to avoid.

Paradoxically, modesty in our claims for aid programs could enhance their impact. They cannot, in any event, substitute for an open political dialogue with the successor states, especially the Russian federation. We must do what we can to diminish the greatest threat to international stability—yesterday's revolutionaries turning into the centralizers of tomorrow, and the leaders of the anti-communist revolution becoming the destroyers of the anti-imperialist one. The convenience of dealing with a familiar center must not blind the democracies to the historic reality that Russian imperialism has too often undermined international stability.

There are many worrisome tendencies. The new Russian republic does not conduct itself as if it were the successor of the traditional Russian empire. Symbolic of its reluctance to accept the breakup of the empire is its refusal, up to now, to establish embassies in the other successor states. The leaders of these new states are, in turn, terrified of the re-emergence of Russian imperialism. If recentralization were attempted, let alone were to succeed, the historic fears of Russia's neighbors would reappear with a vengeance. Suspicion would govern their mutual relationships; arms would multiply; Russia would resent its neighbors' fears and the neighbors would try to protect themselves against Russian hostility; Cold War patterns would re-emerge.

Western countries are unwittingly encouraging this danger. Yeltsin is treated as the linear descendant of Gorbachev and of other rulers of the empire. Aid programs are presented in terms of Russia's needs. Contacts with the other republics—even one so significant as Ukraine—are formalistic and infrequent.

A Political Dialogue

Aid programs must be part of a political dialogue, especially with the Russian republic, and they should be made dependent on the full acceptance of political sovereignty in the relations with the successor states. Considering the membership of these countries in the United Nations, this is hardly an excessive demand. We must include the other republics in a comprehensive program and avoid any implication that Moscow is the voice or the chosen engine for the development of the remainder of the Soviet Union.

Such a political dialogue would sketch the prospects of a new set of relationships. A Russia that renounced domination would end the causes of conflict with the United States; it could become a global partner. A Russia separated from Europe by the Ukraine, Belarus and the Baltic states would allow a degree of cooperation with the European Community unachievable while Europe was trembling before Russian arms. A number of conclusions follow:

—Aid must be based on a precise and realistic concept of how it serves the national interest.

—Economic aid cannot be an end in itself. It should not focus on one successor state but be part of an overall concept encompassing them all.

—It must be deployed to such fields as energy, where there is a prospect of rapid currency earnings, or to the improvement of transportation and agriculture.

U.S. policy must not restrict its field of vision to the former Soviet Union. The principal cause of European conflicts during the past 150 years has been the existence of a no-man's-land between the German and the Russian peoples. Having proclaimed their commitment to the freedom of Eastern Europe for a generation, the industrial democracies cannot abandon these first victims of Soviet aggression. If they do, they will be creating the sources of future conflict. The eastern nations should be related to the European Community as rapidly as possible and be given high priority in any aid program.

"Contrary to widespread perception, the IMF is barely present in Russia."

Increased IMF Intervention Would Strengthen the Republics' Economies

Jeffrey Sachs and David Lipton

The International Monetary Fund (IMF) is a multinational financial organization established to strengthen the economies of member countries. The IMF's task in Russia is to assist in a transition to democracy and a market economy by stabilizing the ruble. According to Jeffrey Sachs and David Lipton, the authors of the following viewpoint, the IMF has left Russia short of funds needed to stabilize the economy. What the republics need, say the authors, is direct IMF involvement in creating new currencies, rescheduling debt, and improving the banking system. Sachs is a professor of economics at Harvard University, Cambridge, Massachusetts. Lipton is a fellow at the Woodrow Wilson Center, Washington, D.C. Both authors are economic advisors to the Russian government.

As you read, consider the following questions:

1. According to the authors, what problems have occurred because of the lack of IMF involvement in Moscow?
2. How should new currencies in the former Soviet republics be handled, according to the authors?
3. Why is it imperative to reschedule the old Soviet debt, according to the Sachs and Lipton?

From Jeffrey Sachs and David Lipton, "Russia's Monetary Madness: The IMF Is Shirking Its Duty to the Fledgling Democracy," *The Washington Post National Weekly Edition*, October 5-11, 1992. Reprinted with permission.

Even as dramatic reforms go forward, Russia's monetary problems remain unresolved: The risks of hyperinflation remain high; the foreign debt is still not restructured; and only two of the 14 non-Russian states have introduced their own currencies. The management of the ruble remains a messy tangle among many new nations that share the currency.

That wasn't supposed to happen. Under the original script, Western governments were to send in the International Monetary Fund (IMF) to help Russia carry out its most urgent economic tasks. Yet something has gone wrong, seriously wrong, with the IMF's role in Russia. And something needs to be done to reform the IMF's effort, or the difficult transition to democracy and a market economy will be jeopardized. . . .

Superficial Presence

The controversies swirling around the IMF tend to focus on whether the institution is too tough in its advice to Russia, but these controversies miss the point. The problem is not toughness, but superficiality. Contrary to widespread perception, the IMF is barely present in Russia.

Remarkably, the IMF does not have a single monetary expert permanently in residence in all of Russia, much less the teams of resident advisers imagined in the public mind. Yes, the staff at headquarters working on Russia has grown significantly through personnel shifts and new recruitment, but the end result where it counts—on the ground in Russia—has been negligible. Only two staff members are based there, but their job is mainly to gather and transmit information to and from the Washington staffers who fly in periodically for a couple of weeks at a time.

The visitors may leave a written document behind, but without anybody in residence to discuss their reports, or, more importantly, to help with implementation, the IMF simply has not done the things it can do to make a difference. It could, for example, show in far more detail how continued heavy subsidization of the military-industrial sector risks hyperinflation and the destruction of the overall reform process.

The absence of a permanent, high-quality IMF staff in Moscow has contributed to one debacle after another. Tellingly, the day before the collapse of the ruble, the IMF expressed confidence in the Central Bank rather than sounding the alarm that its policies were sending the country back toward high inflation. No wonder: The IMF had not had a team in Russia for more than a month.

The first IMF debacle was failing to recognize the urgency of Russia's needs. The IMF senior staff actually told officials of the seven major industrial nations (G-7; the United States, Germany, France, Britain, Canada, Italy and Japan) that Russia's financial needs for 1992 would be modest, around $6 billion. Oddly lackadaisical about Russia's balance-of-payments situation, the IMF greatly overstated Russia's likely exports for 1992, and therefore understated Russia's need for foreign grants and loans. As the facts came in, and new assessments were made, the G-7 announced a $24 billion support package in April 1992.

A Big Challenge

The IMF is facing the biggest challenge of its history. After nearly five decades of grappling with Latin America, Africa, and Eastern Europe, it is now helping the world's largest centrally planned economy build its own version of capitalism. Never before has the IMF dealt with a touchy former superpower with its own massive army and a still-ominous nuclear arsenal. Nor has it ever faced building the financial structure of a huge country from the ground up. . . .

The IMF must prod the country to undergo the pain of economic restructuring without producing a social explosion or a xenophobic backlash that could usher a new dictator to power. If the IMF succeeds, Russia and other former Soviet republics will finally become real members of the world economic community. If the IMF fails, a hostile Russia could again become the West's biggest nightmare.

Rose Brady et al., *Business Week*, September 28, 1992.

Even after that, the IMF remained largely passive in one of its main tasks: rounding up the promised funds in a manner most useful to the reforms. Not only has much of the money, including the crucial $6 billion stabilization fund, not yet materialized, but the IMF has not once given the Russian government a detailed assessment of what is in the $24 billion package—and what will arrive when. The IMF's defense, that it simply doesn't know what the G-7 wants to do, merely shows that the IMF itself has spent little effort in assessing Russia's real needs and educating the G-7.

Another blunder was the IMF's remarkably bad advice on the question of new currencies. The natural solution was a quick introduction of separate currencies in each of the newly independent states, which would be linked with each other through floating exchange rates. Instead, the IMF sent a go-slow signal on monetary independence. In effect, this action meant that each state continued to issue ruble credits, feeding the inflation in the whole region and, in particular, undermining Russia's stabilization effort.

In April 1992, we helped an inflation-weary Estonia launch a new currency to protect itself from the ruble inflation. Once again, the IMF tried to slow the effort. The Estonians pushed ahead, contrary to IMF advice, and introduced a stable, convertible currency in June 1992.

But even after Estonia's success, the IMF has done virtually nothing in the other states to speed the process. Ukraine set Oct. 1, 1992 as a date to introduce its own currency. One might have expected the mobilization of bankers, lawyers and economists to help Russians and Ukrainians draft the requisite foreign exchange legislation and set up a new market to exchange Ukrainian and Russian money. Alas, this action has not happened.

Elsewhere, the story is the same: The uncertainties caused by the delay in rescheduling the old Soviet debt stifle trade and undermine confidence in Russia. It doesn't take a PhD in finance to know that in the middle of hyperinflation and a collapse of imports (from around $81 billion in 1990 to a projected $37 billion in 1992), Russia must husband its foreign exchange for basic imports rather than debt service. . . .

Making It Work

Not everything has gone awry. To its credit, the IMF is the only institution that stresses the importance of monetary discipline, the dangers of high inflation and the mechanisms for monetary control (even if it has missed the boat on redesigning the ruble area). . . .

The key, then, is not to give up on the IMF, but to make it work. To do that, the IMF should present a technical assistance plan worked out in conjunction with the Russian government. Teams of resident financial experts should be placed at the disposal of the Russian Central Bank, the Finance Ministry and other institutions, to quickly resolve pressing problems, including new currencies, debt rescheduling and improvement of the banking system.

Second, the IMF should take the lead in formulating a realistic package of financial assistance, spelling out in detail to Russia and the West the necessary components. Debt rescheduling should be agenda item No. 1, and the IMF should have the guts to press the G-7 to get on with it. There is no use giving the IMF new money if it eventually is to be recycled to pay off old Soviet debts.

"The ruble stabilization program will not achieve its narrow economic objectives."

IMF Intervention Would Not Strengthen the Republics' Economies

Steve H. Hanke

According to Steve H. Hanke, author of the following viewpoint, funds transferred from the International Monetary Fund (IMF) are intended to reduce the supply of and increase the demand for rubles, thereby stabilizing the exchange rate. This policy will fail, says Hanke, because the Russian Central Bank will continue to print rubles faster than Western monetary growth rates. Hanke opposes IMF intervention in the Russian economy, citing Poland and Yugoslavia as examples of IMF failures. He goes on to suggest that IMF funds would lead to wealth for a few speculators, which would offend many Russians and turn sentiments against the current government. Hanke is a professor of applied economics at Johns Hopkins University in Baltimore. He served as the personal economic adviser to the deputy prime minister of Yugoslavia from 1990 to 1991.

As you read, consider the following questions:

1. Theoretically, how would IMF intervention stabilize the ruble, according to Hanke?
2. According to Hanke, why would IMF funds fail to stabilize the ruble?
3. Why does the author believe the Russian Central Bank will continue to print rubles?

After 46 years, Russia, Ukraine and most of the other ex-Soviet republics joined the International Monetary Fund on April 27, 1992. The eagerness of the post-Soviet republics to join the IMF for symbolic reasons is understandable. It is the substance of what membership in the IMF will entail for them that is troubling.

When Moscow signs the formal agreement with the IMF, the $24 billion in aid from the rich G-7 countries promised by President George Bush and Chancellor Helmut Kohl on April 1, 1992 will be made available to the Russian government—including a $6 billion fund for the stabilization of the ruble. The ruble stabilization fund will be transferred to the Russian Central Bank at that bank's request.

The Plan

In principle, that hard currency is to be used only to prop up the value of the ruble. Armed with the IMF's $6 billion, the Russian Central Bank will intervene in the foreign-exchange markets to move the ruble from its current rate of about 150 to the dollar to a higher rate of 40 or 50 to the dollar.

For some months, the experts at the International Monetary Fund and some economists have worked hard to persuade Western governments of the need to transfer some of their taxpayers' wealth to Russia. Although the experts had success with the press and in some political quarters, the Bush administration for a long time avoided being stampeded.

The IMF finally wheeled out the big guns. In a five-page memorandum circulated to 50 power brokers, former President Richard M. Nixon castigated the Bush administration for playing a "pathetically inadequate," "penny ante game" with Russia. That did the trick.

The IMF and some Western economists have argued that stabilization fund intervention is necessary because the ruble's current, market-determined exchange rate is unrealistic. By reducing the supply of and increasing the demand for rubles, central bank intervention is supposed to move the ruble to a more "realistic" level.

The Reality

So much for the theory. Let's examine instead what will most likely happen in Russia, based on the near universal experience of IMF-sponsored stabilization programs and the current political-economic environment in Russia. The Russian Central Bank will continue to print rubles at a rate that exceeds the rate of monetary growth in the West. Anticipating that the "excess supply" problem will continue, foreign-exchange traders will continue to pass rubles to one another like hot potatoes. In consequence, the ruble will continue its free fall.

To reverse the ruble's course, the Russian Central Bank will use dollars in its stabilization fund to purchase rubles in the foreign-exchange markets. As it intervenes, the Bank will print more rubles to replace the rubles that it has purchased. Eventually, the dollars in the stabilization fund will disappear, the stock of rubles will not have been reduced and the foreign-exchange value of the ruble will keep declining.

IMF Aid Will Not Work

In theory, of course, the [West's] aid package [to Russia] is supposed to encourage the Yeltsin government to move forward with reforms. But, paradoxically, assistance is more likely to sap the government's commitment. . . .

It is hard to think of many organizations less deserving of increased funds than the IMF and the World Bank. The multilateral lending institutions have never met a thuggish regime that they didn't like, backing even the grossest Communist dictatorships in Ethiopia and Romania. And both regularly supported virtually every Third World state that experimented with disastrous, statist development policies.

This record is particularly surprising in light of the IMF's record as an economic taskmaster. And while the IMF has been tough with Poland, its efforts have had no obvious effect elsewhere in the world. Indeed, for four decades the Fund has joined with the other multilateral development banks to create a never-ending Socialist dole.

Doug Bandow, *Human Events*, May 2, 1992.

This will, of course, bring forth calls to replenish the stabilization entitlement program. Indeed, Michel Camdessus, the IMF's Managing Director, opened the door for additional funding requests and the fund has not yet even been established.

Little Control

That the Russian Central Bank will be forced to continue to print rubles at a record clip should be clear to even a casual observer. A shakeout of Russia's state-owned enterprises has not yet taken place. Indeed, there has been virtually no restructuring and privatization of those enterprises. Vneshconsult, a Moscow-based consulting firm, estimates that about 80% of the big state-owned enterprises are insolvent. Faced with interest rates of 50% on six month loans, the majority of enterprises can't afford to keep playing what amounts to a Ponzi game. They are refusing to pay back loans or honor bills, and many have already put workers on reduced work schedules. Overdue loans have soared from 34 billion rubles in January 1992 to 676 billion rubles by mid-March 1992.

In an attempt to avert an economic and political shakeout, the Russian Central Bank has already begun to let its much advertised austerity program go by the boards. For example, a government document released on April 3, 1992 indicates that 200 billion rubles in new credits have been extended to bankrupt state-owned enterprises, and that twice as many rubles were printed in March 1992 as in January 1992.

This is a far cry from the claim of Yegor Gaidar, Boris Yeltsin's top economic adviser, that the Yeltsin government had complete control over the ruble supply, and that the government planned to become even more tightfisted in the coming months. However, that was before Mr. Gaidar was forced to resign as Russia's finance minister, and before the Yeltsin government was forced by the Russian parliament to accept some economic compromises.

Bad Record

Consider the precedent of Poland, which is touted as an IMF success story. In late 1989, a Polish stabilization fund was established. On Jan. 1, 1990 it took 9,500 zloties to fetch a dollar. Now a dollar commands 12,800 zloties. Yugoslavia provides yet another, and alas a more relevant, example of a stabilization program gone awry. A member of the IMF since 1945, the government in Belgrade has recently claimed that inflation could reach an annual rate of 100,000%.

The ruble stabilization program will not achieve its narrow economic objectives. More important, it will not achieve its broader political goal: to lend the Yeltsin government a helping hand. To appreciate that, consider who the final beneficiaries of the Russian Central Bank's rubble-support operations will be.

The IMF stabilization fund will flow from Western taxpayers into foreign-exchange speculators' pockets like water running downhill. Those foreign-exchange traders will get rich quickly, offending ordinary Russians, and providing the old communists, who have significant support in the Russian parliament, the popular anger they need to bring down President Yeltsin. Ironically, rather than assisting Boris Yeltsin and his friends, the stabilization fund will provide the parliament with yet another club to beat Mr. Yeltsin's government.

"There is only one remedy: to resume movement forward on the socialist course."

Socialism Would Strengthen the Republics' Economies

Mike Davidow

Mike Davidow is Moscow reporter of the *People's Weekly World*, an American communist newspaper. In the following viewpoint, he argues that the socialist system of the former Soviet Union, although imperfect, is preferable to capitalism. Since Russian president Boris Yeltsin introduced his drastic economic reforms, says Davidow, the benefits of socialism—stable prices, fair wages, civil order, free medicine and education—are being replaced by high prices, unemployment, decreased production, and racial and class conflict. Davidow proposes that the republics adopt a less centralized, more economically balanced socialism than the one that existed under the Soviet system.

As you read, consider the following questions:

1. What does Davidow mean when he says "chaos in the former USSR . . . is the penalty . . . for retrogression"?
2. Why does the author predict that "privatization will result in primitive stores and services"?
3. Why have racial and class conflicts arisen under capitalism, according to Davidow?

Mike Davidow, "Yeltsin's Assault on Socialism," *Political Affairs*, April 1992. Reprinted with permission.

Anti-socialist forces in their August-December 1992 counter-revolution gained political control of the Soviet Union. However, though greatly undermined, the socialist economic structure—the collective farm system, the social ownership of the means of production and distribution, the social responsibilities of the state to which the mass of the people have become accustomed (still enshrined in the existing Constitution), stands in the way of the full restoration of capitalism. Thus, the essence of the Yeltsin-Gaider "economic reform" is political: the final destruction of socialism's economic foundations.

Few things reveal the ideological disorientation that had eaten away at the CPSU [Communist Party of the Soviet Union] more than that many of the leading economists promoting capitalism were party members, among them Yegor Gaider who had worked at *Pravda*. Economic, political and social chaos have followed in the wake of destruction of much of the socialist economic structure. For 7 decades this structure and the relations based on them, were developed; true, with deformities, but historically they constituted a higher stage in the progress of humanity. This is vividly demonstrated in the progressive role the USSR played on the world scene for 7 decades and its positive influence on social development, including in the U.S.

Chaos in the former USSR and the disarray in Eastern Europe is the penalty history is exacting for retrogression. This is causing leaders of the U.S. and West to temper their initial jubilation over their "victory over communism," with growing concern over the "difficulties" of turning the course of history backward from socialism to capitalism. This is the essence of the profound crisis.

Though makeshift adjustments to the crisis can be made, for its resolution there is only one remedy: to resume movement forward on the socialist course, not in returning to pre-1985 years but in making progressive improvements, originally the aim of the socialist forces for correction. The forces for rejection of the socialist course for 6 years conducted a feverish campaign (putting to shame the enemies of the USSR in the West) to erase the historic achievements recognized by the world and to reduce the 7 decades to totalitarianism and repression. Though great moral damage to the Soviet people was done, this mockery of history will not stand the test of time. What has been and is being destroyed by the counter-revolution?

A Planned Society

The essence of socialism is that it is a planned society. This feature has even been envied by the major capitalist states and to the limited degree possible under capitalism, copied by them. The former Five Year Plans were worked out from the ground up. While planning had assumed a too rigid, too centralized character and needed to be made more flexible and decentralized, it was the Five Year Plans which took stock of the vast resources of 15 Republics, put them to the service of the people, trained and allotted cadre and avoided the anarchic disruptions of capitalism. It was the Five Year Plans which amassed and distributed the finances and natural and human resources to overcome to a large degree the backward state of the Central Asian and Caucasian Republics. The industrialization of the USSR (literally pulling itself up by its own bootstraps), the modernization of its agriculture, the creation of a world-recognized corps of scientists, the advanced character of its educational system (whose achievements led our government to provide scholarships for many of today's scientists), all would not have been possible without state planning.

Harvell/The Greenville Piedmont, S.C. Reprinted with permission.

Today this great socialist achievement has been reduced to shambles. The Five Year Plan is no longer in existence. In its place have come the worst anarchic features of primitive capitalism where barter and unchecked speculation reign supreme, where prices in the course of the following week are unpredictable and massive unemployment is replacing guaranteed jobs.

Economic ties built up in the course of 7 decades between thousands of enterprises have been severed. Few economies were so integrated as the Soviet economy due in great part to its planned character. It is true that serious mistakes were made such as the over-concentration on the production of cotton in Central Asia, leading to the neglect of other economic needs of the people. But that called for correction not destruction of the integrated economy. Today many enterprises have been idled by the severance of these economic ties. The miners of Donbas, Ukraine could not work because lumber they used to receive from the Russian Federation was missing. Such disruption contributed to the catastrophic 25% decline in production in 1991 and 15% drop since the beginning of 1992.

The basis of the worker-collective farmer alliance built up in the course of 7 decades was the balance established between them. This was a unique feature of socialism. Agriculture over the years has provided the machinery, equipment, fertilizer and scientific aid on a scale never achieved under capitalism. This balance has been disrupted. The recent Congress of Collective Farmers of Russia charged that the Yeltsin government was impoverishing and undermining the collective farms. It noted that prices of industrial products had increased 10-40 times, while the price of agricultural products had only risen 3-5 times. This is the operation of the capitalist "scissors" which has ruined millions of farmers in the West. In addition, the tax on the value added, including the 30% tax on credits, is working havoc among collective farmers.

The 87 billion rubles in aid voted by the Second Congress of Deputies of the Russian Federation has been reduced to 10 billion. The Yeltsin Administration is openly aiding the small number of private farmers who only account for 0.4% of the value of agricultural products, and discriminating against the overwhelming majority in the collective farms. All aid has been stopped to debt-ridden farms (even the U.S. government extends aid to its hard-pressed farmers), and their land is being distributed to private farmers. The aim to do away with the collective farm system is hardly concealed. This is one of the chief reasons for the steady, sharp decline in farm production and soaring prices. The destruction of the collective farm system can lead to mass hunger. From modern, large scale agricultural production it would be a return to the primitive level of the early 20th century farming.

Stable Prices

One of the pillars of stable Soviet prices in reach of the mass of the people was the state system of purchasing. By plan and contract, agriculture and industry entered into agreement to sell to the state the bulk of their products at fixed prices. Farmers were permitted to sell some of their products in the free market.

Thus, through its network of stores (and via the cooperatives), the state was able to supply the basic needs of the people at controlled prices. A system of state set prices and wages, worked out with the unions, maintained prices within reach of the people, and provided for a steady rise in the living standard. There were obvious inequities in wages and these had to be corrected. Also, the distribution system and services lagged far behind modern norms. Correction here too was needed. Instead of efforts to improve the mechanism we are witnessing the destruction of the state system of purchasing.

Nowhere does anarchy reign more supreme than in the prices which have run wild. Instead of the state, the 400 stock markets, almost 100 times more than in the U.S., and monopolist enterprises arbitrarily set prices 10 to 40 times higher than in days of state control. Wages by comparison rose an average of 3 times. Wages are determined by enterprise egoism with the strongest seizing the largest piece of the economic pie. This is at the expense of state paid employees, and dismissed workers who constitute as much as 40% of the work force.

Thus, in place of planned distribution of the wealth created, it is everyone for himself and the devil take the hindermost. This is encouraged by the Yeltsin Administration and used to divide the working people. The main streets of Moscow have been turned into flea markets with the poor selling to the poor their personal belongings (it is estimated 20% of the population is so engaged). No prices are too outrageous for the commercial stores which have become, in a manner of speaking, a legalized black market. Soon, stores and services are to be sold off to private individuals and firms who are largely yesterday's black marketeers turned into today's speculators. Some are also former factory directors now turned capitalist working in joint ventures with foreign capital.

Gone is the main law of socialism providing for the maximum needs of the people. In its place is the avaricious law of the capitalist market—maximum profit often by restricting production. Moreover, the former USSR is in no position to promote private modern supermarkets and shopping malls. Modern methods like chain marketing require vast amounts of capital. And only the state or foreign monopoly capital can provide it. The present instability can hardly attract such capital. Thus, privatization will result in primitive stores and services. The USSR was beginning to modernize its distribution system. Perhaps a state-lease partnership could have provided the capital and flexibility.

Laws for the People

In the course of 7 decades a socialist legal structure was developed. While suffering from bureaucracy and inadequate development of democracy it was far more concerned with the welfare of the people and moral standards than in capitalist countries. Laws against racism and promoting hatred of nationalities were strictly enforced. There were no Nagorny-Karabakh national strife situations permitted to develop during the years of socialist rule. To attribute the tragedy of national discord now ravaging the former USSR mainly to past wrong practices is to excuse the shameful failure, particularly of Gorbachev, in the name of "democracy," to combat the inflammatory and unlawful activities of anti-socialist national extremists.

Socialist legality has practically been destroyed. In its place is an increasing breakdown of all authority, shielded by a maze of laws largely unknown to the people and not implemented. This is reflected in massive, brutal crime, attacks upon military installations, seizure of large-scale arms, and assaults on military personnel and militia. Three hundred people were killed in such attacks in 1991. This is the terrifying picture of the once cities without fear. The laws against speculation and pornography (still on the statute books) are ignored. Never have Soviet citizens been as insecure economically, politically, socially and physically. And this has been proclaimed as Gorbachev's and Yeltsin's great "democratic revolution!"

A Return to Exploitation

Under tsarism and capitalism, Russia's vast resources were open to foreign exploitation, particularly of British and French capital. This was done away with by the October Revolution. One of the chief aims of the 7-decade effort to undermine the USSR (at an acknowledged cost of $5 trillion) was to restore this one sixth of the globe to capitalist exploitation. U.S. State Secretary James Baker hailed the "victory over communism" as providing a once in a century opportunity for U.S. monopoly capital, and made periodic visits to the independent Republics to oversee the implementation of exploitation. The rich resources of Russia, its gas, oil, precious metals, lumber, brains of its scientists—all are being sold off to the capitalist West at bargain prices. In the name of "independence," inexperienced, money-hungry enterprises have been permitted to sell off their products at ridiculously low prices to battle-wise foreign firms and to freely dispose of their accumulated foreign currency. The result is a critical shortage of much-needed medicines while the currency is wasted on jeans, gadgets and cosmetics.

Perhaps the most painful operation is now being made upon the network of social benefits once admired and in part copied by the West. Free, comprehensive medical care is not only rapidly being replaced by paid medical clinics; Polyclinics and hospitals are being put on a profit basis. The same process is encroaching on free, comprehensive education. Sanitoria which now cost 30,000 rubles for 24 days, were once only 200 rubles. Rest homes as well as restaurants are today beyond the reach of the mass of the people. Nothing more vividly illustrates this rapid loss of socialist gains than what is happening to Soviet nurseries, once the envy of mothers of the world; today it costs from 600 to 800 rubles per month per child. In the socialist past it was only 12 to 20 rubles.

Class Differences Minimized

Class differentiation and the resulting antagonisms are sharpening. Although it was an overestimation of the stage of socialist development to declare, as was done, that all class antagonisms had disappeared and that Soviet society had reached the stage of an "all-people's state," it is true that state planning, control of prices, foreign trade and utilization of its labor and natural resources for the common good contributed to minimizing class differences and restraining class and national antagonisms. In comparison with both national and racial tensions and strife in the capitalist world and certainly with the tragic situation today, the USSR was a land of national and class harmony. Socialist relations, though at an early stage of development, constituted the basis for that harmony.

That there was an undercurrent waiting to be released has been painfully revealed. But with the abandonment of socialism and the step by step march to capitalism these restraints were removed. And to the extent that the still existing socialist base is destroyed, these class and national antagonisms will be exacerbated. From leveling of incomes, counter-revolution is moving Soviet society to the other extreme common to capitalism: new millionaires on the one hand and 80% of the population living at the edge of poverty on the other.

All this has led to the death rate exceeding the birth rate in Russia. This makes a mockery of the appeals for national reconciliation. The tragedy is no one deserves more peace and normal living than the long-suffering Soviet and Russian people. It is painful to say, but a long, hard struggle still lies ahead for the peoples of the former USSR. It is the price history imposes for allowing their leaders to abandon socialism. History demands and will compel movement forward to socialism, to a new more democratic, more effective USSR and that is the road to class and national harmony.

"Socialism is dead as an ideology and . . . exhausted as an economic model. "

Socialism Would Not Strengthen the Republics' Economies

Guy Sorman

Guy Sorman is a French political scientist who has authored six books on economic and political topics. In the following viewpoint, he states that socialism is an archaic and inefficient system. In its stead he prefers liberalism, which he defines as a decentralized government and a free-market economy. Sorman predicts that the breakup of the Soviet Union will cause an unstable situation in which different types of authoritarian economic systems will emerge. This period of authoritarian rule, he believes, is necessary for the republics to make the transition from socialism to liberalism.

As you read, consider the following questions:

1. Why, according to the author, does a market economy create a peaceful society?
2. According to Sorman, what limits result from the "tribal structure" of socialism?
3. Why is authoritarianism necessary for the transition from socialism to liberalism, according to Sorman?

From Guy Sorman, "How to Emerge from Socialism," *New Times*, January 1992. Reprinted with permission.

An anti-communist revolution has taken place in the Soviet Union, although its completion is still a long way off. As to a liberal revolution, it hasn't even started. Such is the impression I got as a "partial observer" of the historic events of the summer of 1991. . . . Let us not forget, however, that in the country in question ideas made history to a greater extent than anywhere else and their importance was sometimes exaggerated. . . . As a result, the Soviet people became hostages for 74 years of a murderous idea. It is the intellectual duty of our times to work for true or at least less fallacious ideas, but chiefly for those which, instead of killing people, vitalize them. . . .

A question arises: is liberalism necessary at all, and are the peoples of the USSR destined for it? I think that sober-minded people can offer no sound alternative to it. One can well imagine, of course, a relapse into communist totalitarianism, but this would be a misfortune for the peoples. Let us face it: socialism is dead as an ideology, and "biologically" exhausted as an economic model. Communism may persist only as a form of clannishness, as a means of protecting material interests. . . .

The Threat of Despotism

However, let us be wary of the illusion that there are only two ways of development—communism and liberalism. There are quite a few other roads, such as nationalist despotism, the economic essence of which can be defined as state capitalism. In a disintegrating USSR, this road may lead to the political and economic structures being usurped by authoritarian regimes and their supporters in every republic. The new despots will certainly regard themselves as more enlightened than their predecessors, and under cover of national interests, will take all the material resources under their control, being convinced that by authoritarian methods they will run the economy more efficiently than the private sector does. The realization of such a model of development, likely in many republics of the present Union, will lead to the oppression of national minorities and perhaps to internecine wars like the one now in progress in Transcaucasia. Such regimes will not solve economic problems. As a matter of fact, the economy can be revived only in a situation where people are motivated by private property ownership and where the class of real entrepreneurs manages enterprises following economic rather than political logic. It is only a change from state to private property ownership, from centralism to autonomy, from political argumentation to economic expediency that makes a slow resumption of growth possible if not obvious. Partocratic rule—in fact, the very idea of partocracy—should be abolished. Temptation by enlightened despotism, by nationalism as ideology and by state capitalism is, in my opinion, the greatest threat to liberalism. Another argument in favour of economic and political decentralization is that foreign aid will prove effective only when Western enterprises enter into direct contacts with real entrepreneurs, in the flesh, rather than with faceless organizations. It is precisely in this sense that Western aid is contingent upon preliminary reforms in the USSR.

Market Economy Brings Peace

Aren't liberalization, decentralization and the republics' independence fraught with the danger of Balkanization, inefficiency and a civil war? They are not if economic considerations prevail over political ones. A revolution is fine, but who is going to harvest potatoes while it is in progress? This is what most citizens are really concerned about. It won't occur to anyone who runs a business or works for fair wages to attack a neighbour. In principle, a market economy makes for non-aggressive peaceful human relations, and whatever conflicts may arise within its framework are unlikely to be violent. The model of the European Economic Community is an example of how different nations of that part of the continent which have so often come into conflicts with one another have succeeded in creating a system of economic exchange which ensures a harmonious combination of national specifics and common prosperity. . . .

Communism seeks to change human nature, while liberalism accepts and respects man for what he is. A Liberal can be a Russian or a Ukrainian, remain true to his ethnicity, profess Russian Orthodoxy, Uniatism or atheism. As for a communist, he must be a communist in the first place and in the last place, too. Contrariwise, liberalism wants everyone to remain himself. Finally, liberalism, as distinct from communism, is not an imported ideology, it is a Russian tradition which can be traced back a long way in Russian history. . . .

Tribal Government

Under cover of the slogan of economic efficiency, collective farms or people's communes have reconstructed tribal structures. The paradox of socialist institutions consists in the following: theoretically, they rest on scientific foundations and on the principle of economic efficiency. Actually, they are archaic, hopelessly obsolete, hence their inefficiency. Of all the forms of the organization of human society, the society of "advanced socialism" is the most reactionary one. Socialism rejects the principal organic features of modern reality: the individualization and infinite division of labour. Being a tribal structure, socialism is incapable of creating wealth; all it can do is redistribute the goods in short supply in accordance with the classical model of any primeval economy. . . .

In its consequences, withdrawal from socialism is easily comparable with the fall of the Roman Empire. What we witness today is not a mere government crisis, but events which transcend the time limits of the lifetime of one generation. The leaders of the USSR, China and East European countries pretend to have triggered these developments; actually, withdrawal from socialism is not directed either by prominent statesmen nor by some outstanding mind. This is partly explained by the non-revolutionary character of what is going on. The communist regimes have crumbled of their own accord, and the process of their destruction has been faster and deeper than it would have been if caused by a coup carried out by organized opposition having an alternative programme. . . .

Socialism Is Regression

Socialism belongs to the pre-history of mankind. Far from being a progressive conception, the socialist ethic is drawn from instinctual sources, and represents the primitive morality of pre-industrial formations, the clan and the tribe, which had to be overcome in order to realize the great wealth-making potentialities of market societies. Modern socialism is thus the return of the repressed. Its values—equality, cooperation, unity—are the survival codes of small, vulnerable groups with knowable goals and shared interests. But the morality of tribal communities proves disastrous when applied to complex economies that depend on geographically dispersed factors of production. In the modern context, the tribal ethos produces social atavisms—the paternalistic politics, fratricidal nationalisms, and economic despotisms that have kept large regions of Africa, Asia, Latin America, and Central Europe trapped in brutal poverty and oppression.

David Horowitz, *National Review*, April 13, 1992.

However, it is still too early for the liberals to celebrate their victory over socialism. What's more, there is the danger of them losing the battle before they have won it, and of a change from real socialism to real liberalism proving impossible! All the liberal politicians in the East have found themselves in a difficult position. . . .

Democracy Now?

Why, indeed, is it so difficult to pursue a genuinely liberal policy which would privatize all the enterprises at once? Isn't it democracy that opposes this by blocking political decisions, bogging them down in endless parliamentary procedures and not countering the interference of various lobbying groups? If so, then it ought to be made perfectly clear that you cannot democratize politics and liberalize the economy simultaneously. In accordance with the same hypothesis, a strong government should compel society to accept liberalization at once.

The truth of this statement is borne out by the historical precedents for such a pattern of transition to liberalism: in Spain, under Franco; in Taiwan, under Chiang Kai-shek; in Korea and Chile, also under dictatorial regimes; in Japan, under the influence of a powerful foreign presence. In all the above-mentioned cases, a certain amount of despotism guaranteed the citizens' real rights and interests at the right time and stimulated the emergence of the middle class. Can we talk about democracy at all where there is no middle class? Backed by its real rights, this middle class then demanded, and got, its political freedom.

Admittedly, such a method of going through two stages—economic liberalization followed by democratization—was indeed the most effective one because it left it to the nations in question to make their own choice between enlightened despotism, liberalism and any other system of government. . . . Considering that people in post-communist societies want political freedom and economic prosperity at one and the same time, let us see whether it is possible to carry out democratization and liberalization simultaneously under such real and unprecedented consequences. . . .

Temporary Authoritarianism

As the first stage, socialist empires will probably be replaced not by liberal societies but, more likely than not, by a variety of authoritarian social forms. Among the forms which are to emerge, two models—authoritarian-capitalist and neo-tribalist will be more common than the rest.

With respect to historical precedents, the former model can be referred to as "Francoist and Korean." New regimes may emerge on the scene, with the authoritarian government coexisting with private capitalism (as was the case in Franco's Spain), or with the military government uniting with state capitalism (as was the case in Korea). In both cases we have a variety of despotism concerned with the progress of a genuine market economy. It is common knowledge that in Korea and Spain these models gradually moved towards real political and economic freedom. This does not mean, of course, that such a model can be exactly reproduced in some other country. Nevertheless, many leaders of Eastern countries think it can, which adds to the likelihood of attempts to imitate Spanish and Korean models. . . .

Obviously, many nations now withdrawing from socialism will tend towards neo-tribalism, which is the ideological form

172

closest to socialism: the step to be made from one to the other is the shortest indeed. Neo-tribalist societies will be authoritarian, although not necessarily becoming as totalitarian as the socialist regimes have been. They will be particularly harsh with minorities and free thinkers, which will result in intense migration flows from the neo-tribalist to the liberal sphere. This will cause a protective reaction in the liberal countries which will rebound on neo-tribalism.

In the liberal spheres, people will become ever more cosmopolitan, migrant, individualist and prosperous. In the neo-tribalist sphere, stagnation will cause a return to collectivism, to ethnic and cultural solidarity. The fall of the standard of living will foster neo-tribalism, which in its turn will impede economic growth, because liberal ethics which stimulates this growth is contrary to neo-tribalist beliefs. The liberal world will be epitomized by the federation of states, and the neo-tribalist world, with its continuous ethnic and religious wars, by the feudal state. . . .

The Fight of a Liberal

How are the nations which have lost all patience to be prevented from getting the impression that all liberalism can bring is political illusions and economic complications? This can be done only by a vigorous effort.

Anyone regarding himself as a liberal must be an active fighter. I was convinced of this during my latest talk with Friedrich von Hayek, who will be referred to one fine day as the shrewdest political thinker of the 20th century. . . . Leaning on his cane, with a watch chain dangling from his waistcoat pocket, he gave me another lesson. "Be a proponent," he told me, "after all, there are so few of us! Capitalism alone can save the majority of mankind from famine!" What does "fight" mean to a liberal? A liberal is an individualist by nature, and there is little fight in them.

To fight means, above all, to cite facts, to explain that the liberal programme of action exists and is just waiting to be fully implemented. To fight means to expose lies and slander which the Leviathan states seek to perpetuate under cover of liberalization. To fight means to oppose the "holy alliance" of Eastern and Western technocrats who are trying, in their own interests, to perpetuate strong states and weak societies. . . . The alliance of political freedom and a market economy is not a new "end of History," and capitalism can, of course, be replaced by something else. The way I see it, liberalism is an attempt to find solutions to the problems of our times with our limited understanding of history.

173

"Currency boards . . . are the best alternative for Russia and the other ex-Communist states."

Currency Boards Would Strengthen the Republics' Economies

Alan Walters

Since the 1991 collapse of the Soviet empire, the exchange rate of the Soviet ruble has been declining steadily. Alan Walters, the author of the following viewpoint, proposes the establishment of currency boards to stabilize the ruble. A currency board would create a new ruble. The board would exchange this ruble against an established currency, such as the U.S. dollar, at a fixed rate. The new ruble would then compete with the old ruble until a gradual stabilization occurred. Walters recalls the successful policies of economist John Maynard Keynes, who instituted a currency board in Russia in 1918. Walters is vice chairman of AIG Trading Corporation, a commodities exchange house in Washington, D.C., and was formerly chief economic advisor to former British prime minister Margaret Thatcher.

As you read, consider the following questions:

1. Why does Walters argue that the old ruble should continue to be printed?
2. In what way will the former Soviet republics stray from the Keynes model, according to the author?
3. How would the currency board enable economic reforms in the former Soviet republics, according to Walters?

From Alan Walters, "A Hard Ruble for the New Republics," *National Review*, February 3, 1992, © 1992 by National Review, Inc., 150 E. 35th St., New York, NY 10016. Reprinted by permission.

In 1918 the Allied forces, mainly British, landed in North Russia (Archangel and Murmansk) in order to support a non-Bolshevik government. The expedition was frustrated, however, by the collapse of the national currency, the ruble. John Maynard Keynes, then managing Britain's war finances, quickly introduced a new parallel hard currency in the form of a new ruble by lending the government £330,000 to provide the reserves for a currency board. Then both Russians and the troops could exchange Bank of England notes at a fixed rate of approximately 40 new-ruble bank notes to the pound, and vice versa, at the currency board. This enabled the British government to buy supplies for the troops, just as it encouraged production, commerce, and trade among Russians. The ruble was as good as sterling. Russians and others could readily accept rubles in exchange for real goods and services, secure in the knowledge that (at least as long as the currency board survived) it would hold its value. During the short life of the Northern government, the new ruble was stable and widely held as a safe store of value, whereas the old currency went the way of all Bolshevik rubles. . . .

The collapse of the existing Russian ruble—currently trading at less than a penny a ruble—is as obvious as it is distressing. Following Keynes, the Russians would create a hard or *new* ruble to compete with the existing or *old* ruble. A currency board would be set up with the *sole* function of exchanging the new ruble against a specified hard currency at a *fixed* rate. As an illustration, suppose it is fixed to the dollar at one new ruble per dollar. Thus you would get, say, 99.5 new rubles in notes and coin for 100 greenbacks, and $99.5 in notes and coin for a hundred new-ruble notes—so that from the spread the currency board recovers its costs. Note that it swaps only *currency and coin*, not deposits, but of course the swap offer on currency will be arbitraged through the free market to deposits of new rubles at banks. The new rubles could be freely held by anyone and would count as legal tender. Similarly, the holding of either dollar notes or accounts would be declared quite legal. Freedom at last.

Financing

What do we need to make this work? First, the currency board needs hard-currency reserves so it can redeem its issue of hard rubles. It should hold at least 100 per cent reserves of dollars against its new-ruble issue. Only then will there be confidence in its promise of redemption of new rubles for dollars. My colleague and collaborator Steve Hanke has suggested that the only way to instill complete trust is to locate the currency board in a haven out of reach of the Russian government, such as Switzerland. Worth thinking about, but likely to be a nonstarter. The only way is for the Russian government or central bank to be aware of the great benefits it will get from having a convertible currency on the premises of the republic.

How much will it cost to equip all the republics with a hard-ruble currency board? That depends on how it is introduced. So let's begin with the outside estimate. Suppose that the new ruble *completely* and *instantly* replaces the old. Then as a most rough calculation, I believe that Russians would wish to hold about 20 billion of new-ruble notes and coin. Thus, to be on the safe side, the currency board would need some $30 billion in reserves. By an odd coincidence this is just about the value of the monetary gold that the Russians claim to have. . . . So the government could lend this gold to form the capital of the currency board. In turn the currency board would sell the gold for dollars—or so as not to rile other gold holders it might simply borrow dollars with the gold as security. The new rubles would be issued to the government. And the government in turn would spend them—preferably by buying up old-ruble notes at an exchange rate freely determined by market supply and demand.

An alternative way of financing the new-ruble issue is for the aid-giving governments of the West to pony up the $30 billion. Again by an odd coincidence this is the amount which was suggested as the appropriate annual aid budget by the Harvard-Yavlinsky group in the "grand bargain" in 1991. For my part I would be opposed to such large sums in aid, for reasons which have been argued so forcefully over the years by Lord Bauer. Furthermore such sums will not be needed in practice. The process of reform would be a gradual one.

Old and New

There would be no wholesale currency conversion from old to new. The old rubles would continue to be printed by the central bank and would continue to circulate and be accepted as legal tender. Why? I believe it is realistic to assume that the Russian republics will not reduce their massive budget deficits to manageable levels overnight or even over years. A major tax reform (mainly the introduction of VAT [value added tax]) is needed, and even with the best will in the world that will take a long time. Nor is the Russian government going to have ready and speedy access to ample loans either from foreigners or from its long-suffering people. The only way to close the budget gap is to print old rubles. (Note that the central bank cannot print new rubles unless it has received dollar notes in exchange.) Granted the large deficits, this would mean that there would be a continuing inflation, probably hyperinflation, in terms of old rubles. People would be induced to cut down their holdings of rapidly depreciating old rubles and switch to the new. Indeed the nice new ruble would drive out the bad old ruble—and incidentally make printing old rubles a worthless occupation. Thus governments would then either have to balance their books or earn a credit rating.

This seems to be contradicted by Gresham's Law—"Bad money drives out good." But Gresham's Law is valid only when the exchange rate between the bad and good is *fixed*. Bad and good money can live together if the exchange rate is determined freely by the market. From our experience in Latin American inflations and reforms, however, one suspects that the old ruble, with its rapidly declining value, will be less and less used except for small transactions.

A Currency Board Will Avert Disaster

If the Commonwealth of Independent States hopes to ever introduce markets, it must replace the ruble with a convertible, stable currency. A sound currency serves as a satisfactory store of value, medium of exchange, and unit of account. An unsound currency such as the ruble does none of these things. . . .

Unfortunately, CIS leaders believe a central bank is the way to make the ruble convertible. Guided by experts from the International Monetary Fund, World Bank, and Harvard University, they are busy learning how to run central banks. That central banking fetish could prove to be disastrous. . . .

There is a better way: a currency board instead of a central bank. A currency board issues notes and coins convertible into a foreign reserve currency at a fixed rate on demand. . . .

More than 60 countries (mainly former British colonies) have had currency boards. All successfully maintained convertibility at a fixed exchange rate.

Steve H. Hanke and Kurt Schuler, *Reason*, March 1992.

But as the new ruble becomes the accepted currency, so foreign capital would flood in to take advantage of the high rate of return and security of currency. Similarly the large quantities of dollars, Deutsche Marks, etc. which are at present in the mattresses or Swiss bank accounts of Soviet citizens would be disinterred, swapped for new rubles, and invested or spent on Russian projects and goods.

Thus although one should be prepared for an eventual new-ruble issue of 30 billion, it would be preferable to use only, say, 5 billion of the gold supply as the government's initial contribution to the dollar reserves. The rest would come from the mattresses and Zurich as the new ruble is seen to be as good as the dollar. Then in a matter of a year or so the Russian people will have a stable money to serve as the basis for their further economic reform program.

Questions

Why go through the rigmarole of a currency board? Why not simply circulate the greenback? Apart from the obvious one of political pride in having one's own currency, there is the risk of loss. A burned dollar bill is a dollar lost to Russia, whereas a burned ruble note can easily be replaced by another. Second, and more important, much of the dollar reserve can be invested in income-bearing assets—and that income will accrue to Russia, whereas circulating greenbacks is making an interest-free loan to the United States. Not good business, at least for Russia.

A second question: If this is so good a system, why have not other countries practiced it? The short answer is: They have—and very successfully. Britain in her heyday, from 1844 to 1931, was on a currency board—and certainly sterling was stable and commanded wide respect. Today, and another heyday, the fastest-growing countries in the world are on currency boards—namely Hong Kong and Singapore.

A third question: Why the dollar? Why not the Deutsche Mark or the yen or even a bastard sort of basket currency such as the European Currency Unit (ECU)? The main reason is a combination of acceptability and simplicity. Although the German and Japanese records on inflation are somewhat better than that of the United States, the difference is small. And neither Germany nor Japan has the liberal and open regime of the United States monetary system. Mixtures of currencies complicate the currency board's business; and so far as I know ECUs are acceptable only at Harrods—not, I fear, the corner shop of every Russian. I conclude that the dollar is best.

I would not want to pretend that currency boards solve all, always. But I do think that they are the best alternative for Russia and the other ex-Communist states. Are they likely? I believe that some attempts will be made to prepare the way for a currency-board system—rather like the reforms we have seen in Poland since January 1990. I fear, however, that—again as in Poland—the reform will attempt to maintain the state's monopoly of the money supply and will not set up the hard ruble as a *parallel* currency. It will, so to speak, harden up the existing soft ruble.

Like the zloty reform in Poland, this will take the form of first declaring convertibility and then pegging the existing ruble to (say) the dollar at (say) 200 to provide a "nominal anchor" for the currency. If this exchange rate is held through hell and high water, then ultimately there will be stability somewhere near the inflation rate of the United States. The trouble is that this requires a most restrained rate of expansion in the quantity of rubles issued. But this requirement will be quite inconsistent with the need for the governments to print rubles to cover their horrendous budget deficits. Ah, you may say, this misses the fact that the rhetoric of the reforms requires low and manageable deficits. Indeed the IMF [International Monetary Fund] insists on such. But the reforms also insist on the great state-owned enterprises being subject to market discipline—and this will mean erstwhile surpluses are converted into swinging losses; and a very large component of public revenue, the taxes on such surpluses, will disappear. The sharp decline of output, always so far associated with the first years of reform, will also balloon the budget deficit. (Is it really necessary to argue here in the United States that all budget deficits are bigger than expected?)

Hard and Soft

If one retains only the newly hardened ruble (200 to the dollar) and the government has to print a large amount of money to cover the deficit, then there will be too many rubles and eventually the currency will have to be depreciated. Once it goes soft its "as good as a dollar" reputation will be gone. It is, of course, *possible* to avoid printing money to cover deficits. The government could borrow, or it could receive "donations" (aid) from a grateful West anxious to conclude a "grand bargain." Alas, the CIS credit ratings are low and are unlikely to improve. And it is unlikely that the West will double the amount donated to the Third World (about $35 billion) to provide what the lobbyists for the "grand bargain" think is appropriate to bail out the former Soviet Union (about 5 per cent of Russia's GNP, or $100 per capita for five years).

I conclude that it is good policy to keep the old inflating ruble, freely floating in a free market, to enable the government to cover its obligations. I believe it would also be useful in avoiding the shock implied in hardening the existing ruble. The parallel hard and soft rubles would ease the transition to a free and open market economy.

Finally, it is worthy of note that Keynes's new ruble was a parallel currency. So I conjecture that Keynes would have approved of the reincarnation of his currency boards. After all it worked in 1918; why not now?

"Privatizing . . . will result in increases in efficiency, higher quality products, increased wages and decreased costs to government. "

Privatization Would Strengthen the Republics' Economies

Leonid Grigoriev

One major step in the transition from Soviet-style socialism to a market economy is privatization—the transference of state-owned property and enterprises to the private sector. In the following viewpoint, Leonid Grigoriev of the Institute of World Economy and International Relations in Moscow argues that privatization needs to occur rapidly in order to stabilize the faltering economies of the former Soviet republics. Despite the obstacles—lack of banking institutions, an inconvertible currency, and resistance on the part of the old bureaucracy—Grigoriev is convinced that the former Soviet republics can achieve private ownership of agriculture, business, housing, industry, and land.

As you read, consider the following questions:

1. Why does Grigoriev propose a "homestead approach" to distribute state-owned land?
2. Why should managers of state farms be given land, according to Grigoriev?
3. What problems with the voucher plan does the author foresee?

From Leonid Grigoriev, "The Former Soviet Republics Confront Privatization: A Russian Analysis," Heritage Foundation *Backgrounder*, October 11, 1991. Reprinted with permission.

One of the most urgent tasks for the republics of the former Soviet Union is to dismantle their inefficient, state-dominated economies and to turn over to private ownership virtually all state-owned agriculture, businesses, housing, industry, and land. This transition from a communist command economy to a market economy—commonly known as privatization—must be undertaken with unprecedented speed, because the Soviet economy is collapsing, and only a growing, robust private sector can save it.

Privatizing the state sector will result in increases in efficiency, higher quality products, increased wages and decreased costs to government. Of course, privatization is not a panacea for all that ails the republic economies. To be effective, privatization must be accompanied by other reforms such as price and trade liberalization, tight control of the money supply to avoid inflation, deregulation, tax reform, and budget cuts.

Recent experience with privatization in Eastern Europe demonstrates that the republic policy makers face formidable obstacles. Foremost among these is the sheer size of the undertaking. By some counts there are approximately 46,000 large state enterprises and 750,000 state-owned shops on the territory of the former Soviet Union. In addition to finding methods for turning these entities over to private ownership, the 50 percent of the housing stock still in government hands and the bulk of agricultural land also need to be privatized. Privatization on such a mass scale has never been attempted.

Technical and economic obstacles to privatization in the republics include the lack of savings, an absence of capital markets and banking institutions, and a currency that cannot be converted into Western "hard" currencies needed for international transactions. Agricultural privatization is a particularly difficult task. Furthermore, the irrationality of Soviet prices, which have been set arbitrarily by the state rather than market forces, makes it nearly impossible to correctly value the state enterprises to be privatized. As if these problems were not enough, political and social obstacles to privatization are sure to arise, including opposition from local officials and the *nomenklatura*—the Soviet Union's entrenched bureaucracy—new problems of envy, the need to privatize in an equitable way, and control over part of the underground economy by the Soviet Union's own "mafia" of organized crime.

Surmountable Obstacles

While the obstacles to privatization in the former Soviet republics are formidable, they are by no means insurmountable. Most of these problems have been encountered in privatization efforts in other parts of the world, and have been overcome by economically sound and politically savvy policies. The lack of capital markets and domestic savings and the problem of how to value enterprises can be overcome by giving away state assets, rather than selling them. The opposition of workers, factory managers, and local officials can be turned around by giving them a stake in promoting the development of a market economy. Some of the giant "agroindustry" state farms can be privatized by turning them into joint-stock companies and giving workers shares in the enterprise.

Finally, the republics should be expected to rely on internal financing and private foreign investment for privatization, not Western government handouts. Foreign firms are already very active in the republics. In the near future, there should be much greater foreign interest in purchasing stakes in the more profitable enterprises. Republics should encourage greater foreign participation in the privatization process because it brings in needed capital and managerial expertise.

An Urgent Task

Without doubt, the peoples of the former Soviet Union will encounter political and technical difficulties in the process of privatization. However, they have no alternative but to embark immediately on this task. The longer they wait, the more difficult it will prove.

The new political situation . . . has resolved the issue of what to do with what is known as "all-union property." Virtually any enterprises or other assets owned by the Soviet central government, or "center," it is widely acknowledged, now will belong to the republics. It also is clear that privatization will be almost entirely the responsibility of the republican governments rather than what remains of the center. While some republics unwisely may choose to go slowly, republican control of privatization on balance should accelerate the process, as has been demonstrated with privatization efforts around the world.

The main danger is that some republics may try to exclude outsiders from bidding on enterprises within their territory. Such a restriction of capital flows would be self-defeating because it would decrease the amount of capital available for purchasing and subsequently modernizing the enterprises, thereby slowing the process. These and other restrictions on capital flows and free trade—such as restricting exports—explicitly should be rejected by the republic governments. Any program of privatization also will require tailored approaches. Policy makers, for instance, face much different political and technical obstacles in privatizing housing than they do in privatizing large industry. . . .

Due to the tremendous inefficiency of collectivized agriculture, fertile regions that once were agricultural exporters, such as the Baltics and Ukraine, now must often cope with food shortages of their own. Privatizing agricultural land will rapidly increase the productivity of farms in all the republics and ensure that reliable supplies of staples reach hungry citizens. In some republics, agricultural privatization is proving relatively easy. Example: Armenia already has privatized 70 percent to 80 percent of its agricultural land. This was possible because the agricultural plots in Armenia were not very large, and therefore could easily be turned over to the peasants who worked the land. In some other republics, particularly Russia, quick agricultural privatization faces significant obstacles.

One problem is the scale of Russia's "agroindustry." The huge size of Russia's state farms, known as *kolkhozes*, is not in itself the problem. In China, beginning in 1978, huge state farms similar to Russia's were privatized quickly by simply dividing up the land and distributing it to peasants. But on many large Russian collective farms there is the added factor, not present in China, of widespread reliance on sophisticated large-scale machinery. Such machinery cannot easily be divided up among the workers of collective farms. Furthermore, many of the large farms will be more efficient economically if they are not broken apart before being turned over to private owners.

U.S. agriculture, for instance, is far more efficient and productive than that of Western European because American farms are much larger, and therefore can take advantage of economies of scale. One solution for the large and relative productive *kolkhozes* is to turn them into joint-stock companies, and to give freely tradable shares in the new company to the workers.

Resistant Managers

Another major obstacle to agricultural privatization is the strong political and economic power of the managers of the agroindustrial enterprises and of local government authorities in rural areas. Their very strong political lobby convinced the Russian parliament to write off about 70 billion rubles of debt owed to the state from the *kolkhozes*. In many cases these debts were owed by healthy agroindustrial enterprises.

These managers and local officials also have significant economic clout. Collective farm managers control the distribution of such supplies as fuel and fertilizer and the allocation of resources. The new, private owners of land will be dependent in the short run on the willingness of these same managers and local officials to sell them supplies. The managers could use this economic power to sabotage the new private farms.

Local authorities and managers of state farms have a great interest in preventing the successful privatization of agriculture because they will lose the powers and privilege they now enjoy.

183

Most of these communist bureaucrats do not have the skills needed for farming on their own and are unlikely to be hired elsewhere in the near term. The only realistic way to blunt the opposition of these powerful opponents of market reform is to turn their opposition around by giving them a financial interest in the success of agricultural privatization. This can be done by giving them land and shares in the privatized *kolkhozes*.

Benefits of Privatization

The major objectives of privatization . . . include creating a sector of private owners, increasing enterprises' efficiency, ensuring social protection for the population and developing social infrastructure, promotion of competition and demonopolization, and encouragement of foreign investment.

Alexander Ivanenko, *New Times*, October 1992.

A final obstacle to rapid agricultural privatization is that many of the agricultural regions in Russia are deteriorating and are very sparsely populated. Demographically, they have aging populations since most of the brightest young people from the countryside—those who will be needed to make the new private farms productive—were recruited to work for the bureaucracies in major cities like Moscow. Young people working in city factories and bureaucracies, many of which need to be shut down anyway, should be encouraged to go back to the land. One way of doing this would be to employ a homestead approach similar to that used in America's old West. Citizens from urban regions would be given the opportunity to stake a claim on formerly state-owned land in return for a promise to cultivate it.

Large State Enterprises

Around 46,000 large enterprises, employing many millions of workers now are coming under the control of republic governments. The majority of these enterprises are inefficient, and produce goods and materials of vastly inferior quality and design to those in the West. To improve efficiency, production, and quality, and to bring these factories up to Western levels, they must be turned over to the private sector. Putting these enterprises in private hands in a relatively short period of time will not be an easy task. In Britain, it took nearly ten years to privatize about two dozen large state-owned enterprises.

There are numerous impediments to privatizing state enterprises in the republics. These include a lack of capital markets, the near impossibility of correctly valuing the enterprises, high inflation—which makes investment inherently more risky—and a shortage of household savings to use to purchase shares in enterprises.

Most of the savings in the former Soviet Union are concentrated in the hands of small percentage of the population. Those who could be classified as "rich"—usually private businessmen or black marketeers—possess more than half of all personal savings. For the bulk of citizens, household savings are not great enough for major investments. Even among the relatively well-off segment of the general population, those with annual incomes in the 300-400 ruble range per capita, average savings are sufficient only to buy one or two major items, such as a car. The majority of the population possesses only enough savings to buy ordinary consumer durables, meet run-of-the-mill unforeseen expenses, and supplement state pension funds for retirement. Such individuals, with their limited resources, cannot be expected to play a major role in the purchase of state assets.

Another potential problem in selling state enterprises to outside investors would be opposition from the managers of the enterprises. Many managers consider themselves the de facto owners of the enterprises that employ them, and would strongly resist the loss of control. The failure of the August 1991 coup reduced the power and size of the existing *nomenklatura*, but many still will attempt to assert control over enterprises and profit from their privatization.

Voucher System?

An often-proposed solution to overcoming all the obstacles to rapid privatization of state enterprises in the republics is to issue vouchers free of charge to every citizen. The vouchers in turn could be used to purchase shares in state enterprises. The Russian parliament approved an initial voucher system on July 3, 1991. These vouchers have been termed "privatization accounts," and can be used by Russian citizens to acquire shares in state and municipal enterprises from local or republic authorities. The voucher system has much to recommend it, yet distributing the vouchers to hundreds of millions of citizens entails enormous administrative problems. Moreover, with little available accurate published information about individual enterprises, the average Russian citizen—in fact, even many financial analysts—will have no idea which enterprises might be good investments, or what their real value should be. The process will more closely resemble a lottery than a market-oriented approach to investment based on potential profitability. Lastly, such an approach would mean that in the short run, ownership of enterprises will be broad and diffuse. Without the presence of strong core owners, the enterprises may continue to operate as inefficiently as they did in the state sector.

A better alternative than having citizens invest directly in state enterprises with vouchers would be to assign large state enterprises to "investment funds." The investment funds would first turn the state enterprises into limited liability, joint-stock companies. The investment funds would be charged with selling or distributing stock in the new joint-stock companies and appointing Boards of Directors to head the companies. The investment funds would be required to sell off their portfolio of state enterprises within a given time period, perhaps ten years. . . .

A Critical First Step

One of the most urgent reforms for the new governments is privatization. Housing, land, agriculture, industry, stores, restaurants, and services all need to be transferred rapidly to the private sector.

While the need for massive privatization is generally acknowledged by most of the new leaders in the republics, privatization faces daunting obstacles that may discourage many leaders from launching an ambitious program. For instance, the lack of a capital market, which allows savings to be transferred efficiently to investment, constrains privatization. Other obstacles are the absence of market institutions, high inflation, a worthless and non-convertible currency, opposition from the *nomenklatura*, and the sheer size of the task in the state-run economy.

To develop appropriate policies, policy makers need to have a clear understanding of the numerous political and economic obstacles to privatization. They must recognize that though the obstacles are formidable, they are not insurmountable. Instead of selling state assets and running into major problems with valuation, for instance, state assets can be given away. Problems with agricultural privatization can be overcome in a number of ways, including turning large agroindustrial complexes into joint stock companies and giving away shares in the new enterprise to the workers.

The experience around the world with privatization—from Britain to Chile to Kenya—demonstrates that heavy political opposition and serious technical difficulties to privatization can be surmounted through creative strategies. The republics of the former Soviet Union can draw important lessons from the success and failures of the worldwide privatization movement and the recent experience in Eastern Europe. Although the course will be a difficult one, privatization in the republics ultimately will be the critical first step to building prosperous economies in the republics of the former Soviet Union.

"Direct employee ownership of enterprises is an ideal solution to the problem of privatization."

Employee Ownership Would Strengthen the Republics' Economies

John Logue and Dan Bell

As the former Soviet republics shift from centralized to market economies, there is debate over the method of privatization—the transference of state-owned property and enterprises to the private sector. The questions center on who should acquire ownership and how possession should be transferred. John Logue and Dan Bell, the authors of the following viewpoint, favor a system of employee ownership, in which enterprises would be purchased with assets and loans, and shares would be distributed and/or sold according to guidelines established by the workers. The authors describe two successful worker-owned enterprises already in existence in Russia. Bell is the network coordinator for, and Logue is director of, the Northeast Ohio Employee Ownership Center.

As you read, consider the following questions:

1. According to the authors, why did buying state enterprises become more desirable than leasing?
2. How does workers' failure to understand employee ownership impede its implementation, according to the authors?
3. Why, according to Logue and Bell, does employee ownership increase production?

From John Logue and Dan Bell, "Worker Ownership in Russia," *Dissent*, Spring 1992. Reprinted with permission.

It was raining when we pulled up in front of a low, nondescript factory in Tver, two hours' drive northeast of Moscow. The Tveris glass plant, built as a state enterprise, was celebrating its first anniversary of employee ownership.

Tveris Glass is one of some hundred firms that, by the time of our visit in July 1991, had opted out of the command economy through direct worker ownership. What "direct worker ownership" means varies from enterprise to enterprise, but the concept of worker ownership is an attractive alternative both to state ownership and to such other forms of privatization as sale to managers and government officials (the "propertization of the nomenklatura"); sale at auction to the Russians with the most rubles, the so-called black market mafia; or sale to foreign investors. "Employee ownership is the most socially acceptable form of privatization," economist Jacob N. Keremetsky told an audience of Soviet managers of employee-owned and -leased businesses, "because it avoids the class conflict inevitable in all the other types of privatization."

The Russian republic's government intends to convert its moribund command economy to a market economy. But who will own what is far from clear. A variety of ownership forms are compatible with the market, ranging from highly concentrated private ownership, through a Jeffersonian pattern of widely dispersed ownership in small businesses, family farms, and employee stock ownership, to state and municipal ownership within a market socialist structure. Each has its adherents among Russian reformers. Choosing *which* mix of ownership forms is to replace monolithic state ownership is a crucial issue in the process of economic reform.

The purpose of our visit to employee-owned plants in the Moscow area in July 1991 was to discuss what Russian firms could learn from the American experience with employee ownership. Although that experience is mixed, some eleven thousand U.S. companies employing over 10 percent of the non-public sector work force have introduced some element of employee ownership through Employee Stock Ownership Plans (ESOPs) since 1974; more than two thousand of those employing more than one million people are estimated to be majority employee-owned. Studies demonstrate that firms that combine significant employee ownership with significant employee participation systematically outperform their conventional competitors. Good business and distributive justice can go hand in hand.

Understanding Worker Ownership

The passage of the Russian republic's privatization legislation in July 1991 lent a sense of urgency to understanding worker ownership, for the legislation gives employees preference in buying enterprises to be privatized. (Legislation calling for giving every citizen a voucher that could be exchanged for shares or real property was also passed. Implementation of the voucher system has, however, been postponed as inflationary.) The conservative opposition to the concept, epitomized by KGB chief Vladimir Kryuchkov's condemnation of direct worker ownership, was swept aside in the aftermath of the August 1991 putsch attempt. The July 1991 legislation is currently being amended. The government's position is to award 25 percent of shares to employees without charge and to sell an additional 10 percent to workers and 5 percent to management at preferential prices. . . .

Direct worker ownership remains terra incognita for most Russians. Leonid V. Leibov, the general director of a group of five furniture plants employing 2,500, put it succinctly: "When we started looking at introducing worker ownership at Mosfurnitura, we had no more idea of how to carry it out than [Mikhail] Gorbachev did when he started perestroika."

The first halting steps toward employee ownership were taken in the early days of Gorbachev's economic reforms. "Work collectives"—employees as a group—were permitted to lease state enterprises on an experimental basis. Employee leasing began on a small scale in the service sector of Estonia in 1985 and was adapted to industrial enterprises around Moscow in fall 1987 by Dr. Valery M. Rutgaizer, an economist then at the All-Union Institute for Public Opinion Research. Leased firms were able to retain their surplus and plow it back into the enterprise in the form of capital improvements, wage increases, and programs to improve the living conditions of the employees. By February 1990, employee-leased firms were estimated to number between 1,200 and 2,000 and to employ between one and two million. Such enterprises saw sharp increases in productivity and benefited from a more entrepreneurial management style.

To Lease or Buy?

While leasing contracts were initially negotiated on the basis of historical profitability, in December 1989 the USSR Supreme Soviet passed a law that changed the terms for setting the lease price to a formula based on a percentage of the firm's asset value. This raised lease fees sharply and diminished leasing's attraction. In January 1990, the Union's Council of Ministers offered an avenue permitting employees to buy industrial assets directly: it created BUTEC People's Concern as an economic experiment combining collective worker ownership of enterprises and market relations. State-owned enterprises that joined BUTEC were permitted to withdraw from the state plan when their work collectives purchased the enterprises' assets. The Law on Property, which took effect on July 1, 1990, provided a more permanent legal basis for this form of ownership.

In BUTEC's first eighteen months, work collectives of some sixty-six state enterprises in light industry, construction, and services—70 percent of them in the Moscow area—took advantage of the BUTEC model to buy their assets. (As of July 1991, BUTEC members also included four hundred new businesses. About eighty state enterprises in sectors where privatization was not permitted were associated members.) Together they employ about twenty-six thousand people; the median employment is about three hundred, small by Soviet standards. While other experiments have been undertaken on an ad hoc basis in individual firms, such as the truck producer Kamaz, the BUTEC model prescribed a systematic framework governing the purchase, operation, and distribution of member enterprises' profits. Although the new privatization law will lead to mass privatization outside BUTEC, the BUTEC experiment provides most of the Russian experience with direct worker ownership.

Work collectives joining BUTEC received the right to purchase the business at the "residual asset value" as determined by a local commission. Although prices have varied with the skill of the negotiators, they have typically been low—encouraging experimentation—since "residual value" permitted deducting imputed payments on the assets' acquisition price through employee labor during the years of state ownership. Funds for purchasing assets were derived from the profits of the enterprise, employee savings, and state bank credits. At the state's discretion, outdated fixed assets could be given to the employees. Purchase payments were divided between the union government and the local government in proportion to the share each had previously received of the profits of the enterprise.

A Nascent Market System

Once the enterprise was purchased, the BUTEC model permitted its value to be divided among the employees individually "according to their personal labor contribution." How an individual's labor contribution was determined was left to the discretion of the enterprise. However, the law specified that the value of the enterprise for individual distribution was set at the initial amount paid plus any portion of the acquisition loan that had been repaid. Any value that has not been paid for, because it was credited to employees for past labor or was a simple grant from the state, would not be distributed among the workers individually though it belonged to them collectively. An employee leaving the enterprise would be entitled to compensation for his individual share.

BUTEC enterprises were permitted to determine their own plans for production, obtain their own sales, deal directly with suppliers, issue securities, hire skilled labor, set wages, and establish their own prices within legal limits "under the guidance of the market," as the regulations implementing the Council of Ministers' decree stated. BUTEC member firms were also entitled to engage directly in foreign trade and to set up a commercial bank to provide credit to the enterprises and to individual employees and to handle foreign currencies. Thus BUTEC enterprises represented a nascent market system, building market relationships from below, though they also could continue to buy from and sell to state enterprises covered by the plan. Their profits belonged to the enterprise (and hence the employees); their direct relation to the state was limited to paying taxes. Rates vary with use: retained earnings used for capital improvements and social development (such as housing) were taxed at 8 percent; remaining income was taxed at 17 percent. What was left could be allocated among employees in bonuses and dividends.

An Employee Ownership Success

The Vakhrusheva mine was a pioneer of privatization. . . . The mine was converted to a shareholding company in September 1991, with an authorized capital of 33 million roubles (about $240,000 at the current exchange rate), calculated on the basis of the written down book value of the mine's assets. . . . The company was established as a closed company, with share ownership strictly limited to employees, and no individual being permitted to own more than 1 percent of the shares. . . . Share ownership certainly seems to provide an incentive for the workers to improve productivity, which has increased by 30 percent, while in the mines which remain under state control productivity has fallen by almost half.

Petr Biziukov and Simon Clarke, *Monthly Review*, November 1992.

Motivations for joining the BUTEC experiment varied. "We were all idealists," says Valery N. Varvarov, BUTEC's personnel director. But idealism was tempered with economic incentives. For the managers we talked to, a crucial motivation was escaping the straitjacket of the state plan. As one put it, in the old system "The art of the manager was to neutralize the bureaucracy and to keep it from hindering your work." In the new, they could escape the command system entirely. . . .

The Tveris Plant

The Tveris plant, which produces consumer glassware and art glass, was built from scratch by its employees a quarter of a century ago. On July 1, 1990, employees bought the firm's two glass plants and auxiliary enterprises (a machine shop, power plant, and hog farm) for six million rubles. This is a modest price for a firm that does thirty million rubles in sales, employs one thousand people, and has an operating income of ten million rubles. Igor Semionov, its director, estimated the firm's real value to be at least fifteen million rubles. The purchase price was calculated as the residual asset value of the plant's 1972 asset inventory. Of the six million ruble purchase price, two million came from cash on hand; the remainder was a three-year bank loan with a 10 percent fixed-interest rate.

Registered initially as a "People's Concern" within BUTEC, Tveris restructured itself as a shareholding society in May 1991, issuing 6,500 shares valued at 1,000 rubles each. Two thousand shares, representing the initial two million ruble payment, were allocated on the basis of seniority and salary to individual employees; some 70 percent of the employees qualified for these shares on the basis of their service records. An additional five hundred shares were made available for direct purchase by employees who could buy them on credit; this represented new equity, and was also distributed to individuals. The remaining four thousand shares are held by the shareholding society collectively; some or all of this bloc may be sold in the future. The firm will initiate an internal market, which will permit employees to buy and sell shares to each other.

A Success

In its first year of employee ownership, Tveris did well. It increased both wages and wage differentials from a range of two hundred to six hundred rubles a month to a range of three hundred to twelve hundred. (The average industrial wage in July 1991 was about 250 rubles per month.) The firm undertook a number of major projects including building a new plant and four and a half million rubles worth of new housing construction for employees. In an effort to insulate Tveris against what Semionov called "the complete anarchy in supply," a small commercial bank and several trading firms were founded to serve as an alternative to state supply and distribution channels.

Semionov first became general director in 1988 in the brief period when directors were directly elected by the workers. Today he is selected by and responsible to a seven-member management board elected by a fifteen-member shareholders' council, which, in turn, is elected by the employee shareholders. The council includes the local trade-union leader. The relative roles of management and council have not been clarified. The council represents the owners and has a right to democratize management. Yet management requires expertise. Semionov has tried to educate his staff on finance, so far with little success. . . .

Stroipolymer, located in Golitsyno, about thirty miles outside Moscow, manufactures laminated polymer construction products, including linoleum, wallpaper, and vinyl wall coverings. In April 1988, it was one of the first plants in the Moscow region to be leased by employees. It did very well; the average wage increased from 220 rubles in April 1988 to 360 in February 1990 for its 700 employees, while the enterprise also constructed sixty apartments and built a clinic. In August 1990 employees bought the plant for twenty million rubles; 5.7 million was deducted from the purchase price for capital improvements made while leasing, one million was paid in cash and 13.3 million was borrowed from the state bank with an eight-year term and an interest rate of initially 5.5 percent. Since employees bought the plant, the average wage had doubled to 700 rubles in July 1991, while employment had been cut to 610. Sales for 1991 were expected to hit between sixty and seventy million rubles with an after-tax profit of about twelve million rubles.

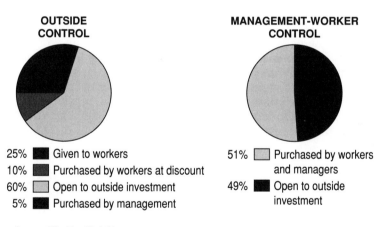

Types of Privatization

OUTSIDE CONTROL

MANAGEMENT-WORKER CONTROL

25% Given to workers
10% Purchased by workers at discount
60% Open to outside investment
5% Purchased by management

51% Purchased by workers and managers
49% Open to outside investment

Source: *The New York Times*

Stroipolymer had the lowest ratio of shareholders to employees that we encountered: only 290 of 610. To be included, one needed two years seniority and a good evaluation of job performance. Share allocation was then based on seniority and wages: the 290 employees who qualified will receive about 70,000 rubles each in shares. To justify the allocation of shares on which the loan has not yet been repaid, workers sign individual contracts agreeing to pay for their shares by pledging the future dividends from these shares.

Ownership and Responsibility

Stroipolymer has sought to promote a culture of ownership since employees leased the plant in 1988. This effort has met with some success. Employees interviewed at random seemed knowledgeable. For example, Anatoly Aleshinkov, a manual worker with thirty years of seniority and ninety thousand rubles in shares, explained to us in some detail how the dividends on his shares, which came out of Stroipolymer's profits, were actually paying for his shares. "But," we asked, "has ownership affected your daily job?" "Previously we were on fixed wages," responded Aleshinkov. "Now when we get greater production, we benefit directly. So now we always try to implement good ideas. That often requires buying new equipment," he added.

Stroipolymer has embarked on a two hundred million ruble capital improvement project that will more than double existing production capacity, add additional products, and increase the firm's participation in joint ventures with foreign companies. Two more apartment buildings for Stroipolymer workers are on the drawing board and sixty detached cottages are planned.

In addition to recognizing the need to educate the workers about ownership, Stroipolymer's Makharinov has been focusing on what he calls *psychological privatization*: getting workers to take ownership and responsibility for their work through decentralization and team decision making. His greatest success has been a group of eight employees involved in producing polymer stabilizers who now run their department as a separate subsidiary. They produced eighteen tons of stabilizers the previous year; now they produce eighteen tons a month.

Theory and Practice

In theory direct employee ownership of enterprises is an ideal solution to the problem of privatization. It can be carried out quickly, provides powerful incentives for workers to increase production and reinvestment, and its labor-based formula for allocating capital fits both ideological and cultural norms.

But will it work in practice? What we saw at Tveris, Stroipolymer, and the four other plants we visited was an impressive demonstration of managerial initiative, improvements in productivity and compensation, a significant expansion of existing production capacity, and the development of new products, businesses, and joint ventures. Production is up, wages are higher, and employees are beginning to accumulate substantial capital.

Yet even in these innovative enterprises, significant . . . problems remain. . . . Perhaps the most intractable immediate problem for employee ownership is the lack of a culture of ownership among Russian workers. When we asked at works council meetings at Tveris and Ordynka (a Moscow-based freight broker with 343 employees), "What proportion of employees understand ownership?" only two of nineteen works council members thought that as many as half the employees understood ownership; the median guess was that only 10 percent understood.

A Transitional Phase?

While the example of Stroipolymer suggests that information and education may create a sense of ownership over time, given the current level of stock ownership among Russian workers, there is a substantial likelihood that individually held employee stock will be resold as soon as the law permits and ownership will rapidly become concentrated. Some Russian economists consider this desirable, and they treat employee ownership as only a transitional phase.

By contrast, the "collective private property" that BUTEC has promoted ties capital ownership to labor input. Although it can be (and is) combined with joint ventures with foreign firms and investors, its underlying premise has been that privatization should spread productive wealth broadly. BUTEC's combination of individual property rights with a collective structure will require some technical adjustments to work over the longer term—for instance, it does not make adequate provision for including new employees—but in these technical areas, some aspects of American Employee Stock Ownership Plans (including the trust structure, allocation formulas, vesting and distribution schedules, the company's obligation to repurchase the stock, and the employee's obligation to give the company the first right of refusal to buy the stock) can be adapted to Russian circumstances to keep the ownership of capital decentralized.

So far the efforts to create a market economy in Russia have yielded much pain and few results. Shelves are empty and prices are rising. Existing enterprises are structured as monopolies, which makes any market system—no matter who owns the enterprises—an easy victim of price fixing. For too many Russians the free market has meant no more than the disappearance of goods from the inexpensive state sector and their reappearance at a much higher price in the private market—for the profit of those carrying out the diversion.

The experiments with employee ownership offer some relief in this bleak picture. In the midst of the general Russian economic debacle, the evidence is overwhelming that employee-owned and -leased enterprises have worked on a small scale. Whether they will work on the continental scale now required remains to be seen.

Periodical Bibliography

The following articles have been selected to supplement the diverse views presented in this chapter.

Oleg Bogomolov — "Who Will Own 'Nobody's Property'?" *Dissent*, Spring 1993.

Rose Brady et al. — "Will Yeltsin Get Thrown from the Train?" *Business Week*, June 22, 1992.

Simon Clarke — "Privatization and the Development of Capitalism in Russia," *New Left Review*, November/December 1992.

Bill Clinton — "A Strategy for Foreign Policy," *Vital Speeches of the Day*, May 1, 1992.

Stephen S. Cohen and Andrew Schwartz — "Privatization in the Former Soviet Empire," *The American Prospect*, Spring 1993. Available from PO Box 383080, Cambridge, MA 02238.

Dorinda Elliott — "Making Russia Private," *Newsweek*, December 14, 1992.

Marshall I. Goldman — "Kapital-ism," *World Monitor*, April 1992.

Boris Kagarlitsky — "New Regime, New Calamities," *New Politics*, Summer 1992.

Sergei N. Khrushchev — "Stop Wasting Aid to Russia," *The New York Times*, March 19, 1993.

Andrew Kopkind — "From Russia with Love and Squalor," *The Nation*, January 18, 1993.

David Lipton — "Reform Endangered," *Foreign Policy*, Spring 1993.

Michael Mandelbaum — "By a Thread," *The New Republic*, April 5, 1993.

Doug Reardon — "Looking for a Strong Man After the Revolution," *The Freeman*, April 1992. Available from The Foundation for Economic Education, Irvington-on-Hudson, NY 10533.

Steven Rosefielde — "The Grand Bargain: Underwriting Catastroika," *Global Affairs*, Winter 1992.

Ann M. Simmons — "Brother, Can You Spare a Ruble?" *Time*, July 13, 1992.

What Measures Would Reduce Ethnic Conflict in the Republics?

THE
BREAKUP
OF THE
SOVIET
UNION

Chapter Preface

The Soviet Union once consisted of an empire of more than one hundred ethnic groups and more than two hundred languages and dialects. For decades the totalitarian communist government forced these groups into one nation by repressing minority customs, languages, and religious practices. Russian was the official language, atheism the official religion, and communism the unifying political ideology.

With the collapse of communism, the peoples of each region are finally free to speak their native languages and practice their unique customs. This freedom, however, has come at a price. For along with the revival of ethnic pride comes the reemergence of long-standing ethnic hatreds. Wars between Christian Armenia and Muslim Azerbaijan and between Ossetian and Abkhazian separatists and Georgian nationalists are just two examples of ethnic conflicts tearing at the fabric of the former empire.

Such animosities are of concern to many observers who believe that ethnic conflict may create economic and political instability and, ultimately, anarchy. For example, Yerevan, the capital of Armenia, was once a vibrant, cultured, modern city. Today it is in ruins, its people without food and fuel because of the war with Azerbaijan. As *Los Angeles Times* reporter Sonni Efron comments, "Armenia was once considered among the most promising of all the former Soviet republics. Now, in this newborn nation it is simply too cold to undress. . . . Three years ago, Western businessmen flocked to Armenia in search of investment opportunities. Now it seems only relief workers and journalists want to go."

Fearing that other former Soviet cities will meet Yerevan's fate, political science experts and others are advocating ways to reduce the current ethnic conflict in the region and to prevent future conflicts from erupting. A collection of these solutions are presented in the following chapter.

"Extreme forms of nationalism . . . will bring nothing but suffering to the Russian people."

Quelling Nationalism Is Necessary

Natalia Narochnitskaya, Vladimir A. Babak, and
Victor Nadein-Rayevski

Natalia Narochnitskaya, Vladimir A. Babak, and Victor Nadein-Rayevski are associated with the Institute of Geopolitics and Forecasting in Moscow and are senior research fellows at the Institute of World Economy and International Relations. In the following viewpoint, the authors explain the roots of Russian nationalism and why it is on the rise. Most of the former Soviet republics, the authors state, gained their independence after the collapse of the Soviet Union. Russia, however, perceives that it gained nothing and lost a significant amount of land, resources, and population. This humiliation has fostered an increasing sense of nationalism among many Russians, who want to reassert their former power. The Russian government must work to quell this movement if it wishes to avoid increased conflict among the republics.

As you read, consider the following questions:

1. Why are the ideas of democracy and nationalism in conflict in Russia, according to the authors?
2. In the authors' opinion, what role has nationalism played in the non-Russian republics?
3. How can the Russian government reduce nationalism, according to the authors?

From Natalia Narochnitskaya, Vladimir A. Babak, and Victor Nadein-Rayevski, "Modern Russian Nationalism," *Mediterranean Quarterly* 3 (4): 94-107. Copyright Duke University Press, 1992. Reprinted with permission of the publisher.

It has become commonplace to associate the future of Russia and the prospects for the changes taking place within it with the success of antitotalitarian transformations in the former Soviet Union as a whole and in the Russian Federation in particular. The success of the current Russian administration and the preservation of its democratically won power likewise are often linked to such transformations. The events of August 1991, however, have significantly accelerated and made evident many complicated processes related to the end of totalitarianism. Specifically Russian features in this political development either have passed unnoticed by observers or have not seemed significant enough for comment.

In almost all of the former Soviet republics, democratic ideas and notions of national revival have been closely interrelated, stepping forward together under the banner of national liberation. As for Russia, emerging and parallel ideas of democracy and national revival have turned out to be incapable of supporting each other and have never really united in a single antitotalitarian movement.

Euphoria and Defeat

The democratic revolution and revived Russian national and patriotic ideas have become increasingly alienated from each other, sometimes even artificially and purposely juxtaposed by political leaders. The tragedy of this dichotomy in Russian politics, a fatal division of the nation, has become especially noticeable since the abortive August 1991 coup, when the political dynamics of the Russian Federation were given a powerful impetus and long-term orientation. The destruction of the institutions of the Soviet state and the decomposition of the USSR have caused euphoria in one part of the society and a feeling of pain and defeat in another part, resulting in increased alienation. These complicated dynamics, together with an obvious weakness of new legislation and an awkwardness of the first democratic phenomena, have led to disappointment and have given a powerful new impetus to what appears to be a rapid escalation—a veritable avalanche—in the growth of Russian nationalism. . . .

The Roots of Nationalism

Present-day Russian nationalism may be correctly identified as a nationalism of defeat: the defeat of the Communist idea and its practice. Closely linked to this is the bitterness of a people's dethroned national pride. They fought and won the Second World War and then realized its cost and real historical result, purchased at the price of that people's blood. They had waged a struggle, they thought, not for the *Socialist* fatherland but for *the* fatherland. Today we see the disastrous defeat of this power in the Cold War and, with this defeat, the liquidation of the outer empire and the destruction of the power itself.

The Russians were more closely related to the Bolshevik system than were the outer republics and suffered the most from its excesses, and the defeat of this system inevitably brought about a syndrome of a defective state of mind that has both a conscious and an unconscious aspiration for some kind of national and social revenge. Russia's people have been brainwashed with an idea of a special missionary role for their nation, which had been called to pave the way to a bright future for the whole of humankind. Now bitterness, disappointment, and, for some time, a sickness of heart have overwhelmed the citizens of Russia as they have learned that the object of their pride, Great Russia, turned out to be great only in its vast spaces and in the range of its misfortunes, and that the attitude of the outside world toward it was one not of the great love spoken about in official propaganda, but of a fear of its enormous military power, associated with the messianic and missionary expansionist ideology of its leaders.

Oppression Feeds Nationalism

Alongside the syndrome of defeat, however, are found the evolving conditions for a natural Russian nationalism that has matured in the depths of the totalitarian system that had made hostages of the Russian people and ruined Russia itself. This Russian nation had to carry the main burdens of industrialization, collectivization, the struggle against fascism, postwar reconstruction, the development of virgin lands, the arms race, and the grandiose pretensions of competition in space.

Yet, old attitudes toward Russian nationalism linked with the Soviet mission persist. In all of the borderlands around the Russian Federation there are still those who picture a growing Russian nationalism as a Great Russian chauvinism. There are, of course, demonstrations of chauvinistic feelings within those layers of Russian society oriented toward empire. However, there is more to this contemporary nationalistic resurgence than chauvinism, and even where this appears, it is less a chauvinism than a new phenomenon for Russia, a nationalism always considered by orthodox Marxists to be an attribute of an oppressed nation. The main moving forces of Russian nationalism of this kind are due to the changed geopolitical situation of Russia along with the growth of anti-Russian feelings in the former republics of the Soviet Union as problems associated with borders, territories, and economics are confronted. . . .

A great number of Russians live within the territories of the newly independent non-Russian republics of the former USSR.

These people have had varying degrees of influence on the economies and cultures of the new states. Now there is the problem of the status of these persons, who may find themselves in an anti-Russian environment and may have bitter feelings about their changed circumstances.

A Dark and Ugly Force

With the demise of the all-powerful Soviet state and the dominant ideology of the Communist Party, other forces—some dark and ugly, others dormant or repressed for decades—have rushed in to fill the void. . . .

Among the most potent of the new forces mobilizing the masses is nationalism—the call that only Georgians should rule Georgia, or the Ukrainian government ban on taking refrigerators and other items deemed of crucial economic importance out of the republic.

The effects of nationalism are seeping into the most unexpected nooks of day-to-day life—for instance, it is now virtually impossible to fly out of Yerevan, Armenia's capital, to other Soviet republics because the Azerbaijani rail blockade of Armenia has badly reduced deliveries of aviation fuel.

The official ideals in the Soviet Union were once "internationalism" and the creation of a uniform *Homo Sovieticus*, although it is true that such pseudoscience served largely to justify the Russification of society and heavy-handed rule from Moscow.

Now, increasingly, there is overt xenophobia and isolationism.

John-Thor Dahlburg, *Los Angeles Times*, October 7, 1991.

Moreover, nationalism in these non-Russian republics, cultivated over many centuries, has now filled the vacuum of ideological emptiness with the banners of social and political renewal. When such nationalism is made state policy, unfortunately, it becomes like any other monopolistic ideological system claiming to find solutions for all social and political problems: it has within it the seeds of diktat and totalitarian rule. We have already witnessed one of the first indications of this feature of nationalism and degeneration in the democratic movement in Georgia at the hands of its former president and the public that supported him. The deeds of Georgian nationalists have already created a refugee problem in South Ossetia and have given a new and dangerous impetus to traditional hostilities between various peoples of the Caucasus. The roots of such conflict are found in diverse religious, socioeconomic, and cultural traditions.

Similar processes have developed in other areas adjacent to Russia, perhaps most dramatically in the Baltic region, where various peoples' fronts have been perceived as hostile forces by local Russian populations. A splash of nationalism among the Russian-speaking groups in the Baltic states is not just an activity inspired by the old Communist party against democratic forces, as local nationalist leaders wish the outside world to believe. It is both a reaction of disagreement by the local Russian population to legislation oriented against them and a fear that they will become an oppressed and persecuted population. Before joining the chorus condemning the nationalist mood of the Russians in the Baltic states, therefore, outsiders must first make sure that these Russians have obtained legislative guarantees of their rights corresponding to international law and the UN Declaration of Human Rights. Absent such guarantees, Russia's commitment of support to the new Baltic leaders and their republics would be premature and would limit Russian diplomatic flexibility.

No Slavic Unity

Significant problems also have been associated with the development of nationalism in Ukraine, problems that are viewed depressingly by Russians. Ukraine's obvious alienation is hard for Russians to understand, given the instinctive Russian belief in the historical logic of the joint development of three Slavonic Christian-Orthodox nations or *pravorosses*: Russia, Ukraine, and Belarus. In this context, the future of Ukrainian-Russian relations is critical for Russia's new international political status. Minus equal partnership with Ukraine, the position of Russia in Europe will be weaker, and it alone will have to face the dynamic Turkic world in the east. The apparently intentional unwillingness of the leaders of Ukraine and Belarus to build their relations with Russia on the ideas of a Slavonic unity, together with Ukraine leaving the union, becomes another indication for Russian nationalists that Great Russia is disintegrating. There are also indications from the Ukrainian government of anti-Russian views that will have to be borne in mind in the making of future Russian policy.

Kazakh nationalism, both anti-Russian and Asian-centered in orientation, can also produce complicated problems. Ideas of creating supranational unions, such as a "Turkic-Russian nation," which have some local intellectual appeal but are perceived quite differently in Russia, appear here together with more nationalistic pan-Turkic proposals.

In general the problem of equal rights for national minorities can serve as an important factor in the responsible growth of

Russian nationalism. It is necessary to note that not one of the republics seeking self-determination is ready to provide an opportunity for self-determination to any of the national minorities living in its territory. This is true of Azerbaijan's oppression of non-Shiite Muslim minorities; of the Central Asian Muslim republics' refusal to grant minorities any territorial rights; of Kazakhstan's claim that any territory crossed by its nomadic ancestors belongs to it; of Georgia's adherence to Caucasian rather than European traditions; and of Moldova's, Ukraine's, and the Baltic states' avowal of European culture while discriminating against those not part of the ethnic majority.

The destruction of the USSR weakened Russia's position vis-à-vis the other republics, and it will also weaken its international position. The countries to both the west and east, especially the east, are very sensitive to and respectful of national power and will seize on Russian weaknesses for their own ends. In this connection, it is probable that following the Japanese claim to the four northern islands held by the Soviet Union since the end of the Second World War, a claim no more valid for Japan than for present-day Russia, China will also raise the matter of revising its Russian frontiers.

These territorial and other concessions are demanded only from a Russia that has already given up the role of "elder brother" in world affairs and has, at the same time, apparently made endless concessions to is future competitors in the division of the Soviet Union's legacy. Such a situation cannot but induce a certain amount of responsive nationalism from Russians who have become the oppressed nation on its own soil: territory that has been shrunk in its size for the benefit of other members of the former Soviet Union. There are quite objective reasons, therefore, for the appearance and growth of Great Russian nationalism today. . . .

What the Government Should Do

A wise appeal by the government to feelings of national pride and consciousness in Russia, special to any nation and closely related to a respect for such power institutions as the army and church, would be an important factor uniting various groups and layers of people. This is especially important in a crisis situation that separates, as a rule, the social basis of any regime. A union with the patriotic movement can prevent that movement from transforming into a powerful opposition force that may have dangerous repercussions for national stability. It is unacceptable to allow growing nationalistic feelings to form a strength independent from established power or opposed to it. The mass potential of this national feeling seems to be very great, and neglecting it, to say nothing of efforts to counteract it, will be tantamount to abdicating the political scene.

Russian leadership thus faces a peculiar task: to incorporate Russian nationalism into its concepts and policies in the form of informed patriotism. This task is not on the present agenda yet, but one should get ready for it. It is also important to account for this nationalism, if for no other reason than ending inattention to and even neglect of the national feelings and aspirations of Russians. These feelings appeared everywhere in the USSR and were exploited in its politics, and the Russian Federation has no alternative but to do the same. Any other alternative will bring catastrophe for leadership. Nationalism will find new leaders and forces and will replace those in power who do not pay much attention to it. There can be no other outcome. If neglected, nationalism will use only its negative potential, as would any other impulse left unaccounted for in a country's politics. . . .

Measures to Quell Nationalism

The revival of Russian nationalism is a reality of current social life. A sophisticated policy, taking into account different trends in the Russian nationalist movement, should be adopted for them.

First, there is the necessity of a thorough educational campaign aimed at revealing these truths to the Russian people:

• Chauvinism has no special monopoly on Russian patriotism.

• The government is sincerely devoted to the national idea and patriotism, but it does not support the destructive ideas propagated by extreme nationalist organizations.

• Extreme forms of nationalism can involve the Russian people in endless and unpromising opposition to other nations and result in a large number of victims and will bring nothing but suffering to the Russian people.

Second, the policy for patriotic movements should be aimed at their dissociation from extremists; the latter should be notified that the propagation of national hostility and violence against other peoples will not be permitted. Patriotic movements should seek the defeat of notorious Fascist organizations that compromise national movements on the whole. . . .

Third, an invitation should be extended for cooperation and wide-ranging dialogue between modern-day "Slavophiles" and "Westerners," "patriots" and "cosmopolitans," in order to improve the political life of the country and to achieve social partnership as well as the rebirth of national culture and traditions within the democratic process.

It is reasonable to start from the premise that Russia is geopolitically, historically, and culturally a keeper of the balance between Europe and Asia. . . . Either closing itself within national traditions or blindly following abstract political schemes is fatal for Russia.

"The nexus between nationalism, marketization and a liberal democratic world order is much stronger than liberal and Marxist critics of nationalism will admit."

Quelling Nationalism Is Unnecessary

Philip Goldman, Gail Lapidus, and Victor Zaslavsky

Many political science experts view nationalism as a negative force that increases conflict and instability in the world. In the following viewpoint, excerpted from their book *From Union to Commonwealth: Nationalism and Separatism in the Soviet Republics*, Philip Goldman, Gail Lapidus, and Victor Zaslavsky disagree with this belief. Nationalism in many of the former Soviet republics, they argue, is tied to political parties demanding democratic reforms, and may therefore be a positive, stabilizing force. Goldman is a doctoral candidate in political science at the University of California, Berkeley. Lapidus is a political science professor at Berkeley and the chair of the Berkeley-Stanford Program in Soviet Studies. Victor Zaslavsky is professor of sociology at the Memorial University of Newfoundland in Canada.

As you read, consider the following questions:

1. How did Soviet policies promote nationalism, according to the authors?
2. Why did political activity in the Soviet Union express itself in national movements rather than in political parties, in the authors' opinion?
3. How can the international community help control the negative consequences of nationalism, according to the authors?

From Philip Goldman, Gail Lapidus, and Victor Zaslavsky, "Introduction: Soviet Federalism—Its Origins, Evolution, and Demise." In *From Union to Commonwealth*, edited by Gail Lapidus and Victor Zaslavsky, with Philip Goldman. New York: Cambridge University Press, 1992. Copyright © Cambridge University Press 1992. Reprinted with the permission of Cambridge University Press.

For decades, obsessive Soviet preoccupation with external security spurred the development of a massive military establishment as well as a gigantic military-industrial complex to support it. But ultimately the primary threat to the stability and territorial integrity of the USSR came from within. The failure of the coup attempt of August 1991 accelerated a process of disintegration which was already under way, and gave new impetus to the demands for independence by many of the constituent republics of the former union. Disintegration now threatens the Commonwealth of Independent States itself, and ethnic minorities in Georgia, Moldova, and Russia are asserting their own claims to statehood.

This viewpoint focuses on the fundamental sources of the Soviet Union's transition from a stable and highly centralized state to a system in chaos, as well as on the forces that will shape the post-coup future of what was once the Soviet Union. Three issues are of key importance: the relationship of the union republics to the center, the relationship of ethnic minorities to the republics in which they reside, and the future political and economic role of the Russian Federation. These relationships, in turn, have been profoundly shaped by the nature of the Soviet system, and particularly by the initial decision to organize the Soviet state on the basis of a hierarchy of ethnoterritorial units.

The Bolsheviks' Federal Model

The historical circumstances which prompted the Bolsheviks to organize the Soviet state according to the principle of national-territorial autonomy have produced outcomes neither intended nor anticipated by its creators. Marxist-Leninist doctrine assumed that the objective laws of history guaranteed mankind's progress towards the unification and eventual fusion of nations. In practice, however, the Bolsheviks ultimately fell back on a federal model in their search for new forms of political organization, a model Lenin had rejected prior to the seizure of power. During Lenin's lifetime, this approach enabled them to preserve the strong and centralized multiethnic state deemed necessary to the final goal of world revolution. In subsequent decades, it facilitated the maintenance of the internal stability of the Soviet multiethnic empire.

The introduction of the federal principle and the proclamation of the right of self-determination, dutifully preserved in all Soviet constitutions, were intended as temporary measures designed to weaken resistance to the formation of the Soviet Union among newly assertive national groups. However, seven decades of Soviet nationality policies resulted in two outcomes antithetical to the officially proclaimed goals of merging nationalities and transcending ethnic distinctions. First, these policies led to the creation and emergence of nations and national identities in many communities which had not achieved ethnic consciousness by 1917. Despite policies intended to weaken or subvert national identities and loyalties, the Soviet period was also one of nation-building for many ethnic groups.

Second, Soviet nationality policies led to the creation of a federation of ethnoterritorial units organized into a complex administrative hierarchy. Ethnicity in Soviet society was institutionalized both on the individual and on group levels. On the individual level, nationality was registered on each person's internal passport, thus establishing a rigid ethnic affiliation for every citizen that passed immutably from one generation to the next. At the group level, the ethnoterritorial basis of political organization established firm links between nationality groups, their territories, and their political administrations. Consequently, the major components of the Soviet Union—its union republics— were in effect turned into peculiar forms of the "tactical nation-state," [as Gregory J. Massell states]. Notwithstanding their far-reaching subjugation by the center, they thereby acquired the preconditions for independent existence, including their own political elites and educated middle classes, their own administratively defined territories inhabited by indigenous populations, and a continuous tradition of cultural production in their own languages. . . .

Perestroika Promoted Nationalism

The accession of Mikhail Gorbachev and the inauguration of reforms centered on glasnost and perestroika led to a cognitive and political revolution which irreversibly changed the nature of the national question in Soviet political life. The appearance of new and potent national movements in various parts of the Soviet Union was an unintended consequence of the "revolution from above" that was introduced by the reformist segment of the Communist Party. . . .

The powerful tendency for political mobilization to express itself in national movements rather than in political parties was the product of two key features of the Soviet system. First, competitive elections stimulated intense political activism primarily at the local level. Much of this early organization was spontaneous and even chaotic; after seventy years of single-party rule, no traditions of pluralist political organization at the grassroots level could be drawn upon. The new political parties lacked prior experience in formulating programs or attracting mass followings, as well as the resources to build coherent structures. Nor could they identify with and articulate the particular interests of various groups and strata since these interests were still in the process of being formed. Because the Soviet Union had evolved as a marketless formation based on nationalized property, a centrally planned economy, and a single-party political regime, it had its own principles and practices of internal differentiation and stratification. This stratification divided the population into a variety of functional groups, distributing rewards and privileges in ways that favored those groups whose activities were deemed crucial for the preservation and reproduction of the Soviet system. When this system began unravelling with the decline of the state which had been responsible for its emergence, nationality became the most potent base of mass political mobilization.

Anti-Russian Sentiments

Several factors help explain this outcome. First, the ethnoterritorial structure of the Soviet system meant that the weakening of the central institutions would enhance the relative status and power of the republics. Second, shared historical grievances and threats to ethnic survival provided powerful bonds within many of them. Third, because the ruling party-state not only enjoyed a monopoly of political power, but was simultaneously responsible for economic and social development, the growing deterioration of Soviet economic and social conditions meant that discontent in the periphery would be directed against the center. Moreover, the incoherence and inner contradictions of Gorbachev's economic policies had particularly devastating consequences for republic and local officials; ever greater responsibilities were devolved upon them while at the same time they were increasingly deprived of the resources needed to deal with them. Because of the centrality of the Russian population in the Soviet empire, and the obvious Russian hegemony in the Soviet state, it was not surprising that growing discontent increasingly took the form of anti-Russian sentiments, linked in a number of cases with separatist aspirations. These emerging orientations among the non-Russian nations of the USSR in turn shaped the character of Russian nationalism. . . .

Perhaps the most dramatic development of recent years has been the transformation of Russian national consciousness from its traditional association with an imperial identity toward a concern with creating a Russian national state. Until quite recently, the dominant strand of Russian nationalism has been anti-Western, focusing on Russian exclusiveness, the uniqueness of the Russian historical path, and the messianic mission of the Russian people. All too often, this impulse was closely associated with the defense of the empire. But . . . there has been a notable shift in recent years away from the former imperial consciousness to a profound disillusionment with empire, accompanied by a widespread conversion to the ideas of liberal Russian nationalism.

The dissolution of the British empire, and French decolonization after World War II, demonstrated that when colonies become a burden and are perceived as liabilities rather than assets, a rapid change in popular attitudes towards empire may occur and the process of decolonization will encounter only limited resistance within the metropole. In the Soviet case, the explosion of anti-Russian sentiments in the non-Russian republics was largely shaped by a general dissatisfaction with the Soviet system and its declining performance. Except among the Russian settler communities in the non-Russian republics, the predominant Russian reaction to these sentiments was less an upsurge in great power chauvinism than a crystallization of Russian nationalism. The notion of a Russia free from its burdensome empire appeared to entice the Russian popular mind, and it became increasingly common for segments of the intelligentsia to envision the Russian future from the standpoint of enlightened national interest. Aleksandr Solzhenitsyn's call before the coup for the voluntary or (if necessary) forceful breakup of the Soviet Union and the creation of a new Slavic state spawned a heated debate and gave a new impulse to the diffusion of Russian national ideas. . . .

Implications for Western Policy

As James Mayall argues, "the three great waves of modern state creation—in Latin America in the nineteenth century, in Europe after 1919, and Asia, Africa, the Caribbean and the Pacific after 1945—have all been associated with the collapse of empires." The collapse of the Soviet empire has raised significant questions about the stance which the West should take towards the emergence of a new state system in the present territory of the Soviet Union. In the United States, two opposing positions emerged, with some analysts and politicians calling for policies actively promoting Soviet disintegration and others advocating policies designed to bolster the Soviet central government and preserving the integrity of the USSR. By the early 1990s, however, it had become increasingly clear that the major problem for both the Soviet population and the international community involved not so much the preservation or disintegration of the Soviet Union, but rather the nature of the changes which would take place in its territory. As Alexei Arbatov lucidly argued, the dangers posed by disintegration were not so pressing as Westerners frequently believed, and those in the Soviet administration and the military who kept "blackmailing the West and the Soviet people alike by doomsday prophecies of chaos and civil war" were primarily interested in preserving their dominant positions in the centralized Soviet regime.

The international community could play only a limited role in facilitating or preventing Soviet disintegration in any case. The breakdown of the Soviet infrastructure and the upsurge of nationalism in the Soviet Union could not be reversed by a simple infusion of capital or by the signing of nuclear arms reductions treaties. Further arms agreements might have reduced the number of weapons in the hands of future leaders, and thereby contributed to greater security, but would have done little to strengthen the center. Furthermore, there was no coherently articulated vision by external actors (including the USA) as to what the future shape of the Soviet Union should have been, other than the fact that the system should aim at embracing liberal economic principles. The enthusiastic support for the Soviet center did wane by late 1991, but there remained real ambivalence about embracing republican leaders such as Yeltsin or Georgia's Zviad Gamsakhurdia.

Nationalism and Democratic Aspirations

Nationalism demonstrates how changes in individual identity and concepts of self resonate with, that is, are both determined by and help to determine, historical change. The notion of Communism as a refrigerator from which ancient animosities have emerged intact does not stand up. In both Eastern Europe and the Soviet Union national feeling was actually fostered by both state authorities and opposition movements for different ends and in different ways.

In an excellent essay on this subject, George Schopflin points to the way Stalinism, through its attack on the major affective bonds of community, manifest in family, religion, and workplace, actually intensified the importance of nationhood for the majority of society as a symbol of the familiar and continuity with the past. Not surprisingly therefore, "nationalism became one of the repositories of social autonomy" and a vehicle for the democratic aspirations of the opposition. In Eastern Europe particularly, nationalism developed a strong association with self-determination and the desire to escape from empire. This sometimes took a chauvinist form but was more often connected with a demand for human rights and an outward-looking internationalist perspective.

Lynne Jones, *Peace & Democracy News*, Winter 1992-93.

Western programs of economic aid may play a significant role over the long term, but should be crafted with some care. Such policies can no longer presume the economic unity and territorial integrity of the old union, but will have to be tailored to the distinctive problems facing specific territorial markets. More-over, because the number of primary actors in the international system has multiplied, and the USA is no longer the central eco-nomic hegemon, coordinating policy towards this region will be a major challenge for the West. . . .

Eric Hobsbawm argues that "the characteristic nationalist movements of the late 20th century are essentially negative, or rather divisive" and do not provide an alternative principle for the political restructuring of the world in the twenty-first cen-tury. The present evolution of Soviet-type societies demonstrates that this type of approach towards nationalism and secessionism in the Soviet Union and Eastern Europe needs to be fundamen-tally reconsidered. The Soviet experience should serve as a re-minder that the nexus between nationalism, marketization and a liberal democratic world order is much stronger than liberal and Marxist critics of nationalism will admit.

Leaders of a number of former Soviet republics rightly believe that their separation from the Soviet Union and their integration into the world market and new international order are one and the same thing. The Baltic states and Ukraine seek incorpora-tion into other supranational communities, like the European Free Trade Association, the emerging Baltic Commonwealth, or the European Community. The Central Asian states seek greater integration with the developing economies of Asia. It is already evident that the Baltic states have not pursued autarkic policies with regard to the non-Baltic states—Lithuania has entered into independent trade agreements with both Ukraine and Russia.

Benefits of Nationalism

Both the nationalist idea and the international system have undergone a major evolution in the course of this century. An international order capable of condemning the irrational and de-structive potential of xenophobic forms of nationalism, and ma-jor violations of human rights and ecological standards, has by and large been created. Regional leaders in the former Soviet Union have clearly been influenced by these international norms in drafting their programs for reform and in seeking membership in international organizations. In these conditions, the national movements in the Soviet Union are not uniformly "essentially negative or rather divisive." On the contrary, the breakup of the Soviet Union may represent a real precondition for greater global cooperation on social, economic, and ecologi-cal issues.

"[Many are] increasingly fearful that Islamic fundamentalism is on the rise in Central Asia and will destabilize the whole region. "

Islamic Fundamentalism Must Be Repressed in the Central Asian Republics

Boris Z. Rumer

Boris Z. Rumer is a fellow at Harvard University's Russian Research Center in Cambridge, Massachusetts, and the author of the book *Central Asia: "A Tragic Experiment."* In the following viewpoint, Rumer warns that the growth of Islamic fundamentalism in the Central Asian republics of the former Soviet Union poses a grave threat to the stability of the region and to the entire world. Just as Islamic fundamentalism brought anarchy and violence to Iran, it could also do so to Central Asia. Rumer concludes that Russia, the European allies, and the United States must work to quell the rise of Islamic fundamentalism in Central Asia.

As you read, consider the following questions:

1. Why is stability in Central Asia so important for the United States, in Rumer's opinion?
2. How will the presidents of the Central Asian republics maintain their commitment to the CIS while continuing to satisfy the nationalist sentiments of their peoples, according to the author?
3. How has the West shown its desire to remain involved in Central Asia, according to Rumer?

From Boris Z. Rumer, "The Gathering Storm in Central Asia," originally published by JAI Press in the Winter 1993 issue of *Orbis: A Journal of World Affairs*. Reprinted with permission.

With the break-up of the USSR, its five Central Asian re-publics—Uzbekistan, Tajikistan, Turkmenistan, Kyrgyzstan, and Kazakhstan—have emerged from more than a century of Russian and Soviet domination. These five countries, which in modern times have never enjoyed the status of independent actors in international politics, have started to define their geopolitical orientation. The outcome, indeed the very process, threatens to alter political and military equations from China to the Persian Gulf.

Even for the distant West, it is difficult to overestimate the importance of Central Asia, for the region directly affects countries and causes that are of strategic concern to the United States and its allies. With an area roughly half the size of the United States, Central Asia borders on Russia, China, Afghanistan, and Iran; and it is separated from Pakistan only by a thin stretch of land. Its population of 50 million is chiefly Turkic, but some of them also have strong ethnic, linguistic, and cultural ties to Iran. The predominant religion is Islam. Economically, the region is poor but possesses extensive and still largely unexplored natural resources, including natural gas, oil, gold, and uranium. Unlike many underdeveloped areas, Central Asia has a significant technical and scientific intelligentsia and facilities of potentially considerable military importance. Not least, the region is home to a large contingent of ex-Soviet military units, with large stocks of weapons and military equipment.

A Geopolitical Vacuum

None of this has gone unnoticed in capitals from Ankara to Islamabad to Beijing, where the sudden geopolitical vacuum in Central Asia has been viewed with ambivalence—both concern about potential instability, but also with an awareness of new opportunities. This new "great game" in the heart of Asia is unfolding not so much among the old colonial powers as among their former minions, many of whom are themselves just emerging from colonial domination and seeking to define their roles in their regions and the world.

Turkey and Iran have been the most active in pursuit of new opportunities in Central Asia, building on ethnic, linguistic, and cultural ties to the region. For Turkey, Central Asia offers an irresistible political opportunity to bolster its international standing. Its ambition is fueled not only by memories of lost empire and a desire to assert Turkish influence among ethnic kin, but also by the hope that leadership in Central Asia would enhance Ankara's standing in Europe.

Iran's interest, based initially on its ties to the Persian-speaking Tajiks, can also be explained by its desire to break out of international isolation. Tehran plainly seeks to establish a sphere of influence in a region of great importance to its neighbors and competitors. Its ambitions are further fueled by a desire to export its own brand of politically active Islam. Although Central Asia has no tradition of such Shiite Islamic fundamentalism, the Iranian creed might well exert strong appeal in a time and place of socio-economic deprivation. . . .

Given their already unstable situations, the Central Asian presidents—even if willing to flirt with Islamic forces—recognize that only Russia can help defend their regimes against the menace of Islamic revival. The latter is not a figment of their imagination; the ominous threat from Afghanistan is already looming on the horizon.

Six Islamic Nations

Thus, the decision to maintain the collective armed forces of the CIS is a critical factor in ensuring stability in the Central Asian region. This vital issue was a major focus at the various summit meetings convened in Central Asia during 1992. The Tashkent conference in May, 1992, for example, dealt with the creation of a regional security system, or a military-political bloc with Russia. At present, the Central Asian presidents are seeking to reach a compromise that would enable them to keep the troops of the former military districts on Central Asian terri-

215

tory, but satisfy nationalist sentiments by giving the troops a "national" status. The Kazakh and Uzbek presidents have explicitly endorsed the model of NATO [North Atlantic Treaty Organization], and the other presidents have indicated their agreement as well. The plan is that each republic should have its own armed forces, but on a relatively small scale. The Uzbek military, for instance, is to number no more than 25,000 to 30,000 troops; the Turkmenistan army will have a mere 2,000. In principle, these troops are to defend their state's fundamental laws and government institutions. In addition to these national military units, the CIS will then station a considerably larger number of forces in Central Asia. . . .

Moscow and Muslims

The leaders of Central Asian states are seeking to obtain as much economic aid from the Middle East as they can, while at the same time professing their desire to maintain their ties with Russia. The reason is clear. The Central Asian leaders need Moscow for defense, but Muslim capital for development. Consequently, to use a Russian peasant saying, they are trying to milk two cows at the same time.

These leaders, to be sure, are cognizant of the tensions and contradictions inherent in this two-edged policy. At the May 1992 meeting in Ashkhabad, attended by the Central Asian presidents but also the heads of state from Iran, Turkey, and Pakistan, the participants were careful to emphasize that their agreements were not directed against Russia. Nursultan Nazarbaev of Kazakhstan declared that "we are strengthening our relations with other countries, but our first priority is exclusive relations with Russia, with whom we foresee a continuation of close ties in our life and politics." He added, with particular emphasis, that "I am approaching this meeting, and economic cooperation in general, without any religious bias whatsoever."

Nevertheless, the Islamic powers—Iran, Saudi Arabia, and, Turkey—have actively competed for influence in the area. For example, Iran has taken several steps to solidify its economic ties with Central Asia. Currently, it is developing plans to lay pipelines and railroad tracks from Turkmenistan, thereby connecting Central Asia with Tehran. The Saudis have also been actively courting the leaders of Central Asia. The Saudi foreign minister visited Uzbekistan, Tajikistan, and Turkmenistan in February 1992, and reportedly discussed the possibilities of forming a single "Organization for Economic Cooperation." Riyadh, obviously, is by no means indifferent to Iran's active involvement in the area and therefore has good grounds to give high priority to its relations with the states of Central Asia. Significantly, the member states of the Union for Cooperation—Saudi Arabia, Kuwait, the United Arab Emirates, Qatar, Bahrain, and Oman—immediately recognized the independence of the Central Asian republics. . . .

Fears from the West

The question of Islam in Central Asia is not of interest only to the immediate area. The Atlantic Community and the United States are both increasingly fearful that Islamic fundamentalism is on the rise in Central Asia and will destabilize the whole region, with serious consequences for European and world security. Now that Moscow has lost control over its former colonies, it would be extremely short-sighted for Washington to leave unsupervised a region seething with passions, not to mention one possessing an arms arsenal of considerable proportions. Former Secretary of State James Baker's trip to the new states of Central Asia in early 1992 (followed by the visits of other Western officials); the inclusion of these states in the Conference on European Security and Cooperation; the economic aid granted by the European Commission—all testify to the West's interest in the region and its refusal to cede Central Asia to the Muslim East.

VIEWPOINT

4

"We will never allow Islam to become a political force like Iran has."

Islamic Fundamentalism Poses No Threat to the Central Asian Republics

Colin Barraclough

Because the Central Asian republics of the former Soviet Union are largely Muslim, many have assumed that these republics will become dominated by Islamic fundamentalism. Colin Barraclough asserts in the following viewpoint that this assumption is wrong. The Soviets repressed religion for decades, the author states. Consequently, few Central Asians are devout Muslims. In addition, he maintains, many Central Asians who find the West's values and high standard of living appealing have no desire to follow the ascetic path of Islamic fundamentalism. Barraclough, a writer, is a contributor to the weekly conservative newsmagazine *Insight on the News*.

As you read, consider the following questions:

1. What happened after the collapse of the Soviet Union that led many in the West to fear the growth of Islam in the Central Asian republics, according to Barraclough?
2. Why, in the author's opinion, is Turkey especially thankful for the independence of the Central Asian republics?
3. Why does Barraclough believe the Central Asians will resist a religious revolution?

Central Asia always was remote. When 19th century Britain and Russia played out their great colonial game, fighting covert and subtle battles to carve out spheres of influence in the region, few parts of the world were less accessible. When Russia pushed the British as far back as Afghanistan, the region was lost to the outside world. Even after the collapse of the Soviet Union, Western countries viewed its five Muslim republics as too remote to deserve much attention. "Central Asia is a black hole," observes one British diplomat.

Will the Void Be Filled by Islam?

The collapse of the Soviet structure, though, left a power vacuum in Central Asia's republics that many feared would be filled by a swing toward Islamic radicalism, Iranian style. Pockets of fervent religiosity indeed sprang up in the countryside, and stories abounded of religious opposition to the communist governments, modeled along the lines of the Afghan *mujahideen*. The local economies, dependent on a ruble in free-fall against the dollar, disintegrated. Shortages of butter, sugar and coffee were frequent; a burgeoning black market arose as well as staggering inflation.

And Iran began to nose around the region, seeking to export its own brand of religious fervor. Religious authorities in Pakistan, for their part, resurrected the dream of their former president, Mohammad Zia-ul-Haq (who was killed in 1988): an Islamic power bloc from Kashmir to the Bosporus, encompassing all of Central Asia. To the West, it seemed, the spread of radical Islam was unstoppable.

Today, however, life in the newly independent Muslim republics of Central Asia—Kazakhstan, Kyrgyzstan, Tijikistan, Turkmenistan and Uzbekistan—continues to be as secular as ever. Few local women cover their heads and most prefer to wear Western clothes or colorful print dresses. The men regularly celebrate festive occasions with Russian vodka, and, although some observe important religious holidays, few pray openly or even fast during the holy month of Ramadan.

Free of their Soviet masters, these Central Asians are searching the outside world for a model for change. Iran and Pakistan clamored for the job. But the choice of the Central Asians themselves seems not to be the robe and cloth of religion, but rather the secular blend of Western values, hard currency and comparatively high technology of Turkey.

"We all have the Turkic language," explains Ubaidulla Abdurazzakov, Uzbekistan's foreign minister. "Our president said he's very fond of the Turkish model. Of course, we won't accept everything from Europe. We'll keep our own language and culture, but we'll accept Turkey's progressiveness." He will also presumably accept $250 million in Turk Eximbank credits granted by Turkey to Uzbekistan. . . .

Turkey's New Mission

For Turkey, the republics are God-sent. Uncertain of its position in the modern world, Turkey long has vacillated between East and West. The end of the Cold War removed the country's importance as a frontline member of NATO [North Atlantic Treaty Organization]. Flirting with the European Community produced a slap in the face as Europeans recoiled from the idea of any Muslim country, however benign, inside Europe's sacred portals. The sudden opening of Central Asia's Turkic-speaking, Muslim republics has given Ankara a new sense of mission.

At the same time, Iran's moves into the region are fast becoming bogged down. Iranian diplomats and businessmen speak of a culture clash that is proving tough to overcome. "Culturally, it's very different here," says Hossein Matinrad, managing director of Iranian-based Mashhad Carton Co., speaking of Turkmenistan. "It makes it very difficult to trade. They don't understand Farsi or English. Besides, no one wants to make decisions. There is no central decision making authority. Everyone has to have the agreement of someone else."

Nasr Marami, operational manager of Iran-based Saderat Bank's new branch in Ashkhabad, echoes Matinrad's concerns. "No one has any knowledge of banking or trade. We just cannot rely on local people." Even Iranian diplomats staffing newly opened embassies seem uncertain about their reception.

To the West, however, Iran is still the overriding worry. Since the Ayatollah Khomeini rode to power in 1979 on a wave of fiery fundamentalism, the merest whisper of Islamic revolution has sent Western officials running for their Crusader flags. Iranian influence in Lebanon, Afghanistan and, more recently, Sudan, has merited considerable concern in Washington and other Western capitals. To analysts in the U.S. Department of State, Central Asia has looked like a sitting duck for Iranian expansion. All its people needed, it seemed, was a nudge from Tehran for them to rise to the call of the latter-day Khomeinis.

"We have to deal with these people now," says one Western diplomat in Ashkhabad. "Our time is running out. We don't want them to go to the other side." Desperate to stymie such a move toward Iran, the State Department has opened embassies in all five Central Asian capitals.

It probably needn't have worried. Cultural, linguistic and religious differences between Iran and the Central Asian states already were hampering Iran's attempts to gain influence. Most Central Asians, except for the Tajiks, speak Turkic languages unconnected to Farsi. Most follow the Sunni branch of Islam, shunning the Shiite practices of the Iranians. Uzbeks and Turkmen are descended from the Mongolian tribes that spawned 14th century conqueror Tamerlane, whereas the Iranians' ancestry stretches back to the Zoroastrian emperors of the southern Iranian province of Fars.

Weak Attachments

The Kazakhs' attachment to Islam is far from strong. Most became Muslim only in the early 19th century. As a largely nomadic people, they retained many pagan practices and beliefs even after adopting Islam; and their knowledge of the newly acquired religion remained sketchy. The other factor working against fundamentalism in Kazakhstan is that 47 per cent of the republic's citizens are European, mostly Russian, Ukrainian or German, and they are concentrated in the north. Any move towards Islamisation will result in the Europeans threatening to break away and joining Russia with which northern Kazakhstan shares a long frontier.

Like Kazakhs, the mainly nomadic Kyrgyz too were late converts to Islam. Hence the Islamic movement in Kyrgyzstan is weak except in the southern province of Osh which, being part of the Fergana Valley, has been home to settled clans, mostly Uzbek. Traditionally, women of such nomadic or semi-nomadic tribes as the Kyrgyz and the Turkmen have gone about their business unveiled.

Early reports on the Turkmen tribes in the mid-19th century by the Russian soldiers noted their lack of religious fanaticism. When the only mosque in the capital, Ashgabat, was destroyed by an earthquake in 1948, it was not rebuilt. For the next 40 years this city of 350,000 Muslims had no mosque at all.

Dilip Hiro, *Middle East International*, February 5, 1993.

Privately, Uzbeks will say that they do not much like the Iranians, which probably explains the frosty welcome they give most Iranian newcomers. More important, Iran lacks one thing desperately needed in Central Asia: money. Iran has barely started to rebuild its economy since its destructive eight-year war with Iraq ended in 1988. Oil exports, which shrank due both to increased wartime consumption and Iraqi raids on the massive Iranian refinery at Kharg Island, are still a fraction of their prewar level. Inflation and a plummeting currency have further curtailed Tehran's foreign spending.

Moreover, unrest in five major Iranian cities alerted President

Hashemi Rafsanjani's government to the consequences of economic failure. Rafsanjani is pushing privatization programs intended to bully the economy into shape, but lifting subsidies on fuel and basic foodstuffs made his program appear inflationary. At such a crucial juncture, he is distracted from foreign endeavors.

Failures of Pakistan

Even Pakistan, long considered a "tame" Islamic republic by the West, has not been able to match Turkey's penetration of Central Asia. Telecommunication between the two regions is almost impossible, and continued fighting in Afghanistan has cut the only land bridge. Since the fall of Kabul's communist government, thousands of civilians have died in the Afghan capital from factional fighting among Muslim rebels. Until peace comes to a country plagued by tribal warfare for most of its 250-year history, Pakistan's communications with the Central Asian republics will be limited to Pakistan International Airlines' once-a-week flight into Tashkent.

Even these flights have become a joke. Ostensibly a business link to Central Asia, they mainly ferry Islamabad's jet-setters to the fleshpots of Tashkent; seats are fought over by those wishing to escape the strictures of their Islamic republic for Tashkent's cheap wine and women. . . .

Seventy years of Soviet domination deeply affected Central Asia. Deprived of the freedom to practice their religion for such a long time, many Central Asians never picked up the habit of attending mosque or reciting prayers. "It was very difficult before," explains a resident official at Ashkhabad's central mosque. "We used to gather in private homes, and the militia would come and break up the meetings. People are not used to the freedom yet. They are not going to the mosques."

The few mosques left open after 70 years of Moscow's rule remain underused, attended by a mere handful of believers at Friday prayers. The government of Saudi Arabia is building a mosque in Ashkhabad, authorities say, but few expect attendance to be more than a few hundred. The hinterlands will doubtless be a more fruitful site for proselytizing. Even Stalin at his most repressive could not rid Uzbekistan's Fergana Valley, 120 miles southeast of Tashkent, of its fundamentalist bent. And some Islamic groups have consolidated support there and in other rural areas. Religious parties in Tajikistan, the only Farsi-speaking republic, even succeeded in toppling President Rakhman Nabiyev in September 1991, though forces loyal to him continue to fight the new government.

But outside of Tajikistan, religious movements have not spread to cities, and religious parties still are banned from politics

222

throughout the republics, a legal holdover from the Soviet period. Also militating against the success of fundamentalist parties, says a researcher in anthropology in Ashkhabad, is the fact that the people have "just won their freedom from one form of repression. They don't want to submit to another."

Any attempt at religious revolution in the cities is sure to be resisted. The larger cities in Central Asia—Tashkent, Alma-Ata and Ashkhabad—are filled with thousands of ethnic Russians whose influence on the local Uzbek, Kazakh and Turkmen populations has been profound. The Russian language is universally understood, although some Central Asians are now refusing to speak it, and Russian culture permeates the lives of Central Asia's intellectuals. Some women, especially those of Russian extraction, fear that a wholesale swing toward Islam would threaten their comparatively autonomous position in society. They are a constituency for increased ties to the West, though a nervous one. "I don't know what will happen here," says Irena, an ethnic Russian Aeroflot hostess. "We're learning Uzbek, we're wearing longer dresses. Maybe we'll have to wear the veil soon."

Even many non-Russian women have long since lost the habit of staying home to bring up good Islamic families. "Prices are too high for women not to work," says Uzbek teacher Munira Arifbaev. "No family could afford to live without the income that the wife brings home."

Some Leaders Favor Progress

Surprisingly, perhaps, some Islamic leaders acknowledge that strict religious dogma will not pluck their region from its dire post-Soviet economic straits. Some even endorse moves toward a progressive, high-tech society. . . .

Imam Amangelde, the highest religious authority in Turkmenistan, speaks approvingly of the products laid out before him at a recent exhibition of Western technology in Ashkhabad. "Under the Soviet Union, we had no quality," he says. "Now we want high quality in agriculture, in the telephone system, even fax machines. I agree these products will change our lives, but the change will be for the better.". . .

The Uzbek government in particular has been watchful of the spread of Islam. It is eager to avoid a repeat of antigovernment riots in the Fergana Valley, when police arrested hundreds of demonstrators.

"Fundamentalism is a problem for the Islamic countries," says Uzbek Foreign Minister Abdurazzakov. "We will never allow Islam to become a political force like Iran has. But we must watch out because we are surrounded by countries where Islam is very tough."

"The United States should be even-handed in its dealings with [the Central Asian republics] . . . and offer inducements to the peaceful resolution of conflicts."

U.S. Policies Could Reduce Conflict in the Central Asian Republics

Firuz Kazemzadeh

Firuz Kazemzadeh is a history professor at Yale University in New Haven, Connecticut. He teaches courses on the expansion of the Muscovite state, the formation of the Russian empire, relations between the Russians and other nationalities, and the separatist movements of those groups conquered by the Russians. In the following viewpoint, Kazemzadeh describes the people and history of the Central Asian republics. Because of the many diverse ethnic and religious groups in the republics, there is a great potential for conflict, Kazemzadeh states. He concludes that the United States can help ameliorate this conflict by helping to resolve disputes and by being an example of peace, democracy, and tolerance.

As you read, consider the following questions:

1. Why, in the author's opinion, did Russia conquer Central Asia so easily in the 1860s?
2. How likely is it that Central Asia will become democratic, in Kazemzadeh's opinion? Explain his reasoning.
3. How should the United States address human rights abuses in Central Asia, according to the author?

From Firuz Kazemzadeh, "United States Policy Toward Central Asia," a speech delivered to the House of Representatives Committee on Foreign Affairs, Subcommittee on Europe and the Middle East, April 28, 1992.

Central Asia is not well known in the Western world. Even the term itself has no universally accepted definition. Some have included in it not only the five republics of Kazakhstan, Kyrgyzstan, Uzbekistan, Turkmenistan, and Tajikistan, but Afghanistan, Sinkiang, and even Tibet. This broader definition may be more useful since it indicates a relationship between areas inside and outside the former Soviet Union.

Central Asia is a region of great complexity. It is inhabited by many peoples and tribes, speaking many languages, and belonging to many and varied cultural traditions. Its history is long and rich. Alexander the Great passed through Central Asia on one of his many campaigns in Iran. The presence of the Greeks is certified to this day by the reliefs they carved out of rocks in the Pamirs. Soon after the founding of Islam, Arab conquerors brought their religion to Central Asia where it rapidly supplanted Zoroastrianism, Buddhism, and Christianity. It was from Central Asia that Muslims staged their incursions into India, planting the banner of Islam over much of that subcontinent. Central Asia was for centuries the battleground of nomads and sedentary peoples, of barbarism and civilization. It was dealt painful blows by Genghis Khan and Tamerlane. Yet medieval Central Asia also produced great poets, philosophers, astronomers, mathematicians, artists, and architects. The last two centuries have not been kind to Central Asia. Isolation from the rest of the world, disunity, constant warfare, despotism, and religious fanaticism turned the once prosperous lands into deserts, ruined the economy, impoverished cultural life, and prevented modernization.

The Absorption of Central Asia

When Russia, having first absorbed the Kazakhs, began her great advance into the heart of Central Asia in 1864, she met virtually no resistance from the weak and backward societies ruled by the Khans of Khiva and Kokand, and the Amir of Bukhara. It took Russia less than a quarter of a century to turn Central Asia into a tightly controlled colony.

The collapse of the Soviet Union is one of the most striking and significant events in history. An empire built over four centuries disintegrated in a few short years. No one can predict with any certainty what lies ahead for the millions of its former subjects. At best one can make only educated guesses. It should be constantly kept in mind that the past of the peoples of the former Soviet Union has not been uniform. If Estonia and Latvia had briefly existed as independent countries in the years between the two world wars, Lithuania, Georgia, and Armenia had known long periods both of independence and of foreign subjugation. Azerbaijan was independent for no more than two years, while the republics of Central Asia had never existed as nation states, their various peoples from time to time forming part of loosely held dynastic dominions of tribal chieftains.

The Central Asian Republics

Kazakhstan   *Population:* 16.4 million
                Capital: Alma-Ata
                Ethnic Makeup: 40 percent Kazakh; 38 percent Russian;
                                6 percent German; 5 percent
                                Ukrainian; 2 percent Uzbek.

Kyrgyzstan   *Population:* 4.3 million
                Capital: Bishkek (formerly Frunze)
                Ethnic Makeup: 52 percent Kirghiz; 22 percent Russian;
                                13 percent Uzbek; 3 percent Ukrainian;
                                2 percent German.

Tajikistan   *Population:* 5.1 million
                Capital: Dushanbe
                Ethnic Makeup: 62 percent Tajik; 24 percent Uzbek;
                                8 percent Russian; 1 percent Kirghiz;
                                .08 percent Ukrainian.

Turkmenistan   *Population:* 3.5 million
                Capital: Ashgabat
                Ethnic Makeup: 72 percent Turkmen; 9 percent Uzbek;
                                9 percent Russian; 1 percent Ukrainian.

Uzbekistan   *Population:* 19.8 million
                Capital: Tashkent
                Ethnic Makeup: 71 percent Uzbek; 8 percent Russian;
                                5 percent Tajik; 4 percent Kazakh;
                                0.9 percent Kirghiz; 0.8 percent
                                Ukrainian; 0.2 percent German.

NOTE: Figures do not add up to 100 percent because some populations are unaccounted for or are of mixed heritage.

Source: *Journal of Democracy,* January 1993.

The present political map of Central Asia is the product of the Soviet Commissariat of Nationalities whose first and only head was Joseph Stalin himself. Carelessly to generalize about the many peoples which inhabited the U.S.S.R. is to invite error. It would be equally erroneous to assume that the population of Central Asia constitutes a uniform mass of Muslims or Turks. The differences among the peoples of Central Asia are vast. Although most speak Turkic languages, these are not mutually intelligible, Turkmen and Uzbek being no closer one to the other than Italian is to Spanish. The Tajiks, of course, speak Persian, an Indo-European language unrelated to Turkic.

The Kazakhs, known in the days of the Tsars as Kirghizes, were, until recently, nomads. Their ancestors were converted to Islam nearly a thousand years later than were the peoples of the southern rim that had been part of the Iranian Sassanid empire. There were no cities, no great mosques, schools, or libraries in the land of the Kazakhs. They had no learned clergy educated in Arabic and Persian classics, their Islam sat lightly on them and preserved ancient shamanic elements. Islamic law, the sharia, was not generally applied, legal matters being settled largely through adat, custom. The Kazakhs were the first to experience the impact of Russia. Their culture was ill prepared to resist Russian influence. In fact the Kazakh intelligentsia came into being as a result of the absorption of Kazakh lands into the Russian Empire and the introduction of the Kazakh tribal elite to Russian education. Moreover, the vast plains where the Kazakhs roamed attracted Russian settlers who gradually equalled the Kazakhs in numbers. Stalin's collectivization and industrialization were a disaster for the Kazakhs. Perhaps as many as one third of the entire population starved to death, further increasing the ratio of non-Kazakhs to Kazakhs. Today the Kazakhs are a minority in their own land.

Compare this with the situation among the Uzbeks and the Tajiks. Their cities, Tashkent, Samarkand, Bukhara, were centers of Islamic learning. Persian was the native language of the Tajiks and the second language of many Uzbeks. Their mullahs knew Arabic, and the qadis, judges, applied the sharia in courts. Their religious and cultural identity was strong and largely impervious to Russian influence. They lived in compact settlements, and the Russians among them to this day constitute a small minority. Thus one should not expect the post-communist revival of Islam to take the same form or to have the same effect in Kazakhstan as in Uzbekistan or Tajikistan. Unless 60 percent of the population leave the republic, Kazakhstan will not be an Islamic state. No matter what the official rhetoric, the Russian element will continue to exercise a decisive influence, since the Russians, and in this instance other Slavs and all Europeans can be counted as Russians, constitute not only the majority of the population but also the majority of the technological, bureaucratic, and military elites. In fact, in Central Asia Kazakhstan is a special case not to be judged by the same standards or to be confused with the other Central Asian republics. . . .

Small Hope for Democracy

In judging foreign governments we tend to apply to them criteria derived from our own history. Unfortunately, it is unrealistic to expect Central Asian states rapidly to develop into democracies. Democracy is a tender plant that has existed for only very short periods of time among very limited numbers of people even in the West. At present Central Asian republics are governed essentially by the same men who ran them on behalf of Moscow. Whereas a particular leader may be overthrown or voted out, the old ruling apparatus is in place and will remain in place for the foreseeable future. There is even less of an alternative to the old communist cadres in Central Asia than there is in Russia. This does not mean that Central Asian republics are condemned to have despotic regimes. There may develop governments with powers that are not unlimited. It would be fruitless, however, to try to predict what form such governments would take except that they all will use the rhetoric of democracy, have elections, and claim to be governments of laws and not of men.

The states of Central Asia have a lively interest in relations with the outside world, most of which until a few years ago was terra incognita to them. They have no diplomatic traditions, no trained staffs, and no experience. Yet foreign powers have already rushed in to establish embassies, conclude treaties, promote commercial relations, and exercise political influence. Central Asia is of immediate interest to China, Afghanistan, Pakistan, Iran, and Turkey. . . .

The U.S. and Central Asia

What of the United States? What role should America play in the virtually unknown world of Central Asia? What interests does she have in a part of the world which until the Soviet invasion of Afghanistan in 1979 did not exist for the American public? It is clear that in a world shrunk to a global village the United States cannot disregard developments in Central Asia any more than it can disregard developments in Eastern Europe, the Far East, or the Mediterranean basin. Although Central Asian republics are not, and are unlikely to be, a threat, unless armed with nuclear weapons, local troubles might easily escalate into serious regional conflicts that would endanger the peace of the world. Thus the United States would inevitably have to concern itself with the maintenance of peace in Central Asia.

Since inter-ethnic antagonisms and rivalries would be the most likely causes of problems among the republics of Central Asia, the United States should be even-handed in its dealings with them, offer mediation, promote stability, and offer inducements to the peaceful resolution of conflicts. At the same time the United States should be careful not to become too deeply involved in parochial quarrels, not to interfere in local affairs, except by offering friendly advice, and not to attempt to impose solutions that would help create anti-American feelings in countries where none exist at present.

Caution and moderation should guide America's policies in a part of the world of which she knows so little, and with whose history, languages, and traditions she is quite unfamiliar. Above all, the United States should not play favorites and sacrifice long range prospects of cooperation and peace for short term gains. Faithfulness to the best political principles and traditions of our own country is bound to make a profound impression whereas short-sighted opportunism would undermine its position. Once the perception of America's integrity in the promotion of peace, tolerance, and democracy is tarnished, it can be restored only slowly and with great effort. None of this means that American diplomatic recognition, or financial and technical aid should either not be given or given unconditionally. The United States may legitimately expect that those whom it helps live up to certain minimal standards of civilized behavior embodied in the various charters, declarations, and treaties under the United Nations.

While one cannot expect the newly independent Central Asian republics to provide their citizens with guarantees of human and political rights equal to those enjoyed by the Swiss or the Danes, one should make it clear that American commitment and support do depend on the treatment a given state affords its citizens. The United States may have to tolerate the existence in Central Asian republics of laws and practices that would be considered intolerable at home, e.g. rigorous libel laws, certain limitations on the franchise, the establishment of religion, certain forms of punishment that most Americans would see as cruel. It should not, however, disregard outright denials of freedom of speech and press, the establishment of dictatorships, or cases of religious and ethnic persecution. . . .

Interest in America

Among the educated classes in Central Asia there is now a great deal of interest in the United States. Anti-Americanism so familiar in so many parts of the world, has not affected the populations that have lived for more than a century under Russian rule. The United States should devise a plan for acquainting the peoples of the newly independent republics with American history and culture. Student exchanges, cooperation with academic and scientific institutions, visits by musical groups and individual performers would undoubtedly be welcomed, provided the sensitivities of the local population are taken into account.

Conducting relations with the republics of Central Asia will not be easy. Yet the United States stands at a propitious moment for influencing the future of that remote and very significant part of the world.

"To separate off the Ukraine from greater Russia today would mean to cut across the lives of millions of individuals and families."

Uniting Ukraine and Russia Would Reduce Conflict

Alexander Solzhenitsyn

Alexander Solzhenitsyn was a dissident in the Soviet Union for many years. He exposed the cruelty of the Soviet labor camp system in his book *The Gulag Archipelago*, for which he won the Nobel Prize for Literature in 1970. He was expelled from the Soviet Union in 1974. In the following viewpoint, excerpted from his book *Rebuilding Russia*, Solzhenitsyn argues that Russia, Ukraine, and Belarus (which the author refers to as Byelorussia) should be a united country. These regions, he maintains, were once the core of old Russia, and the peoples of these regions share a common heritage. The independence movements that led Ukraine and Belarus to separate from Russia he contends have no validity. Uniting these regions will prevent conflict and create stability in the republics, he concludes.

As you read, consider the following questions:

1. Why was the issue of nationalities the first to be dealt with after the collapse of the Soviet Union, in the author's opinion?
2. What evidence does Solzhenitsyn give to show that Russia, Ukraine, and Belarus are in reality one region?
3. What is the author's attitude concerning the republics that surround Russia, Ukraine, and Belarus?

Excerpts from *Rebuilding Russia* by Alexander Solzhenitsyn. Copyright © 1991 by Alexander Solzhenitsyn. Reprinted by permission of Farrar, Straus & Giroux, Inc.

Can there still be any one among us who is unaware of our troubles—the loss of a third of our population in the ineptly, almost suicidally waged Patriotic War; the destruction of the peasant class and the soil which can no longer yield adequate harvests; our befouled environment; the depletion of our natural wealth and once luxuriant forests?

We have saddled our women with backbreaking, impossibly burdensome labor, torn them from their children, and have abandoned the children themselves to disease, brutishness and the mere semblance of education. Our health care is utterly neglected, there are no medicines, and we have even forgotten the meaning of a proper diet. Millions lack housing and a helplessness bred of the absence of personal rights permeates the entire country.

Yet human beings are so constituted that we can put up with such ruination and madness, even when they last a lifetime. But God forbid that anyone should dare to offend or slight our nationality. Then nothing can restrain us in our state of chronic submission. With furious courage, we snatch up stones, clubs, spears, and guns and fall upon our neighbors, intent on murder and arson.

Such is man: Nothing has the capacity to convince us that our hunger, our poverty, our early deaths, or the degeneration of our children can take precedence over national pride.

And that is why in Russia's first tentative steps toward recovery and reconstruction we are forced to begin not with our unendurable wounds or debilitating suffering but with the problem of nationalities.

Socialism Ruined Relationships Among Nationalities

Within what geographical boundaries shall we heal our afflictions or die? Who today considers himself part of the future Russia?

In the course of three-quarters of a century, to the sound of incessant proclamations trumpeting "the socialist friendship of peoples," the communist regime has managed to neglect, entangle, and sully the relationships among peoples to such a degree that one can no longer see the way back to the peaceful coexistence of nationalities. [After the departure of the peripheral republics there should remain a core entity] called *Rus*, as it was designated in olden times (the word Russian had for centuries embraced Little Russians [Ukrainians], Great Russians, and Byelorussians), or else *Russia*, a name used since the eighteenth century.

If it is true that Russia has for decades been giving its lifeblood to the republics, then our separation from the periphery will not produce economic losses, but will instead allow us to conserve physical strength.

At the beginning of this century, the eminent political thinker Sergei Kryzhanovsky foresaw that "the Russian heartland does not possess the reserves of cultural and moral strength necessary to assimilate the peripheries. That [effort] weakens the Russian national core."

The Western Republics

With the severing off of the peripheral republics a Russian Union (Russia, the Ukraine, Byelorussia) is now free to pursue its precious inner development, at long last turning diligent attention toward itself instead of outward toward the *empire*.

But even the Russian entity of which I speak would contain a hundred different nationalities and ethnic groups ranging in size from the tiny to the very considerable.

And this is the very threshold from which we can and must

manifest great wisdom and understanding, marshalling all the resources of our hearts and minds to the task of consolidating a fruitful commonwealth of nations, affirming the integrity of each culture and the preservation of each language.

Ukraine Should Remain

I am well-nigh half Ukrainian by birth. And I grew up to the sound of Ukrainian speech. I spent the greater part of my front-line military service in sorrowful Byelorussia, where I became poignantly attached to its melancholy, sparse landscape, and its gentle people.

Thus I am addressing both nations as one of their own.

And in any case our people came to be divided into three branches only by the terrible calamity of the Mongol invasion and by Polish colonization.

All the talk of a separate Ukrainian people existing since something like the ninth century and possessing its own non-Russian language is a recently invented falsehood.

We all sprang from precious Kiev, from which "the Russian land took its beginning"—as Nestor put it in his chronicle—and from which we received the light of Christianity.

The same princes ruled over all of us: Yaroslav the Wise apportioned Kiev, Novgorod, and the entire expanse stretching from Chernigov, to his sons; Vladimir Monomakh was simultaneously Prince of Kiev and Prince of Rostov and Suzdal. The administration of the Russian Orthodox Church exhibited the same kind of unity.

The Muscovite state was of course created by the same people who made up the Kievan Rus. And the Ukrainians and Byelorussians in Poland and Lithuania considered themselves Russian and resisted Polonization and conversion to Catholicism. The return of these lands to Russia at the time was universally perceived as an act of reunification.

It is indeed painful and humiliating to recall the directives issued during the reign of Alexander II (in 1863 and 1876), when the use of the Ukrainian language was banned, first in journalism and then *belles-lettres* as well. Although this prohibition did not remain in force for long, it was an example of the unenlightened rigidity in questions of administrative and Church policy that prepared the ground for the collapse of the Russian state structure.

However, it is also true that the fussily socialistic Ukrainian Rada of 1917 was created by an agreement among politicians and was not elected by popular vote. And when the Rada declared the Ukraine's secession from Russia, it did so without soliciting the opinion of the population at large.

In the past, I have had occasion to respond to emigre Ukrainian nationalists who kept trying to convince America that "com-

233

munism is a myth; it is really the Russians who are seeking world domination, not the communists."

Well, communism is the kind of myth of which both Russians and Ukrainians got a firsthand taste in the torture chambers of the Cheka from 1918 onward. The kind of myth that confiscated even seed grain in the Volga region and brought twenty-nine drought-ridden Russian provinces to the murderous famine of 1921-22. The same myth that later thrust the Ukraine into the similarly pitiless famine of 1932-33. As common victims of the communist-imposed collectivization forced upon us by whip and bullet, have we not been bonded by this common bloody suffering?

As late as 1848, Galicians in Austria-Hungary referred to their national council as "the Chief Russian Rada." But then in a severed Galicia, and with active Austrian encouragement, a distorted Ukrainian language was produced, unrelated to popular usage and chock-full of German and Polish words.

This was followed by the attempt to force Carpatho-Russians away from their habit of using the Russian language, and by the temptations of radical Pan-Ukrainian separatism, which manifests itself in bursts of farcical ignorance such as the assertion that St. Vladimir was "Ukrainian," or in such vehement statements as "let communism live so long as the Muscovites perish."

Separation Harms Families

How can we fail to share the pain and anguish over the mortal torments that befell the Ukraine in the Soviet period? But does that justify the ambition to lop the Ukraine off from a living organism?

To separate off the Ukraine from greater Russia today would mean to cut across the lives of millions of individuals and families; the two populations are thoroughly intermingled. There are entire regions where Russians predominate; many individuals would be hard put to choose between the two nationalities. Many others are of mixed origin, and there are plenty of mixed marriages.

Brothers! We have no need of this cruel partition. The very idea comes from the darkening of minds brought on by the communist years. Together we have borne the suffering of the Soviet period, together we have tumbled into this pit, and together, too, we shall find our way out.

As Mikhail Dragomanov has phrased it, our cultures are "indivisible, yet unmixable." An avenue must be opened—amicably and joyfully—for the free manifestation of Ukrainian and Byelorussian culture not only on their two territories but among the Great Russians as well.

No forced Russification—but no forced Ukrainization either.

There must be an untrammeled development of parallel cultures and school instruction in either language, according to the parent's choice. . . .

Beyond the Ukraine and Byelorussia, the Russian state will inevitably remain a multicultural one, despite the fact that this is not a goal we wish to pursue.

For substantial groups like the Tatar, Bashkir, Udmurt, Komi, Chuvash, Mordva, Mari and Yakut peoples, there would seem to be virtually no choice, because it is simply impractical for one state to exist when it is surrounded on all sides by a second one.

Other nationalities will have an external border, and if they should wish to separate, no impediment can be placed in their way. But, on the condition that all their unique national characteristics—culture, religion, and economic structure—are preserved, it may make sense for them to remain in Russia.

As the creation of many small state structures in the twentieth century shows, a great burden is placed on them in terms of supporting a plethora of governmental agencies, diplomatic missions, and armies; the process also cuts them off from large territories that provide outlets for trade.

Thus, for example, the mountain people of the Caucuses, a group distinguished by their loyalty to the Russian throne before the Revolution, will no doubt wish to weigh carefully the advantages and disadvantages of separation.

It is not the large Russian *union* that needs to have the smaller peripheral nations joined to itself; it is, rather, they who may have the greater need to join up. Should they wish to be with us more credit to them.

"Ethnic cleavages . . . can be a source of democratic strength and renewal."

Democracy Can Reduce Ethnic Conflict

Rita Jalali and Seymour Martin Lipset

In the following viewpoint, Rita Jalali and Seymour Martin Lipset analyze ethnic conflict in the former Soviet Union and other nations. After examining how different political and economic structures affect ethnic conflict, they conclude that democracy in the former Soviet republics and other nations can help reduce ethnic conflict and promote stability. Jalali, a sociologist, teaches at Michigan State University in East Lansing. Lipset is the Hazel Chair of Public Policy at George Mason University in Fairfax, Virginia, and senior fellow at the Hoover Institution at Stanford University in California.

As you read, consider the following questions:

1. Why did many political science experts once believe that ethnic conflict would decline with industrialization, according to Jalali and Lipset?
2. Describe the attitudes of Vladimir Lenin, Joseph Stalin, Nikita Khrushchev, Leonid Brezhnev, and Mikhail Gorbachev concerning ethnic minorities, as detailed by the authors.
3. What is the economic competition model of ethnic conflict, and why is it faulty, in the authors' opinion?

From Rita Jalali and Seymour Martin Lipset, "Racial and Ethnic Conflicts: A Global Perspective." Reprinted with permission from *Political Science Quarterly* 107 (Winter 1992-93): 585-606.

Race and ethnicity provide the most striking example of a general failure among experts to anticipate social developments in varying types of societies. Until recently, there was considerable consensus among many Marxist and non-Marxist scholars that ethnicity reflected the conditions of traditional society, in which people lived in small communities isolated from one another and in which mass communications and transportation were limited. Many expected that industrialization, urbanization, and the spread of education would reduce ethnic consciousness, and that universalism would replace particularism. Marxists were certain that socialism would mean the end of the ethnic tension and consciousness that existed in pre-socialist societies. Non-Marxist sociologists in Western countries assumed that industrialization and modernization would do the same. Assimilation of minorities into a large integrated whole was viewed as the inevitable future.

It is now clearly established that the assimilationist assumptions are not valid. Most parts of the globe have been touched by ethnic conflict. While the postcolonial countries continue to experience the effects of ethnic polarization, ethnic passions have now engulfed regions of the world that until recently were thought to have solved the "nationality" problem. Ethnic conflict now threatens most former communist countries and has led to the political fragmentation of Yugoslavia and the Soviet Union. From the movements for autonomy in Canada, the United Kingdom, Spain, and France to the strivings for a more formally pluralistic society in the United States, ethnic and racial cleavages have become a part of the political landscape of many of the Western industrialized countries. . . .

Ethnic Conflict in the Former USSR and Eastern Europe

The dismemberment of the last of the great multinational empires also threatens to create chaos and disorder in Eastern Europe and beyond. Starting with the conquest of Kazan in 1552, the growth of the Russian empire took place over 360 years. As a result of this expansion, the empire dominated over people from several different language, religious, and ethnic backgrounds. During this period Russian treatment of the minorities changed frequently—from tolerance to forced assimilation and discrimination. By the late nineteenth century, Orthodoxy had become the state religion. Other non-Christian and non-Orthodox religions were discriminated against, particularly if their spiritual centers were located outside the territory of the empire like the Catholic and Muslim faiths.

Before the revolution, conversion to Orthodoxy was the chief means for assimilating minorities. Later, Marxism became the instrument of fusion. The original Marxist theory considered ethnic minorities an unnecessary distraction, if not inhibitors, to economic and political progress. Classic Marxist reasoning justified historically the ethnic domination over economically less productive peoples by developed groups because it was considered to be a historically useful mission: the integration of less productive cultures—such as Mexicans, Algerians, and Asian Indians—into industrially advanced ones helped to produce capitalism in stable agrarian societies. As Carlos Moore points out, Marx's systematic condemnation of "inferior races" included a belief that their nationalist movements could easily become obstacles for agrarian societies in the process of becoming industrialized. To Marx and Engels the struggles of the then politically oppressed blacks, Asians, Slavs, and Latins were distractions from the "real" issue of class struggle.

Ideology

Marx and Engels lashed out against Bohemia and Croatia for seeking freedom from German (Austrian) imperialism. Writing about the situation in the Austro-Hungarian Empire, Engels recognized three of its peoples as destined for a progressive role— Germans, Poles, and Magyars. Then, in an unfortunate turn of phrase, he emphasized "the chief vocation of all the other races and peoples, great and small, is to perish in the revolutionary holocaust."

On the formal ideological level, the communist regimes that had come to power since 1917 rejected Marx's and Engel's idea of absorbing minority and backward peoples into the cultures of more advanced societies. Lenin proposed that national minorities in the Soviet Union should have as much autonomy as possible and the right to secede. Lenin suffered a disabling stroke before he could elaborate on the "nationality" policy. When Joseph Stalin came to power, he ignored Lenin's views on this subject. Although he claimed to support the development of cultures that were "national in form, socialist in content," under his rule the rights of the national minorities, guaranteed under the Soviet constitution, were frequently violated.

While the nationalism of the majority with its state-building and unifying potential was treated with empathy, the nationalisms of the minorities were considered divisive and, therefore, suppressed. The republics were subjected to brutal, colonial Russification. Linguistic and cultural assimilation were promoted through Russian schools. Whole ethnic groups were deported—the Tatars of the Crimea, the Germans of the Volga, the Chechentsy of the Caucasus. Terror managed to keep the lid on ethnic aspirations for several decades. Under Nikita Khrushchev and Leonid Brezhnev, Stalin's nationality policy was implicitly dropped. [According to Teodar Shanin,] "The live-and-let-live practices placated many officials of non-Russian ethnic groups. Lobbies representing native interests became increasingly entrenched."

The advent of *glasnost* under Mikhail Gorbachev unleashed movements for secession. The Union of Soviet Republics is dead and the fourteen non-Russian republics are now independent, although most have joined a loose commonwealth. However, since many of the republics contain ethnic minorities, independence has not ended ethnic tensions in the region. . . .

Ethnic Mobilization

Contrary to the expectations of many Marxist and non-Marxist scholars, the process of modernization itself brought about an increase in ethnic consciousness. As Walker Connor has pointed out, while the notion of popular sovereignty legitimated demands for national self-determination, modernization acted as a catalyst for ethnonationally inspired demands. In Europe, prior to World War II, when there were fewer roads and cars, local radio rather than state-wide television was in operation, and income and education levels were much lower than today. "Brittany's culture appeared safe from French encroachment. . . . [M]ost Walloons and Flemings seldom came into contact . . . with members of the other group." With substantial increases in communication and intergroup contact the divisive sense of ethnonational uniqueness has been reinforced rather than dissipated.

Most theories of ethnic mobilization assume that modernization has played an important role in stimulating the ethnic movements of recent times. They diverge in the factors they identify as causally more significant in the development and persistence of ethnically based movements. Thus Michael Hechter, puzzled with the rise of nationalist movements in the industrialized West, argues that capitalist forms of development create economic disparities between core and peripheral regions and produce ". . . a cultural division of labor: a system of stratification where objective cultural distinctions are superimposed upon class lines. High status occupations tend to be reserved for those of metropolitan culture; while those of indigenous culture cluster at the bottom of the stratification system." This type of a stratification system ultimately gives rise to nationalist movements in the periphery. However, the evidence of stronger nationalist movements in relatively prosperous, peripheral regions of some countries, like Quebec, the Basque region, Catalonia, Flanders, and to a lesser extent, Estonia and Slovenia, casts serious doubts on Hechter's internal colonial thesis.

A model of ethnic mobilization that has enjoyed much popularity in recent years is economic competition. The basic arguments are derived from the ecological theories of Frederick Barth and his associates and Michael Hannan. Proponents of the economic competition model argue that "modernization increases levels of competition for jobs, housing, and other valued resources among ethnic groups" and that *"ethnic conflict and social movements based on ethnic (rather than some other) boundaries occur when ethnic competition increases."* Studies using this approach have found that ethnic party support is much higher in developed, urbanized, and industrial regions than in underdeveloped ones. Development leads to a rise rather than a decline in ethnic mobilization, because it provides resources to ethnic groups in the periphery, increasing their bargaining position and organizational capacity for action. The literature on the class basis of ethnic movements is also supportive of the theory, for it shows that movement activists tend to be more educated, are more well-to-do, and have higher occupational status than others among their ethnic groups.

Political Reforms Can Promote Peace

Electoral reforms (like heterogenous constituencies and incentives to pool votes across ethnic lines) that force ethnic parties to form coalitions with rival groups are techniques that help to maintain peace between ethnic groups. . . . The key is to have institutional arrangements that provide political incentives for accommodation and that penalize extremism.

The economic competition model has also been applied to explain the rise of national consciousness in the Ukraine. In a book written before the ethnic turmoil of the Gorbachev era, Bohdan Krawchenko notes "the question of competition is crucial in explaining the rise of national consciousness" in Ukraine following the economic growth of the 1950s and 1960s. "With mobilized individuals, expectations race ahead of the real possibilities. These were the same people who had to compete with Russians for employment, and the rivalry led to an exacerbation of ethnic tensions."

Profit and Ethnic Lobbies

Similarly, Teodar Shanin implies that economic growth in the Soviet Union's ethnic peripheries created more opportunity to amass individual fortunes, both legally and through corruption. All this facilitated the formation of ethnic lobbies in the post-Stalin era. Industrialization and urbanization led to an increase in the number of local non-Russian cadres and intelligentsia who had to compete with the Russian workers. "As a result nationalist tensions were building up."

The economic competition model is, however, not without its weaknesses. First, as Sarah Belanger and Maurice Pinard point out, theories with this perspective "fail to compare countries experiencing conflict with others experiencing accommodation." They cannot explain why Switzerland, a highly developed country, has little ethnic tension between the French and German-speaking Swiss, although the competition between these two groups should be very high as their socioeconomic positions are equal. It also cannot explain the escalation of ethnic conflict in Sri Lanka and its decline in Malaysia. Cases like these bring up the most prominent defect in all models of ethnic processes that focus primarily on economic explanations—their neglect of political variables. In many ethnic movements, institutional structures and state policies play a major role in shaping and conditioning the emergence of such movements.

In the case of Ukrainian dissent, for example, Alexander Motyl argues that the rise of nationalist sentiments in the pre-*glasnost* era was primarily the product of political circumstances, foremost of them being Khrushchev's de-Stalinization and Brezhnev's partial re-Stalinization of Soviet state and society. Others have similarly observed that by implementing policies that recognized and institutionalized ethnic differences— "creating administrative units along national lines, giving national languages official status, and recruiting local political elites from the indigenous populations"—the Soviet authorities unwittingly helped to establish the infrastructure for nationalism during the post-Stalinist era.

The cases of Switzerland, Sri Lanka, and Malaysia also illustrate that specific political mechanisms chosen to regulate ethnic conflict can often affect the likelihood and intensity of such conflicts. Before the nineteenth century the relations among the three major language groups in Switzerland (German, French, and Italian) were characterized by conflict. If ethnic tension is now muted, this may be because the Swiss have a political system that has institutionalized ethnic pluralism, allowing each of the three major language groups proportional equivalence in power sharing extending from the Federal Council to the bureaucracy and the armed forces. . . .

Political Management of Ethnic Diversity

The proposition that no nation in the world is free from some form of violation of human rights in the form of ethnic, religious, or racial discrimination (unless it is one of the few totally homogeneous in these terms, such as Iceland) is by now accepted as a fact. Much more often than not, people resist and resent those who differ from themselves in race, culture, and religion. Many have sought to institutionalize privileges for members of their groups. In modern times, both rulers and the masses have turned to virulent expressions of bigotry in response to social tensions, to threats perceived by those in power, and to insecurity stemming from economic or status uncertainty. The most extreme racist effort, the Holocaust of European Jewry, occurred in modern times. Anti-Semitism was also the policy of some communist states which, like the former Soviet Union, restricted the rights of Jewish citizens. Racism still prevails in many African states, where the politics of ethnicity continue to determine who rules. Uganda eliminated East Indian minorities, among others.

The white-dominated society of South Africa began to dismantle its segregation and other discrimination policies against the majority black population only after international pressure was brought to bear on it. Ethnic divisions have also undermined the apparent unity of countries as diverse as Belgium, Canada, the United Kingdom, Spain, Cyprus, Pakistan, Malaysia, Lebanon, Nigeria, and Zaire.

What steps have proved effective in containing these divisive forces? How has ethnic conflict been managed in multiethnic polities? Some scholars have argued that consociational democracies provide a model of conflict management for segmented societies. In such democracies the political leaders of the major subcultures "cooperate in a grand coalition to govern the country." Such coalitions have been successfully formed in Austria, Belgium, the Netherlands, and Switzerland.

The Power of Federalism

Dependence on elite conciliation makes consociationalism less effective in Third World countries. Federalism, on the other hand, has proved to be a useful device to reduce ethnic conflicts in many countries—from economically advanced countries like Switzerland to developing ones like India. Federalism works because it transfers the target of political mobilization from the national to the provincial centers, shifts conflicts in homogeneous provinces to intraethnic divisions, and gives ethnic groups local autonomy. . . .

Secession or partition is rarely an adequate solution, because most regions of a country are ethnically heterogenous and partition can involve a costly process of exchanging populations and dividing land and natural resources, often resulting in loss of many human lives and continuing border conflicts. . . .

In the former Soviet Union, where deportations, industrialization, and Moscow's settlement policies made most republics ethnically mixed, secession and independence may not be the solution to the ethnic problems. The ethnic and national groups in the Soviet Union were not always confined to the titular political administrative unit. Nor was the titular nationality necessarily a majority in its administrative unit, a fact that creates major tensions in the newly independent republics.

In Georgia, the first non-Baltic Soviet republic to formally declare independence, 30 percent of the population belong to a wide variety of minorities. In recent years conflicts have developed with Abkazians and Ossetians. The dispute with the Ossetian minority has often turned violent. In 1990, the Georgian legislature formally declared an end to the longstanding local autonomy of South Ossetia after the Ossetian assembly voted to remain part of the former Soviet Union.

In the Moldavian republic (where only 64 percent of the population is Moldavian), the Turkic-speaking Gagauz proclaimed independence, claiming they were being discriminated against by the Romanian-speaking Moldavian majority. In Azerbaijan, Armenians want the Nagorna-Karabakh region to be united with Armenia. Since some of these republics are now under the control of authoritarian leaders, minorities are likely to encounter further repression. . . .

Ethnic Loyalties Can Be Beneficial

Is democracy viable in a multiethnic society? There is plenty of evidence from African and Asian countries that demonstrates that intense ethnic loyalties endanger democracy. Yet many ethnically heterogenous societies have succeeded in managing conflict within a democratic framework. Ethnic cleavages do not necessarily lead to violence. Indeed, one could argue that they can be a source of democratic strength and renewal, for [as Larry Diamond, Juan J. Linz, and Seymour Martin Lipset assert,] "ethnic peace may require greater decentralization, distribution, rotation, and representation of power than authoritarian regimes have been able to provide.". . .

As a comparative study of the democratic experience in twenty-six developing nations concludes, "when ethnic leaders are allowed to share power, they generally act according to the rules of the game, but when the state responds to ethnic mobilization with exclusion and repression, violence festers." Indeed, the fact that interethnic relations are more peaceful in the West than in the Third World does not result from differences in ethnic groups in the different regions. The differences appear to rest in the nature of the Western political structures, which have incorporated multiple ethnic expressions and channeled ethnic conflict into more peaceful and constructive directions.

Periodical Bibliography

The following articles have been selected to supplement the diverse views presented in this chapter.

Mike Edwards   "A Broken Empire," three-part article on Russia, Kazakhstan, and Ukraine, *National Geographic*, March 1993.

Ken Gluck   "The New Russian Imperialist," *The Nation*, September 14, 1992.

Paul A. Goble   "Russia and Its Neighbors," *Foreign Policy*, Spring 1993.

Leon T. Hadar   "What Green Peril?" *Foreign Affairs*, Spring 1993.

Dilip Hiro   "Islamist Strengths and Weaknesses in Central Asia," *Middle East International*, February 5, 1993. Available from 1700 17th St. NW, #306, Washington, DC 20009.

Shireen T. Hunter   "The Muslim Republics of the Former Soviet Union: Policy Challenges for the United States," *The Washington Quarterly*, Summer 1992. Available from 113 E. Centre St., Nutley, NJ 07110.

Henry A. Kissinger   "The New Russian Question," *Newsweek*, February 10, 1992.

Peter Klebnikov   "Ethnic Troubles in Georgia," *The World & I*, January 1992.

Vladimir Klimenko   "Ethnicity Issues Define New Political Agendas," *In These Times*, March 18-24, 1992.

John Kohan   "Five New Nations Ask: Who Are We?" *Time*, April 27, 1992.

Andrei Kortunov   "Relations Between Former Soviet Republics," *Society*, March/April 1993.

David Nissman   "The National Reawakening of Azerbaijan," *The World & I*, February 1992.

Martha Brill Olcott   "Central Asia on Its Own," *Journal of Democracy*, January 1993. Available from the Johns Hopkins University Press, 2715 N. Charles St., Baltimore, MD 21218.

Victoria Pope   "Back to the Future in Central Asia," *U.S. News & World Report*, March 8, 1993.

For Further Discussion

Chapter 1

1. How do George Urban and John P. Maynard view the effects of U.S. policies on the stability of the former Soviet Union? What conflicting attitudes toward U.S. government and society are expressed by the authors' arguments?

2. How does Edwin Meese III interpret former U.S. president Ronald Reagan's actions at Reykjavik in 1986? How do Daniel Deudney and G. John Ikenberry describe the same event? Which analysis is more convincing? Why?

3. Michael Mandelbaum cites a description of Soviet society during the civil war of 1918-1921. How effective is he at connecting this description with the more contemporary context of Mikhail Gorbachev's reforms? How might the passage support Francis Fukuyama's argument about the ending of terror?

4. Michael Mandelbaum and Francis Fukuyama both refer to elections that took place in 1990, five years after the initiation of Gorbachev's reforms. Which author more effectively interprets the election results to illustrate the role of Gorbachev's reforms in the collapse of the Soviet Union? Why?

Chapter 2

1. In viewpoint one, Daniel Ellsberg warns that the breakup of the Soviet Union will increase nuclear proliferation. How does William Walker respond to the fears expressed by Ellsberg and others? On what points does Walker agree with Ellsberg, and on what points does he disagree?

2. Elliott Abrams states that Japan and Germany can never become world superpowers, while Zoltán Grossman believes that they will. What reasoning do the authors give for their opinions? Which argument is more persuasive and why?

3. Writers employ a variety of tactics to persuade readers. While some rely on facts, others appeal to the reader's emotions, values, or fears. What tactics does George Bush use to convince readers of his point? Do you find his arguments compelling? Why or why not?

Chapter 3

1. Dimitri K. Simes and Paul A. Goble both describe the possible dangers from nuclear weapons in Ukraine. Which author's assessment of the situation is more convincing? Why?

2. How does the optimistic tone of Warren M. Christopher's speech reflect his goal to solicit American support for aid to Russia?

3. How does the tone of Steven Rosefielde's argument, which originally appeared in a scholarly journal, differ from Christopher's?

4. The Center for Defense Information argues that the large U.S. nuclear arsenal encourages nuclear proliferation by sending the message that nuclear weapons are desirable. The American Defense Institute says nuclear proliferation justifies a substantial U.S. nuclear arsenal. Which position do you find more convincing? Should nuclear arms be reduced? Why?

Chapter 4

1. Henry A. Kissinger says that proponents have made "excessive claims" about Western aid's potential to promote democracy in the former Soviet Union. Which, if any, of Richard Nixon's arguments could be considered excessive claims?

2. Richard Nixon says that Western aid to the republics would be an investment in peace. Henry A. Kissinger says it might create tensions. Which argument do you find more convincing? Why?

3. Mike Davidow praises socialism, while Guy Sorman criticizes it. What evidence does each author offer to support his position? How does each author attempt to persuade the reader?

Chapter 5

1. Nationalism, which has often been a powerful force in world politics, now seems to be asserting itself in the former Soviet republics. Do Natalia Narochnitskaya, Vladimir A. Babak, and Victor Nadein-Rayevski perceive nationalism as a positive force? How do their views differ from those of Philip Goldman, Gail Lapidus, and Victor Zaslavsky? Narochnitskaya, Babak, and Nadein-Rayevski are all scholars in Moscow, while Goldman, Lapidus, and Zaslavsky live in the West. How might this affect the authors' views concerning the possible threat of nationalism?

2. Why might Iran seek to promote Islamic fundamentalism in Central Asia, in Boris Z. Rumer's opinion? Explain Rumer's concerns about Islamic fundamentalism in Central Asia. How does Colin Barraclough dismiss such fears?

3. Alexander Solzhenitsyn was born in Russia, raised in Ukraine, and spent some of his adult life in Belarus. How might his experiences affect his views concerning the future of the three republics? How might the view of a native Ukrainian differ from Solzhenitsyn's?

4. Why does federalism reduce ethnic conflict, according to Rita Jalali and Seymour Martin Lipset? How might the concept of federalism enable Georgia, Moldova, and other former Soviet republics to reduce their ethnic tensions?

Organizations to Contact

The editors have compiled the following list of organizations that are concerned with the issues debated in this book. All have publications or information available for interested readers. For best results, allow as much time as possible for the organizations to respond. The descriptions below are derived from materials provided by the organizations. The list was compiled upon the date of publication. Names, addresses, and phone numbers of organizations are subject to change.

ACCESS
1730 M St. NW, Suite 605
Washington, DC 20036
(202) 785-6630

ACCESS is a nonprofit, non-advocacy clearinghouse for information on international security and peace issues. Through its extensive computerized database of more than sixteen hundred organizations and thousands of experts, it directs educators, journalists, legislators, foundations, and the general public to a wide range of views on regional conflicts, arms control and disarmament, relations among alliances, military spending, nuclear proliferation, and other international issues. ACCESS publications include *Resource Briefs*, which appears six to eight times a year; *Security Spectrum*, published three to four times a year; directories; and special reports. The former Soviet Union is a frequently covered topic in these publications.

American Enterprise Institute for Public Policy Research (AEI)
1150 17th St. NW
Washington, DC 20036
(202) 862-5800

AEI is a conservative research and education organization that studies national and international issues, including U.S. relations with the former Soviet republics. It promotes the spread of democracy and believes the United States should continue to be a world leader. The institute publishes the monthly periodicals *The American Enterprise* and *AEI Economist*, the bimonthly *Public Opinion*, and various books.

Americans for Human Rights in Ukraine
43 Midland Pl.
Newark, NJ 07106
(201) 373-9729

Americans for Human Rights in Ukraine works to increase public awareness of human rights abuses in Ukraine and the progress of democratization in the republic. It helps support victims of religious, ethnic, and human rights abuses; sponsors seminars; operates a speakers bureau; and maintains biographical archives. The organization publishes an annual report and semiannual newsbriefs.

Armenian National Committee
427 Colorado St., Suite 103
Glendale, CA 91204
(818) 500-1918

The committee believes eastern Turkey belongs to Armenia. It works to force the return of this land and to increase public awareness concerning Turkish atrocities against Armenians. In addition, it provides the public with current information concerning events in Armenia. The committee publishes pamphlets, brochures, position papers, and a quarterly newsletter.

Arms Control Association
11 Dupont Circle NW, Suite 250
Washington, DC 20036
(202) 797-4626

The association is a nonpartisan group that works to educate the public on the value of arms control. It publishes the monthly periodical *Arms Control Today*, fact sheets, and a primer on arms control.

The Brookings Institution
1775 Massachusetts Ave. NW
Washington, DC 20036-2188
(202) 797-6000

The institution, founded in 1927, is a public policy think tank that conducts research and education in foreign policy, economics, government, and the social sciences. It publishes the quarterly *Brookings Review*, the biannual *Brookings Papers on Economic Activity*, and various books, including *In Search of a New World Order*.

Cato Institute
224 Second St. SE
Washington, DC 20003
(202) 546-0200

The Cato Institute is a libertarian public policy research foundation dedicated to stimulating foreign policy debate, including debate on U.S. relations with the former Soviet republics and America's role in the world since the collapse of the Soviet empire. It publishes the triannual *Cato Journal*, the periodic *Cato Policy Analysis*, and a bimonthly newsletter, *Cato Policy Review*.

Center for Citizen Initiatives-USA
3268 Sacramento St.
San Francisco, CA 94115
(415) 346-1875

The center, formerly the Center for U.S.-U.S.S.R. Initiatives, works to strengthen relations between Americans and the peoples of the former Soviet republics. It sponsors agricultural, environmental, and economic programs to assist the republics in creating better societies. The center publishes three bimonthly newsletters and a variety of brochures.

Center for Foreign Policy Development
Box 1948
Brown University
Providence, RI 02912
(401) 863-3465

The center conducts research on U.S. national security policy, with a special focus to the former Soviet Union and nuclear weapons issues. It brings together scholars, politicians, and the public to discuss ways to reduce the risk of nuclear war while defending American values and interests and to form recommendations for a nonpartisan, nonideological foreign policy. In addition to books, monographs, papers, and conference reports, the center publishes the periodic *Perspective* and the periodic newsletter *Update*.

Council on Foreign Relations
58 E. 68th St.
New York, NY 10021
(212) 734-0400

The council is a group of individuals with specialized knowledge of foreign affairs. It was formed to study the international aspects of American political and economic policies and problems, including the special problems of U.S. relations with the former Soviet Union. It publishes the renowned journal *Foreign Affairs* five times a year.

Foreign Policy Association (FPA)
729 Seventh Ave.
New York, NY 10019
(800) 628-5754
(212) 764-4050
fax: (212) 302-6123

The Foreign Policy Association is a nonprofit, nongovernmental educational organization dedicated to the belief that in a democracy, a concerned and informed public is the foundation for an effective foreign policy. FPA publications provide facts and unbiased, balanced analyses of foreign policy issues, including topics on the former Soviet republics. Publications include the annual *Great Decisions* and books in the Headline Series, such as *The Soviet Breakup and U.S. Foreign Policy* and *The U.S.S.R. and Eastern Europe: The Shattered Heartland.*

The Heritage Foundation
214 Massachusetts Ave. NE
Washington, DC 20002
(202) 546-4400

The foundation is a conservative public policy research institute dedicated to the principles of free enterprise, limited government, and individual liberty. Its scholars write numerous articles on foreign policy issues, including U.S. relations with the former Soviet states. Among its publications are the periodic *Backgrounder* and the monthly *Policy Review*.

Hudson Institute
PO Box 26919
Indianapolis, IN 46226
(317) 545-1000

The institute studies public policy aspects of national and international economics. It supports the view that the United States must continue to lead the world economically and politically now that the Soviet Union is no more. Publications include the quarterly *Hudson Institute Report*, research papers, and books.

Institute for Policy Studies
1601 Connecticut Ave. NW
Washington, DC 20009
(202) 234-9382

The institute's national security program provides factual analyses and critiques of America's foreign policies, including its policies with the former Soviet Union. Its goal is to provide a balanced view of international relations. The institute publishes books, reports, and briefs.

International Monetary Fund (IMF)
700 19th St. NW
Washington, DC 20431
(202) 623-7000

The International Monetary Fund is an organization with more than 165 member countries pledged to assist one another with information and financial support to create a prosperous world economy. Member nations contribute to a pool of currencies from which all may borrow to meet their international financial obligations. The IMF seeks to promote international trade and to raise the income and employment levels of member nations. It publishes a wide range of periodicals, books, and reference works, including *A Study of the Soviet Economy*, *The Economy of the USSR*, and an entire series of economic reviews of the former Soviet states.

International Security Council
1155 15th St. NW, Suite 502
Washington, DC 20005
(202) 828-0802

The council, composed of military officers, government officials, political scientists, economists, and historians, works to raise public awareness of U.S. security interests, especially concerning the former Soviet republics. It conducts bimonthly seminars dealing with issues of international security, such as terrorism and the nuclear threat. The council publishes background papers and the quarterly *Global Affairs*.

ISAR
1601 Connecticut Ave, NW, Suite 301
Washington, DC 20009
(202) 387-3034

ISAR (formerly the Institute for Soviet-American Relations) is a non-profit organization dedicated to bettering U.S. relations with the former Soviet republics. It has a special interest in environmental issues in the former Soviet Union. ISAR publishes the quarterly journal *Surviving Together*.

Kyrgyzstan Embassy
1511 K St. NW, Suite 705
Washington, DC 20005
(202) 347-3732
fax: (202) 347-3718

The embassy is Kyrgyzstan's representative in the United States. It provides the public with information in the form of reports, briefs, speeches, and periodicals on Kyrgyzstan and its relations with the United States.

National Conference on Soviet Jewry
10 E. 40th St., Suite 907
New York, NY 10016
(212) 679-4577

The conference is a coalition of forty-five national Jewish organizations and local Jewish community councils and federations in more than three hundred communities. Its goal is to help Jews emigrate from the former Soviet republics and to promote the rights of Jews remaining in the region. The conference conducts seminars and provides the media, university groups, Congress, and government agencies with speakers, data, and photographic materials. In addition to monographs, reports, educational guides, pamphlets, and bibliographies, it publishes the periodic *National Conference on Soviet Jewry—Activity Report* and the biweekly *National Conference on Soviet Jewry—Newsbreak*.

Russian-American Exchange Program
345 Franklin St.
San Francisco, CA 94102
(415) 563-4731

The Russian-American Exchange Program is an organization that seeks to further cooperation between the United States and Russia. To accomplish this goal, it sponsors exchange programs for professionals; seminars for the American public; and informal dialogues between U.S. and Russian scientists, political leaders, and scholars. The organization publishes materials about its programs as well as brochures and pamphlets on strengthening U.S.-Russian relations.

Russian Embassy
Information Department
1706 18th St. NW
Washington, DC 20009
(202) 232-6020

The embassy is Russia's representative in the United States. It provides the public with information in the form of reports, briefs, speeches, and periodicals on Russia and Russian-American relations.

Ukrainian Congress Committee of America, Inc. (UCCA)
203 Second Ave.
New York, NY 10003
(212) 228-6840
fax: (212) 254-4721

Founded in 1940, the UCCA is a nonprofit organization of Ukrainians in America. It has seventy branches throughout the United States and a public affairs office in Washington, D.C. The UCCA publishes the *Ukrainian Quarterly*, a journal of Ukrainian and international affairs, and numerous monographs covering a wide range of topics concerning Ukraine. It welcomes inquiries regarding Ukraine and the Ukrainian-American community.

Ukrainian Embassy
3350 M St. NW
Washington, DC 20007
(202) 333-0606

The embassy is Ukraine's representative in the United States. It provides the public with information in the form of reports, briefs, speeches, and periodicals on Ukraine and Ukrainian-American relations.

U.S. Department of State
Office of Public Communications, Public Information Service
Bureau of Public Affairs
Washington, DC 20520
(202) 647-6575

The Department of State advises the president in the formulation and execution of foreign policy. It publishes speeches and testimonies by government officials. Write or call for a list of publications.

World Policy Institute
777 United Nations Plaza
New York, NY 10017
(212) 490-0010

The institute, affiliated with the New School for Social Research in New York City, is a public policy research organization that studies national security issues and foreign affairs. Publications of the institute include the quarterly *World Policy Journal*, books, monographs, and pamphlets.

Bibliography of Books

Anders Åslund

Gorbachev's Struggle for Economic Reform. Ithaca, NY: Cornell University Press, 1991.

Harley D. Balzer

Five Years That Shook the World: Gorbachev's Unfinished Revolution. Boulder, CO: Westview Press, 1991.

Michael R. Beschloss and Strobe Talbott

At the Highest Levels: The Inside Story of the End of the Cold War. Boston: Little, Brown & Co., 1993.

James H. Billington

Russia Transformed: Breakthrough to Hope. New York: Free Press, 1992.

Ian Bremmer and Ray Taras, eds.

Nations and Politics in the Soviet Successor States. New York: Cambridge University Press, 1993.

Walter D. Connor

The Accidental Proletariat. Princeton, NJ: Princeton University Press, 1991.

Craig A. Copetas

Bear Hunting with the Politburo: A Gritty First-Hand Account of Russia's Young Entrepreneurs—And Why Soviet-Style Capitalism Can't Work. New York: Simon & Schuster, 1993.

Robert Cullen

Twilight of Empire: Inside the Crumbling Soviet Bloc. New York: Atlantic Monthly Press, 1991.

Anthony Dolan

Undoing the Evil Empire: How Reagan Won the Cold War. Washington, DC: AEI Press, 1993.

John Lewis Gaddis

The United States and the End of the Cold War: Implications, Reconsiderations, Provocations. New York: Oxford University Press, 1992.

Patrick Glynn

Closing Pandora's Box: Arms Races, Arms Control, and the History of the Cold War. New York: Basic Books, 1992.

Patrick Glynn, ed.

Unrest in the Soviet Union. Washington, DC: AEI Press, 1989.

Marshall I. Goldman

What Went Wrong with Perestroika. New York: W.W. Norton, 1991.

Mikhail Gorbachev

The August Coup: The Truth and the Lessons. New York: HarperCollins, 1991.

Mikhail Gorbachev

Perestroika. New York: Harper & Row, 1988.

James L. Hecht, ed.

Rubles and Dollars: Strategies for Doing Business in the Soviet Union. New York: HarperCollins, 1991.

Ed A. Hewett and
Clifford G. Gaddy

Open for Business: Russia's Return to the Global Economy. Washington, DC: Brookings Institution, 1992.

David W. Hunter

Western Trade Pressure on the Soviet Union. New York: St. Martin's Press, 1991.

International
Monetary Fund and
World Bank

A Study of the Soviet Economy. Paris and London: Organization for Economic Cooperation and Development, 1991.

Robert Jervis and
Seweryn Bialer, eds.

Soviet-American Relations After the Cold War. Durham, NC: Duke University Press, 1991.

Anthony Jones and
William Moskoff

Ko-ops: The Rebirth of Entrepreneurship in the Soviet Union. Bloomington: Indiana University Press, 1991.

Anthony Jones and
William Moskoff, eds.

The Great Market Debate in Soviet Economics. New York: M.E. Sharpe, 1991.

Kerry M. Kartchner

Negotiating START: Strategic Arms Reduction Talks and the Quest for Strategic Stability. New Brunswick, NJ: Transaction Books, 1991.

Vladimir Krasnov

Russia Beyond Communism: A Chronicle of National Rebirth. Boulder, CO: Westview Press, 1991.

Walter LaFeber

America, Russia, and the Cold War, 1945-1990. New York: McGraw-Hill, 1991.

Gail W. Lapidus
and Victor Zaslavsky
with Philip Goldman

From Union to Commonwealth: Nationalism and Separatism in the Soviet Republics. New York: Cambridge University Press, 1992.

Michael Ledeen

Superpower Dilemmas: The U.S. and U.S.S.R. at Century's End. New Brunswick, NJ: Transaction Books, 1992.

Yegor Ligachev

Inside Gorbachev's Kremlin. New York: Pantheon Books, 1993.

Michael MccGwire

Perestroika and Soviet National Security. Washington, DC: Brookings Institution, 1991.

Michael Mandelbaum,
ed.

The Rise of Nations in the Soviet Union. New York: Council on Foreign Relations Press, 1991.

Stanislav Menshikov

Catastrophe or Catharsis? The Soviet Economy Today. London: Inter-Verso, 1991.

Bohdan Nahaylo and
Victor Swoboda

Soviet Disunion: A History of the Nationalities Problem in the USSR. New York: Free Press, 1990.

Don Oberdorfer — *The Turn: From the Cold War to a New Era—The United States and the Soviet Union, 1983-1990.* New York: Poseidon Press, 1991.

Merton J. Peck and Thomas J. Richardson, eds. — *What Is to Be Done? Proposals for the Soviet Transition to the Market.* New Haven, CT: Yale University Press, 1992.

Paul Craig Roberts and Karen LaFollette — *Meltdown: Inside the Soviet Economy.* Washington, DC: Cato Institute, 1990.

Avraham Shama, ed. — *Perestroika: A Comparative Perspective.* Westport, CT: Praeger, 1992.

Eduard Shevardnadze — *The Future Belongs to Freedom.* New York: Free Press, 1991.

Anatoly Sobchak — *For a New Russia: The Mayor of St. Petersburg's Own Story of the Struggle for Justice and Democracy.* New York: Free Press, 1992.

Alexander Solzhenitsyn — *Rebuilding Russia.* New York: Farrar, Straus & Giroux, 1991.

Nicolas Spulber — *Restructuring the Soviet Economy.* Ann Arbor: University of Michigan Press, 1991.

Hillel Ticktin — *Origins of the Crisis in the USSR: Essays on the Political Economy of a Disintegrating System.* New York: M.E. Sharpe, 1992.

Lev Timofeyev — *Russia's Secret Rulers: How the Government and the Criminal Mafia Exercise Their Power.* New York: Alfred A. Knopf, 1992.

Joan Barth Urban, ed. — *Moscow and the Global Left in the Gorbachev Era.* Ithaca, NY: Cornell University Press, 1992.

Murray Weidenbaum — *Small Wars, Big Defense: Paying for the Military After the Cold War.* New York: Oxford University Press, 1992.

Stephen White — *Gorbachev and After.* New York: Cambridge University Press, 1992.

World Bank — *Russian Economic Reform: Crossing the Threshold of Structural Change.* Washington, DC: World Bank, 1992.

Index

258

259

Nuclear Nonproliferation Treaty
(NPT), 71-75, 129, 134, 137, 138
nuclear proliferation
  James Baker on, 63, 64, 66
  threat of
    increased by Soviet Union
      breakup, 62-69, 71, 81-82,
      138-139, 147
      con, 70-75
  U.S. policies encourage, 129-130
nuclear weapons
  as useless, 132-134
  Commonwealth of Independent
    States and, 63-69, 70-75, 103-104,
    109-110, 129, 137
  compared to conventional weapons,
    133
  end of cold war and, 63, 68, 74
  necessity of eliminating, 38-40, 43,
    129-134
  numbers of, 129-133, 136
  uses for, 67, 68, 71

Oberdorfer, Don, 34
Operation Desert Storm, 92

Pakistan
  Central Asian republics and, 219,
    222
  nuclear weapons and, 129
perestroika
  role in Soviet collapse, 19, 52
plutonium, Soviet stockpiles of, 63,
  65-66
Poland
  currency reform in, 178
  IMF aid and, 160
  liberation of, 32-33
  Pope John Paul II and, 32, 33
  Solidarity labor union, 32, 33, 48
popular culture
  effect on Soviet Union, 42
privatization
  need for foreign investments, 182
  obstacles to, 181
  Russia and, 117, 125-126, 145
  voucher programs, 185-186, 189
  worldwide experiences, 183, 184,
    186
  would strengthen Republics'
    economies, 180-186

racism, worldwide, 242-243
Radio Free Europe
  role in Soviet collapse, 20-21
Radio Liberty
  role in Soviet collapse, 20-21
Reagan, Ronald

role in Soviet collapse, 28-36
  con, 37-43
  liberation of Poland and, 32-33
  opinions on nuclear weapons,
    38-39, 43
  speeches on communism, 29-30
  U.S. arms programs and
    caused Soviet collapse, 19-20, 31
    con, 38
Republics (of former Soviet Union)
  anti-Russian sentiments in, 209-210
  Central Asian
    countries included in, 214, 215,
      219, 225
    democracy in, 227-228
    history of, 225-227
    Islamic fundamentalism must be
      repressed in, 213-217
      con, 218-223, 227
    military weapons in, 214
    religion practiced in, 219,
      221-223, 225
    U.S. policies could reduce conflict
      in, 224-229
    women's roles in, 219, 221, 223
  economies of
    currency boards would
      strengthen, 174-179
    employee ownership would
      strengthen, 182, 185-186,
      187-195
    IMF intervention would
      strengthen, 153-156
      con, 157-160
    privatization would strengthen,
      180-186
    socialism would strengthen,
      161-167
      con, 168-173
    Western aid would strengthen,
      143-147
      con, 148-152
  need for free trade, 182
  privatization of industry in, 184-186
  privatizing agriculture, 181, 182-184
  Russians living in, 201-202
  tax strikes and, 49
  see also Commonwealth of
    Independent States
Reykjavik
  summit meetings at, 34-35, 39
Rosefielde, Steven, 121
ruble
  collapse of, 154, 175
  creation of new currency, 175-179
  G-7 aid and, 123
  stabilization of, 154, 155, 158, 160
Rumer, Boris Z., 213

261